SYSTEM ON CHIP DESIGN LANGUAGES

System on Chip Design Languages

Extended papers: best of FDL'01 and HDLCon'01

Edited by

Anne Mignotte
L3i/INSA,
Lyon, France

Eugenio Villar
University of Cantabria,
Spain

and

Lynn Horobin
Accelera,
U.S.A.

KLUWER ACADEMIC PUBLISHERS
BOSTON / DORDRECHT / LONDON

A C.I.P. Catalogue record for this book is available from the Library of Congress.

ISBN 978-1-4419-5281-3

Published by Kluwer Academic Publishers,
P.O. Box 17, 3300 AA Dordrecht, The Netherlands.

Sold and distributed in North, Central and South America
by Kluwer Academic Publishers,
101 Philip Drive, Norwell, MA 02061, U.S.A.

In all other countries, sold and distributed
by Kluwer Academic Publishers,
P.O. Box 322, 3300 AH Dordrecht, The Netherlands.

Printed on acid-free paper

TABLE OF CONTENTS

CONTRIBUTORS

J-B. Bégueret, J. Bhasker, D. Bierbaum, D. A. Burgoon, D. Brophy, S. Bublitz, L. Cai, J. Carrabina, C. N. Coelho, C. E. Cummings, R. Damaðevièius, M. Darianian, V. Ðtuikys, M. Edwards, H-J Eikerling, R. Ernst, S. Essa, A. Fakhfakh, H. D. Foster, W. Frey, D. Gajski, P. Green, Ch. Grimm, E. Grimpe, F. A. Hamid, M. Jersak, T. J. Kazmierski, H. Lévi, M. D. McKinney, Ch. Meise, P. J. Menchini, N. Milet-Lewis, P. Oehler, M. Olivarez, M. O'Nils, F. Oppenheimer, G. Pelz, G. D. Peterson, E. W. Powell, L. Ribas, P. Ruhanen, J. Saiz, W. Schardein, R. Schmid, B. L. Snyder, J. A. Sundragon Waitz, B. Thörnberg, W. Thronicke, L. M. Voßkämper, S. Wadsworth, K. Waldschmidt, R. Wittmann, G. Ziberkas, D. Ziegenbein

PREFACE

This book is the third in a series of books collecting the best papers from the three main regional conferences on electronic system design languages, HDLCon in the United States, APCHDL in Asia-Pacific and FDL in Europe. Being APCHDL bi-annual, this book presents a selection of papers from HDLCon'01 and FDL'01.

HDLCon is the premier HDL event in the United States. It originated in 1999 from the merging of the International Verilog Conference and the Spring VHDL User's Forum. The scope of the conference expanded from specialized languages such as VHDL and Verilog to general purpose languages such as C++ and Java. In 2001 it was held in February in Santa Clara, CA. Presentations from design engineers are technical in nature, reflecting real life experiences in using HDLs. EDA vendors presentations show what is available – and what is planned- for design tools that utilize HDLs, such as simulation and synthesis tools.

The Forum on Design Languages (FDL) is the European forum to exchange experiences and learn of new trends, in the application of languages and the associated design methods and tools, to design complex electronic systems. FDL'01 was held in Lyon, France, around seven interrelated workshops, Hardware Description Languages, Analog and Mixed signal Specification, C/C++ HW/SW Specification and Design, Design Environments & Languages, Real-Time specification for embedded Systems, Architecture Modeling and Reuse and System Specification & Design Languages.

In this volume you will find a coherent set of selected contributions from both events addressing five hot topics in system design:

- Results from the HDL standardization process
- Contributions to analog modeling, design and synthesis
- Practical experiences in system design based on different languages, such as VHDL, SystemC, and SpecC and using EDA Web services
- Simulation and verification methodologies for complex systems
- Different formalisms for system specification
- Modeling techniques for real-time systems

We hope you would find this selection of papers of interest for your activity either as a student, a lecturer, a designer or a manager in the domain of electronic system design.

Anne Mignotte, Eugenio Villar and Lynn Horobin

PREVIOUS BOOKS

Jean Mermet (Editor), "Electronic Chips & Systems Design languages", Kluwer, 2001.

Jean Mermet, Peter Ashenden and Ralf Seepold (Editors), "System-on-Chip Methodologies and Design Languages", Kluwer, 2001.

HDL standardization

Chapter 1

VHDL 2001: What's New

J. Bhasker
Cadence Design Systems
7535 Windsor Drive, Suite A200
Allentown, PA 18195
jbhasker@cadence.com
610-398-6312, 610-530-7985

Paul J. Menchini
Menchini & Associates
P.O. Box 71767
Durham, NC 27722-1767
mench@mench.com
919-479-1670

Abstract: VHDL-2001 is here! This paper highlights the changes that have been made to the language in the 2001 revision. While there have been no new features added to the language, a number of inconsistencies in the previous version have been addressed and resolved, and finally several features have been identified for removal from future versions of the language. In total, 26 Language Change Specifications were approved for inclusion in VHDL 2001. Some recommend that no changes be made, so fewer than 26 changes were, in fact, made. This paper presents the important changes made that are of more practical value to a designer who uses VHDL.

Additionally, while changes to shared variables were approved as an IEEE standard in 1998, most users will see it first-hand in the VHDL 2001 standard. Accordingly, we also review the new version of shared variables in this paper.

1. MOTIVATION

The current version of VHDL[1] was formally approved as an IEEE standard in 1993. While other standardization efforts [2][3][4][5][6][7] have added to the total language environment and others are underway, the basic language definition has not been updated since then, with just one exception.

The one exception has been the re-engineering of shared variables [8] in VHDL. VHDL '93 contains shared variables that can be simultaneously accessed by multiple processes. Unfortunately, there is no synchronization provided for such access, which can lead to destructive interference [9]. In order to correct this problem, the Shared Variables Working Group was set up. They have recently completed their efforts. While not, strictly speaking, part of the VHDL 2001 effort, their work will be reviewed here as most of the VHDL community is as yet unfamiliar with these changes.

Since IEEE rules require that all IEEE standards be recertified at least every five years, it is time for VHDL to be, at minimum, reballoted.

The VASG (the IEEE committee that "owns" VHDL) has taken this opportunity to make a number of small changes to VHDL. While there were a large number of significant changes to VHDL between the 1987 and 1993 standards, the VASG felt that, given the number of these changes, only minimal changes, in the nature of "bug fixes", were appropriate for the next version.

A. Mignotte et al. (eds.), System on Chip Design Languages, 3–10.
© 2002 *Kluwer Academic Publishers.*

As of this writing, VHDL 2001 [10] has passed ballot, with the ballot comment resolution process underway. By the time of HDLCon 2001, it is expected that it will have been presented to the IEEE for final approval.

The remainder of this paper discusses the most important changes in VHDL 2001 from the user's perspective, then concludes with a glimpse of the future.

2.   CHANGES

This section first covers the changes to shared variables. The major changes to VHDL 2001 from the typical user's perspective are then covered. For details of these changes, see references [8] and [10].

2.1   Shared Variables

VHDL '93 allows unsynchronized access to shared variables. For example:

```
entity SVExample is end;
architecture VHDL93 of SVExample is
    shared variable V: Integer := 0;
begin
P1: process
    begin
        V := V+1;
        wait;
    end process P1;
P2: process
    begin
        V := V-1;
        wait;
    end process P2;
end architecture VHDL93;
```

One might expect that the value of V is perforce zero at the end of the execution of this model, but this result can be guaranteed only under the most fortuitous of circumstances. In fact, without any assumptions as to the access to V, one cannot guarantee either that the value of V will be in [−1, 1] or that the value will be the same after every execution of the model, even within the identical environment.

Since one of the prime goals behind the development of VHDL is portability, such a situation was untenable. The SVWG, after an extensive requirements collection, analysis and ranking process, completely revamped shared variables, implementing them as *monitors* [11]. The example now becomes:

```
architecture Monitors of SVExample is
    type CounterType is protected
        procedure increment(
            by: Integer := 1);
        procedure decrement(
            by: Integer := 1);
    end protected CounterType;
    type CounterType is protected body
        variable Counter: Integer := 0;
```

```
        procedure increment(
            by: Integer := 1) is
        begin
            Counter := Counter + by;
        end procedure increment;
        procedure decrement(
            by: Integer := 1) is
        begin
            Counter := Counter - by;
        end procedure decrement;
    end protected body CounterType;
    shared variable V: CounterType;
begin
P1: process
    begin
        V.increment;
        wait;
    end process P1;
P2: process
    begin
        V.decrement;
        wait;
    end process P2;
end architecture Monitors;
```

2.2   Buffer Ports

Unlike in Verilog, in VHDL, ports of mode **out** may not be read within the design entity containing the port. VHDL provides the **buffer** port for this purpose. A buffer port contributes a driving value to its associated network and may also be read internally to a design entity. (The effect of a **buffer** port is to generate an implicit buffer between the "inside" of the port and the "outside" of the port. Another way of describing a **buffer** port is that it looks like an **out** port from the "outside" and an **inout** port from the "inside.")

The value read from a **buffer** port is always the value contributed to the network, unlike the case of the **inout** port. In order to guarantee this condition, VHDL places a number of restrictions on **buffer** ports. In particular, **buffer** ports may not be associated as actuals with formals of mode **out**. This restriction makes the following example illegal:

```
entity RSLatch is
    port(   R, S:          in      Bit;
            Q, Qbar:  buffer Bit);
end entity RSLatch;
architecture Illegal of RSLatch is
    component NOR2 is
      port( I1, I2: in   Bit;
            O:    out   Bit);
    end component NOR2;
begin
    C1: NOR2 port map(R, Qbar, Q);
    C2: NOR2 port map(S, Q, Qbar);
end architecture Illegal;
```

The problem is that the output ports of the NOR gates cannot be connected to the **buffer** ports of the latch, so the final port association in either instantiation is illegal.

This restriction means that, in practice, vendors must supply two libraries of standard components to modelers, one with **out** ports, and one with **buffer** ports. In practice, this is never done. Thus, **buffer** ports are seldom utilized; instead, modelers typically either explicitly buffer their outputs or use **inout** ports when the output must also be read.

The following table summarizes the VHDL '93 interface object interconnection rules:

		Formal				
		in	out	inout	buffer	linkage
A c t u a l	in	x		x	x	
	out		x	x		
	inout			x		
	buffer				x	
	linkage	x	x	x	x	x

In this table, an x indicates that the indicated formal-to-actual connection (e.g., "Formal => Actual" in a port map, generic map or subprogram parameter list) is permitted in VHDL '93.

The following table summarizes the new interface object interconnection rules of VHDL 2001:

		Formal				
		in	out	inout	buffer	linkage
A c t u a l	in	x		x	x	
	out		x	x	X	
	inout			x	X	
	buffer		X	X	x	
	linkage	x	X	x	x	x

Here, the **X**s indicate the additions for VHDL 2001.

2.3 Floating-Point Format

VHDL provides the REAL data type as an abstract way of representing floating-point operations and values. Originally, no requirements on format, and therefore on range, precision and accuracy were specified; instead, the floating-point implementation of the processor manipulating the VHDL description was intended to be used.

This lack of requirements was appropriate in the early 1980s (when VHDL was first developed), as processors had a wide variety of floating-point formats. However, this lack of specification results in portability issues for a model running on multiple, otherwise compliant implementations.

Presently, most existing processors have adopted one of two floating-point formats: either IEEE Std 754 [12] or IEEE Std 854 [13]. Accordingly and in order to enhance the portability of models, VHDL

2001 requires that implementations represent floating-point values utilizing one of these two standards. An additional requirement is that a minimum representation size of 64 bits be utilized. Such a requirement, equivalent to the *double* type of C, ensures an adequate range and precision of floating-point numbers for modern applications.

2.4   Default Binding Indication

VHDL, utilizes a two-step binding process. (Note that, starting with VHDL '93, one-step binding is also possible via the direct instantiation of design entities and configuration declarations.) In the first step, a component in instantiated and its generics and ports bound with values and with actual signals.

In the second step, a design entity is bound with each instance, and the generics and ports of the design entity bound with their respective counterparts on the instance. In the absence of explicit rules for a given instance, a set of default binding rules, codified as a *default binding indication*, are specified.

The default binding rules are intended to specify "the obvious" binding when no explicit binding information is specified—for example, the instance is to be bound to an entity interface with the same name as the instance by default.

However, because of the interaction with other rules of VHDL, most notably the visibility rules, such obvious rules have been surprisingly hard to write down so that they work as intended. As a result, nearly every vendor has provided custom extensions to the default binding rules, resulting in decreased model portability.

Thus, VHDL 2001 extends the default binding rules in an attempt to capture and standardize on at least the most common of these extensions.

In particular, in VHDL 2001, the entity interface need not be directly visible (except for the effect of the component declaration of the same name). In VHDL 2001, it is sufficient that an entity interface be in the same library as the design unit in which the component is declared. For example:

```
entity C is
  ...
end entity C;
architecture CA of C is
  ...
end architecture CA;
entity E is
end entity E;
use Work.C;   -- see below
architecture A of E is
  component C is
    ...
  end component C;
begin
  L: C port map(...);
end architecture A;
```

To be legal in VHDL '93, the use clause in the context clause of the architecture A is required, although many implementations would bind C(CA) to the instance L even in the absence of the use clause. However, in VHDL 2001, the use clause is no longer required; C(CA) will be bound to L with or without the use clause.

2.5   Incremental Binding

In VHDL '87, it was possible to supply binding information for a given instance either with configuration specifications at the place of the instance (*hard binding*) or with a configuration declaration as a separate design unit (*soft binding*), but it is not possible to use both methods on a given instance.

VHDL '93 introduced *incremental binding*, where one could use a configuration declaration to override certain aspects of the binding information for a given instance that was previously specified by a configuration specification. In particular, one could bind previously unbound ports and either bind previously unbound generics or change the value bound to a previously bound generic. Incremental binding offered new flexibility in configuring systems, where the initial binding could be used as the default, and rebinding could be used to override the defaults for specific, local needs.

Unfortunately, there were a number of mistakes in the VHDL '93 specification of incremental binding, defects that have been addressed and (we trust) repaired in VHDL 2001. No new capabilities have been added.

2.6   Concatenation

VHDL '87 had a simple set of rules for determining the bounds and direction of the index of the result of concatenation. Unfortunately, these rules often led to impermissible values for the indices of a concatenation result; for example, negative bounds for a bit vector concatenation could result:

```
constant k1: bit_vector(1 downto 0) := "10";
constant k2: bit_vector(0 to 1) := "01";
constant k3: bit_vector := k1 & k2;
```

The bounds for k3 in VHDL '87 are 1 **downto** -2, which is illegal.

To repair such problems, VHDL '93 introduced new rules for determining the bounds and direction of the index of the result of concatenation. Unfortunately, these rules were over-specified; hence, there were a few instances where there appeared to be more than one applicable rule. VHDL 2001 repairs this minor defect, and again provides one, simple set of rules for determining the index of the result of concatenation, without the problems inherent in the VHDL '87 set of rules. Otherwise, no new capabilities have been added. (In the above example, the bounds of k3 become 0 **to** 3 in both VHDL '93 and VHDL 2001.)

2.7   Declarative Regions

VHDL defines its visibility rules (which specify the meaning of a given name in a given context) solely in terms of *declarative regions*, which are "name spaces" associated with specific VHDL constructs. Declarative regions may nest, which leads to the hierarchical nature of VHDL descriptions.

In VHDL '93, entity interfaces and their corresponding architectures form a single *declarative region*, as do package interfaces and their corresponding bodies, etc. Configuration declarations also form their own declarative regions. Thus, each design unit forms the root of a hierarchy of declarative regions, so that all names within a design unit have a specific context in which to interpret them. Unfortunately, VHDL does not define a global declarative region surrounding the declarative region associated with a given design unit, so it is unclear how to interpret the library names and use clauses appearing in the context clause of a design unit, as well as the name of the design unit itself—there is apparently not a declarative region in which these names appear. This has been a long-standing problem with VHDL, one that each vendor has addressed in his own way.

Again in the interests of portability of models, VHDL 2001 repairs this defect. There is now an outermost declarative region, initially devoid of names, that surrounds each design unit. Additionally, for detailed technical reasons, architecture bodies now form their own declarative region, one that is nested within the declarative region associated with the entity interface corresponding to the architecture. Such changes should have minimal impact on users' models, but merely serve to ensure that all vendors interpret VHDL identically and allow models to work the same across all vendors' tools.

2.8   'Instance_Name and 'Path_Name

VHDL'93 introduced two attributes, 'Instance_Name, and 'Path_Name, that provide standard hierarchical names for named items in a VHDL model. Unfortunately, the VHDL '93 definition of these attributes contained a few errors of omission and commission, defects that have been repaired in VHDL 2001. No new capabilities have been added.

2.9   Features Marked for Deprecation

There are two features of VHDL that seem to be of little use. Accordingly, although still present in VHDL 2001, they are marked as deprecated and may be removed from future versions of VHDL.

Linkage Ports. VHDL is a purely digital, stimulus-response language. Nevertheless, the designers recognized that mixed, analog-digital systems might be of future importance, so they included **linkage** ports as an experimental way of hooking analog models into a VHDL description. Indeed, at least two early VHDL simulators implemented **linkage** ports for this purpose.

VHDL-AMS[7] does not use **linkage** ports as its way of interconnecting the digital and analog parts of models; neither do any modern VHDL tools implement **linkage** ports. Accordingly, the experiment that is **linkage** ports seems to be concluded and they have been marked as deprecated.

Replacement Characters. In the early 1980s, there were extant many computers that did not implement full, seven-bit ASCII character sets. Accordingly, these computer systems could not represent certain characters, such as '|', '"' and '#', that are necessary to the composition of VHDL models. Therefore, VHDL allows replacements for these characters, with constraints.

Today's computers implement full, seven-bit ASCII, and, indeed, eight-bit character sets, often ISO 8859-1 [14]. In fact, VHDL's character type is now based on ISO 8859-1. So there seems to be little reason to retain the replacement characters and their ensuing complications, and the replacement characters have been marked as deprecated in VHDL 2001.

3.   THE FUTURE

There is much work on other, HDL-like representations, such as SLDL and Open Systems C. Nevertheless, VHDL seems likely to continue to be central to many design methodologies for the foreseeable future.

Accordingly, the VASG continues to look for ways to enhance and improve VHDL. In fact, a low-level effort has been underway even as VHDL 2001 has been balloted. While it is too early to report any results, this effort is likely to intensify once VHDL 2001 is approved.

To join this effort, please visit http://vhdl.org/vasg and help keep VHDL the preeminent medium for systems design!

4.   REFERENCES

1. ———, *IEEE Standard VHDL Language Reference Manual*, IEEE Std 1076-1993, IEEE Standards, New York, New York, USA, 1994.
2. ———, *IEEE Standard for VHDL Multi-Valued Logic Types*, IEEE Std 1164-1995, IEEE Standards, New York, New York, USA, 1995.
3. ———, *IEEE Standard for VITAL: Application-Specific-Integrated Circuit (ASIC) Modeling Specification*, IEEE Std 1076.4-1995, IEEE Standards, New York, New York, USA, 1995.
4. ———, *IEEE Standard VHDL Mathematical Packages*, IEEE Std 1076.2-1996, IEEE Standards, New York, New York, USA, 1996.
5. ———, *IEEE Standard Synthesis Packages*, IEEE Std 1076.3-1997, IEEE Standards, New York, New York, USA, 1997.
6. ———, *IEEE Standard for Waveform and Vector Exchange (WAVES)*, IEEE Std 1029.1-1998, IEEE Standards, New York, New York, USA, 1998.
7. ———, *IEEE Standard VHDL Analog and Mixed-Signal Extensions*, IEEE Std 1076.1-1999, IEEE Standards, New York, New York, USA, 1999.
8. ———, Supplement to *IEEE Standard VHDL Language Reference Manual*, IEEE Std 1076a-1999, IEEE Standards, New York, New York, USA, 1999.
9. Hoare, C.A.R., *Communicating Sequential Processes*, Prentice-Hall, Upper Saddle River, New Jersey, USA, 1985.
10. ———, *Draft IEEE Standard VHDL Language Reference Manual*, IEEE P1076-2000/D4, IEEE Standards, New York, New York, USA, 2000.
11. Hoare, C.A.R., *Monitors: An Operating System Structuring Concept*, Communications of the ACM, 12(10), October, 1974.
12. ———, *IEEE Standard for Binary Floating-Point Arithmetic*, IEEE Std 754-1985 (Reaffirmed 1990), IEEE Standards, New York, New York, USA, 1990.
13. ———, *IEEE Standard for Radix-Independent Floating-Point Arithmetic*, IEEE Std 854-1987, IEEE Standards, New York, New York, USA, 1987.
14. ———, Information Processing—8-bit single-byte coded graphic character sets—Part 1: Latin Alphabet No. 1, ISO 8859-1 : 1987, ISO Central Secretariat, Geneva, Switzerland, 1987.

Chapter 2

Verilog-2001 Behavioral and Synthesis Enhancements

Clifford E. Cummings
cliffc@sunburst-design.com
Sunburst Design, Inc. Sunburst Design, Inc.
14314 SW Allen Blvd.
PMB 501
Beaverton, OR 97005

Abstract: *The Verilog-2001 Standard includes a number of enhancements that are targeted at simplifying designs, improving designs and reducing design errors.*
This paper details important enhancements that were added to the Verilog-2001 Standard that are intended to simplify behavioral modeling and to improve synthesis accuracy and efficiency. Information is provided to explain the reasons behind the Verilog-2001 Standard enhancement implementations

1.   Introduction

For the past five years, experienced engineers and representatives of EDA vendors have wrestled to define enhancements to the Verilog language that will offer increased design productivity, enhanced synthesis capability and improved verification efficiency.

The guiding principles behind proposed enhancements included:
1. do not break existing designs,
2. do not impact simulator performance,
3. make the language more powerful and easier to use.

This paper details many of the behavioral and synthesis enhancements that were added to the Verilog-2001 Standard[1], including some of the rational that went into defining the added enhancements. This paper will also discuss a few errata and corrections to the yet unpublished 2001 Verilog Standard.

Immediately after the header for each enhancement, I make predictions on when you will likely see each enhancement actually implemented by EDA vendors.

A. Mignotte et al. (eds.), System on Chip Design Languages, 11–33.

Glossary of Terms

The Verilog Standards Group used a set of terms and abbreviations to help concisely describe current and proposed Verilog functionality. Many of those terms are used in this paper and are therefore defined below:

- ASIC - Application Specific Integrated Circuit
- EDA - Electronic Design Automation.
- HDLCON - International HDL Conference.
- IP - Intellectual Property (not internet protocol).
- IVC - International Verilog Conference - precursor to HDLCON when the Spring VIUF and IVC conferences merged.
- LHS - Left Hand Side of an assignment.
- LSB - Least Significant Bit.
- MSB - Most Significant Bit.
- PLI - the standard Verilog Programming Language Interface
- RHS - Right Hand Side of an assignment.
- RTL - Register Transfer Level or the synthesizable subset of the Verilog language.
- VHDL - VHSIC Hardware Description Language.
- VHSIC - Very High Speed Integrated Circuits program, funded by the Department of Defense in the late 1970's and early 1980's [2].
- VIUF - VHDL International Users Forum - the Spring VIUF conference was a precursor to HDLCON when the Spring VIUF and IVC conferences merged.
- VSG - Verilog Standards Group.

2.   What Broke in Verilog-2001?

While proposing enhancements to the Verilog language, the prime directive of the Verilog Standards Group was to not break any existing code. There are only two Verilog-2001 behavioral enhancement proposals that potentially break existing designs. These two enhancements are described below.

31 open files

Verilog-1995[3] permitted users to open up to 31 files for writing. The file handle for Verilog-1995-style files is called an MCD (Multi-Channel Descriptor) where each open file is represented by one bit set in an integer. Only the 31 MSBs of the integer could be set for open files since bit 0 represented the standard output (STDOUT) terminal. The integer identifier-name was the file handle used in the Verilog code.

MCDs could be bit-wise or'ed together into another integer with multiple bits set to represent multiple open files. Using an MCD with multiple valid bits set, a designer can access multiple open files with a single command.

In recent years, engineers have found reasons to access more than 31 files while doing design verification. The 31 open-file limit was too restrictive.

At the same time, engineers were demanding better file I/O capabilities, so both problems were addressed in a single enhancement. The file I/O enhancement requires the use of the integer-MSB to indicate that the new file I/O enhancement is in use. When the integer-MSB is a "0", the file in use is a Verilog-1995-style file with multi-channel descriptor capability. When the integer-MSB is a "1", the file in use is a Verilog-2001-style file where it is now possible to have 2**31 open files at a time, each with a unique binary number file-handle representation (multi-channel descriptors are not possible with the new file I/O-style files.

Any existing design that currently uses exactly 31 open files will break using Verilog-2001. The fix is to use the new file I/O capability for at least one of the current 31 open files. It was necessary to steal the integer MSB to enhance the file I/O capabilities of Verilog.

'bz assignment

Verilog-1995 and earlier has a peculiar, not widely known "feature" (documented-bug!) that permits assignments like the one shown below in Example 1 to assign up to 32 bits of "Z" with all remaining MSBs being set to "0".

```
assign databus = en ? dout : 'bz;
```

Example 1 - Simple continuous assignment using 'bz to do z-expansion

If the databus in Example 1 is 32 bits wide or smaller, this coding style works fine. If the databus is larger than 32 bits wide, the lower bits are set to "Z" while the upper bits are all set to "0". All synthesis tools synthesize this code to 32 tri-state drivers and all upper bits are replaced with and-gates so that if the en input is low, the and-gate outputs also drive "0"s.

The correct Verilog-1995 parameterized model for a tri-state driver of any size is shown Example 2:

```
module tribuf (y, a, en);
  parameter SIZE = 64;
  output [SIZE-1:0] y;
  input  [SIZE-1:0] a;
  input             en;

  assign y = en ? a : {SIZE{1'bz}};
endmodule
```

Example 2 - Synthesizble and parameterizable Verilog-1995 three-state buffer model

In Verilog-2001, making assignments of 'bz or 'bx will respectively z-extend or x-extend the full width of the LHS variable.

The VSG determined that any engineer that intentionally made 'bz assignments, intending to drive 32 bits of "Z" and all remaining MSBs to "0" deserved to have their code broken! An engineer could easily make an assignment of 32'bz wherever the existing behavior is desired and the assignment will either truncate unused Z-bits or add leading zeros to the MSB positions to fill a larger LHS value.

Minimal risk

The VSG decided that there would be minimal impact from the file I/O enhancement that could not be easily solved using the new Verilog-2001 file I/O enhancement, and the 'bz assignment enhancement is not likely to appear in the code of any reasonably proficient Verilog designer, plus there is an easy work-around for the 'bz functionality if the existing silly behavior is actually desired!

3.   LRM Errors

Unfortunately, adding new functionality to the Verilog language also required the addition of new and untested descriptions to the IEEE Verilog Standard documentation. Until the enhanced functionality is implemented, the added descriptions are unproven and might be short on intended enhancement functionality detail. What corner cases are not accurately described? The VSG could not compile the examples so there might be syntax errors in the newer examples.

One example of an error that went unnoticed in the new IEEE Verilog-2001 Standard is the Verilog code for a function that calculates the "ceiling of the log-base 2" of a number. This example, given in section 10.3.5, makes use of constant functions. The clogb2 function described in the example from the IEEE Verilog Standard, duplicated below, has a few notable errors:

```
//define the clogb2 function
function integer clogb2;
  input depth;
  integer i,result;
  begin
    for (i = 0; 2 ** i < depth; i = i + 1)
      result = i + 1;
    clogb2 = result;
  end
endfunction
```

Example 3 - Verilog-2001 Standard constant function example from section 10 with errors

Errors in this model include:

(1) the input "depth" to the function in this example is only one bit wide and should have included a multi-bit declaration.

(2) the result is not initialized. If the depth is set to "1", the for-loop will not execute and the function will return an unknown value.

A simple and working replacement for this module that even works with Verilog-1995 is shown in Example 4:

```
function integer clogb2;
  input [31:0] value;
  for (clogb2=0; value>0; clogb2=clogb2+1)
    value = value>>1;
endfunction
```

Example 4 - Working function to calculate the ceiling of the log-base-2 of a number

4.   Top Five Enhancements

At a "Birds Of a Feather" session at the International Verilog Conference (IVC) in 1996, Independent Consultant Kurt Baty moderated an after-hours panel to solicit enhancement ideas for future enhancements to the Verilog standard.

Panelists and audience members submitted enhancement ideas and the entire group voted for the top-five enhancements that they would like to see added to the Verilog language. These top-five enhancements gave focus to the VSG to enhance the Verilog language.

Although numerous enhancements were considered and many enhancements added to the Verilog 2001 Standard, the top-five received the most attention from the standards group and all five were added in one form or another. The top-five enhancements agreed to by the audience and panel were:

#1 - Verilog generate statement
#2 - Multi-dimensional arrays
#3 - Better Verilog file I/O
#4 - Re-entrant tasks
#5 - Better configuration control

Many enhancements to the Verilog language were inspired by similar or equivalent capabilities that already existed in VHDL. Many Verilog designers have at one time or another done VHDL design. Any VHDL capability that we personally liked, we tried adding to Verilog. Anything that we did not like about VHDL we chose not to add to Verilog.

Multi-Dimensional Arrays
Expected to be synthesizable? Yes. This capability is already synthesizable in VHDL and is needed for Verilog IP development.
When? Soon!

Before describing the generate statement, it is logical to describe the multi-dimensional array enhancement, that is essentially required to enable the power of generate statements.

Multidimensional arrays are intended to be synthesizable and most vendors will likely have this capability implemented around the time that the Verilog 2001 LRM becomes an official IEEE Standard.

In Verilog-1995, it was possible to declare register variable arrays with two dimensions. Two noteworthy restrictions were that net types could not be declared as arrays and only one full array-word could be referenced, not the individual bits within the word.

In Verilog-2001, net and register-variable data types can be used to declare arrays and the arrays can be multidimensional. Access will also be possible to either full array words or to bit or part selects of a single word.

In Verilog-2001, it shall still be illegal to reference a group of array elements greater than a single word; hence, one still cannot initialize a partial or entire array by referencing the array by the array name or by a subset of the index ranges. Two-dimensional array elements must be accessed by one or two index variables, Three dimensional array elements must be accessed by two or three index variables, etc.

In Example 5, a structural model of a dual-pipeline model with one 2-bit data input is fanned out into two 2-bit by 3-deep pipeline stages and two 2-bit data outputs are driven by the two respective pipeline outputs. The flip-flops in the model have been wired together using a 3-dimensional net array called data. The data-word-width is listed before the identifier data, and the other two dimensions are placed after the identifier data.

The connections between flip-flops are made using all three dimensions to indicate which individual nets are attached to the flip-flop data input and output, while connections to the ports are done using only two dimensions to tie the 2-bit buses to the 2-bit data input and output ports of the model.

```
module dualpipe_v2k (dout1, dout0, din, en, clk, rst_n);
   output [1:0] dout1, dout0;
   input  [1:0] din, en;
   input        clk, rst_n;

   wire   [1:0] data [1:0] [3:0];          3-dimensional wire-array

   assign data[1][0] = din;                Word assignment -
   assign data[0][0] = din;                two index variables

   dff u000 (.q(data[0][1][0]), .d(data[0][0][0]), .clk(clk), .en(en[0]), .rst_n(rst_n));
   dff u010 (.q(data[0][2][0]), .d(data[0][1][0]), .clk(clk), .en(en[0]), .rst_n(rst_n));
```

```
dff u020 (.q(data[0][3][0]), .d(data[0][2][0]), .clk(clk), .en(en[0]), .rst_n(rst_n));

dff u001 (.q(data[0][1][1]), .d(data[0][0][1]), .clk(clk), .en(en[0]), .rst_n(rst_n));
dff u011 (.q(data[0][2][1]), .d(data[0][1][1]), .clk(clk), .en(en[0]), .rst_n(rst_n));
dff u021 (.q(data[0][3][1]), .d(data[0][2][1]), .clk(clk), .en(en[0]), .rst_n(rst_n));

dff u100 (.q(data[1][1][0]), .d(data[1][0][0]), .clk(clk), .en(en[1]), .rst_n(rst_n));
dff u110 (.q(data[1][2][0]), .d(data[1][1][0]), .clk(clk), .en(en[1]), .rst_n(rst_n));
dff u120 (.q(data[1][3][0]), .d(data[1][2][0]), .clk(clk), .en(en[1]), .rst_n(rst_n));

dff u101 (.q(data[1][1][1]), .d(data[1][0][1]), .clk(clk), .en(en[1]), .rst_n(rst_n));
dff u111 (.q(data[1][2][1]), .d(data[1][1][1]), .clk(clk), .en(en[1]), .rst_n(rst_n));
dff u121 (.q(data[1][3][1]), .d(data[1][2][1]), .clk(clk), .en(en[1]), .rst_n(rst_n));

assign dout1 = data[1][3];
assign dout0 = data[0][3];
endmodule
```

Bit assignment - three index variables

Example 5 - Verilog-2001 structural dual-pipeline model using multidimensional wire arrays for connections

The Verilog Generate Statement
Expected to be synthesizable? Yes
When? Soon.

Inspired by the VHDL generate statement, the Verilog generate statement extends generate-statement capabilities beyond those of the VHDL-1993 generate statement.

In VHDL there is a for-generate (for-loop generate) and an if-generate statement. In Verilog-2001 there will be a for-loop generate statement, an if-else generate statement and a case generate statement.

The genvar index variable

After much debate, the VSG decided to implement a new index variable data type that can only be used with generate statements. The keyword for the generate-index variable is "genvar." This variable type is only used during the evaluation of generated instantiations and shall not be referenced by other statements during simulation. The VSG felt it was safest to define a new variable type with restrictive usage requirements as opposed to imposing rules on integers when used in the context of a generate statement.

Per the IEEE Verilog-2001 Draft Standard, a Verilog genvar must adhere to the following restrictions:

- Genvars shall be declared within the module where the genvars are used.
- Genvars can be declared either inside or outside of a generate scope.
- Genvars are positive integers that are local to, and shall only be used within a generate loop that uses them as index variables.
- Genvars are only defined during the evaluation of the generate blocks.
- Genvars do not exist during simulation of a Verilog design.
- Genvar values shall only be defined by generate loops.

- Two generate loops using the same genvar as an index variable shall not be nested.
- The value of a genvar can be referenced in any context where the value of a parameter could be referenced.

The Verilog generate for-loop, like the Verilog procedural for-loop, does not require a contiguous loop-range and can therefore be used to generate sparse matrices of instances that might prove useful to DSP related designs.

The Verilog if-else generate statement can be used to conditionally instantiate modules, procedural blocks, continuous assignments or primitives.

The Verilog case generate statement was added to enhance the development of IP. Perhaps a model could be written for a multiplier IP that chooses an implementation based on the width of the multiplier operands. Small multipliers might be implemented best one or two different ways but large multipliers might be implemented better another way. Perhaps the multiplier model could chose a different implementation based on power_usage parameters passed to the model.

A FIFO model might be created that infers a different implementations based on whether the model uses synchronous or asynchronous clocks.

Enhanced File I/O
Expected to be synthesizable? No
When? Soon.

Verilog has always had reasonable file-writing capabilities but it only has very limited built-in file-reading capabilities.

Standard Verilog-1995 file reading capabilities were limited to reading binary or hex data from a file into a pre-declared Verilog array and then extracting the data from the array using Verilog commands to make assignments elsewhere in the design or testbench.

Verilog-1995 file I/O can be enhanced through the PLI and the most popular package used to enhance Verilog file I/O is the package maintained by Chris Spear on his web site[4]. Any Verilog simulator with built-in standard PLI can be compiled to take advantage of most of the Verilog-2001 file I/O enhancements today.

Chris' file I/O PLI code was the starting point for Verilog-2001 file I/O enhancements, and since Chris has already done most of the work of enhancing file I/O, it is likely that most Verilog vendors will leverage off of Chris' work to implement the new file I/O enhancements.

Re-entrant Tasks and Functions
Expected to be synthesizable? Maybe?
When? Probably not soon.

Verilog functions are synthesizable today and Verilog tasks are synthesizable as long as there are no timing controls in the body of the task, such as @(posedge clk). The #delay construct is ignored by synthesis tools.

This enhancement might be one of the last enhancements to be implemented by most Verilog vendors. Most existing Verilog vendors have complained that this enhancement is a departure from the all-static variables that currently are implemented in the Verilog language. Automatic tasks and functions will require that vendors push the current values of task variables onto a stack and pop them off when the a recursively executing task invocation completes. Vendors are wrestling with how they intend to implement this functionality.

This enhancement is especially important to verification engineers who use tasks with timing controls to apply stimulus to a design. Unknown to many Verilog users, Verilog-1995 tasks use static variables, which means that if a verification task is called a second time before the first task call is still running, they will use the same static variables, most likely causing problems in the testbench. The current work-around is to place the task into a separate verification module and instantiate the module multiple times in the testbench, each with a unique instance name, so that the task can be called multiple times using hierarchical references to the instantiated tasks.

By adding the keyword "automatic" after the keyword "task," Verilog compilers will treat the variables inside of the task as unique stacked variables.

What about synthesis? Tektronix, Inc. of Beaverton Oregon has had an in-house synthesis tool that was first used to design ASICs starting in the late 1980's, and that tool has had the capability to synthesize recursive blocks of code also since the late 1980s. The recursive capabilities made certain DSP blocks very easy to code. Some creative synthesis vendor might find some very useful abilities by permitting recursive RTL coding; however, it is not likely that recursive tasks will be synthesizable in the near future.

Configurations
Expected to be synthesizable? Yes, Synthesis tools should be capable of reading configuration files to extract the files need to be included into a synthesized design. When? This could be implemented soon.

Configuration files will make it possible to create a separate file that can map the instances of a source file to specific files as long as the files can be accessed with a UNIX-like path name. This enhancement should remove the need to employ 'uselib directives in the source model to change the source files that are used to simulate specific instances within a design.

The 'uselib directive has never been standardized because it requires a designer to modify the source models to add directives to call specific files to be compiled for specific instances. Modifying the source files to satisfy the file mapping requirements of a simulation run is a bad idea and the VSG hopes that usage of the 'uselib directives will eventually cease. The configuration file also offers an elegant replacement for the common command line switches: -y,

-v and +libext+.v, etc. These non-standard command line switches should also slowly be
replaced with the more powerful Verilog-2001 configuration files.

5.   More Verilog Enhancements

In addition to the top-five enhancement requests, the VSG considered and added other powerful
and useful enhancements to the Verilog language. Many of these enhancements are described
below.

ANSI-C style port declarations
Expected to be synthesizable? Yes.
When? Almost immediately.

Verilog-1995 requires all module header ports to be declared two or three times, depending on
the data type used for the port. Consider the simple Verilog-1995 compliant example of a simple
flip-flop with asynchronous low-true reset, as shown in Example 6.

```
module dffarn (q, d, clk, rst_n);
  output q;
  input  d, clk, rst_n;
  reg    q;

  always @(posedge clk or negedge rst_n)
    if (!rst_n) q <= 1'b0;
    else        q <= d;
endmodule
```

Example 6 - Verilog-1995 D-flip-flop model with verbose port declarations

The Verilog-1995 model requires that the "q" output be declared three times, once in the module
header port list, once in an output port declaration and once in a reg data-type declaration. The
Verilog-2001 Standard combines the header port list declaration, port direction declaration and
data-type declaration into a single declaration as shown in Example 7, patterned after ANSI-C
style ports. Declaring all 1-bit inputs as wires is still optional.

```
module dffarn (
  output reg q,
  input      d, clk, rst_n);

  always @(posedge clk or negedge rst_n)
    if (!rst_n) q <= 1'b0;
    else        q <= d;
endmodule
```

Example 7 - Verilog 2001 D-flip-flop model with new-style port declarations

This enhancement is a more compact way of making port declarations and should be easy to implement for simulation and synthesis soon.

Parameter passing by name (explicit & implicit)
Expected to be synthesizable? Yes.
When? Almost immediately.

Verilog-1995 standardized two ways to change parameters for instantiated modules, (1) parameter redefinition and (2) defparam statements.

(1) Parameter redefinition is accomplished by instantiating a module and adding #(new_value1 , new_value2 , ...) immediately after the module name.

Advantage: this technique insures that all parameters are passed to a module at the same time that the module is referenced.

Disadvantage: all parameters must be explicitly listed, in the correct order, up to and including the parameter(s) that are changed. For example, if a module contains 10 parameter definitions, and if the module is to be instantiated requires that the seventh parameter be changed, the instantiation must include seven parameters within the parentheses, listed in the correct order and including the first six values even though they did not change for this instantiation. It is not permitted to simply list six commas followed by the new seventh parameter value.

(2) Using defparam redefinition is accomplished by instantiating a module and including a separate defparam statement to change the instance_name.parameter_name value to its new value.

Advantage: this technique gives a simple and direct correspondence between the instance-name, parameter-name pair and the new value.

Disadvantage: defparam statements can appear anywhere in the Verilog source code and can change any parameter on any module. Translation - when compiling a Verilog design, none of the parameters in any module are fixed until the last Verilog source file is read, because the last file might hierarchically change every single parameter in the design! A "grand-child" module might change all of the parameters of the "grand-parent" module, which might pass new parameter values to the "parent/child" module. It gets ugly and probably slows the compilation of a Verilog design.

Verilog-2001 adds a superior way of passing parameters to instantiated modules, using named parameter passing, using the same technique as named port instantiation.

Advantage #1: Only the parameters that change need to be referenced in named port instantiations. The same advantage that exists when using defparam statements.

Advantage #2: All parameter information is available when the module instantiation is parsed and parameters are passed down the hierarchy; they do not cause side-effects up the hierarchy.

This is the best solution for IP development and usage.

The current defparam statement will not be fully usable in some Verilog-2001 enhancements and the VSG hopes that the addition of named parameter redefinition will eventually cause defparam statement usage to die.

Vendors might want to flag defparam statements as Verilog-2001 compiler errors with the following message:

```
"The Verilog compiler found a defparam statement in the source code at (file-
line#). To use defparam statements in the Verilog source code, you must include the
switch +Iamstupid on the command line which will degrade compiler performance.
Defparam statements can be replaced with named parameter redefinition as define by the
Verilog-2001 standard"
```

Signed Arithmetic
Expected to be synthesizable? Could be(?)
When? Synthesis vendor dependent.

The signed arithmetic enhancement removes a frequent complaint about Verilog, that the design has to explicitly code signed arithmetic functionality into the model.

Any vendor that already handles synthesis of signed arithmetic operations should be able to take advantage of this enhancement to facilitate signed arithmetic design tasks.

'ifndef & 'elsif
Expected to be synthesizable? Yes.
When? This could be implemented soon.

The 'ifdef / 'else / 'endif conditionally-compiled-code compiler directives have been a part of the Verilog language since before the Verilog-1995 Standard. Two additions have been added to help generate conditionally compile code: 'ifndef and 'elsif.

The 'ifdef set of compiler directives have been synthesizable by most synthesis tools for a long time and they became synthesizable by Synopsys tools starting with Synopsys version 1998.02 (full usage within Synopsys tools requires that the switch hdlin_enable_vpp be set to true). The 'ifndef switch adds a small simplification to Verilog code where the intent is to compile a block of code only when a specific text macro has not been defined.

```
'ifdef SYNTHESIS
'else
  initial $display("Running RTL Model");
'endif
```

Example 8 - Verilog-1995 coding style to replicate the Verilog-2001 'ifndef capability

```
'ifndef SYNTHESIS
  initial $display("Running RTL Model");
'endif
```

Example 9 - Using the new Verilog-2001 'ifndef compiler directive

Since the 'ifndef and 'elseif statements are used to simply determine when code should be compiled, these compiler directives could easily be implemented in both simulation and synthesis without much effort.

Exponential Operator
Expected to be synthesizable? Yes, if the operands are constants.
When? This could be implemented soon.

The ** (exponential) operator is a straightforward way of determining such things as memory depth. If a model has 10 address bits, it should have 1024 memory locations.

If the two operands of the ** operator are constants at compile-time, there is no reason a synthesis tool could not calculate the final value to be used during synthesis.

Local Parameters
Expected to be synthesizable? Yes.
When? This could be implemented soon.

Parameters, local to a module, that cannot be changed by parameter redefinition during instantiation is another enhancement to the Verilog-2001 Standard. Local parameters are declared using the keyword localparam.

This enhancement is needed by IP developers who want to create a parameterized design where only certain non-local parameters can be manually changed while other local parameters are manipulated within a design based on the parameters that are passed to a particular design instance. Restricting access to some parameters helps to insure that a IP users cannot inadvertently set incompatible parameter values for a particular module. The memory models in

Example 10 and Example 11 both use local parameters to calculate one of the memory parameters based on other memory parameters.

Comma separated sensitivity list
Expected to be synthesizable? Yes.
When? Almost immediately.

Verilog-1995 uses the keyword "or" as a separator in the sensitivity list. New users of the Verilog language often ask the question, "can I use **and** in the sensitivity list?" The answer is no.

The "or" keyword is merely a separator between signals in the sensitivity list and nothing more. The Verilog sensitivity list is one of the few places where Verilog is more verbose than VHDL. I personally found this to be offensive!

VHDL separates signals in the sensitivity list with a comma character, which most Verilog users would agree is a better separator token. For this reason, the comma character has been added as an alternate way of separating signals in a Verilog sensitivity list.

Because this enhancement is really just a parsing change, it should be very easy to implement. There is no reason this capability should not be available by all Verilog vendors as soon as the Verilog-2001 Standard is released by the IEEE.

The Verilog code for a parameterized ram model in Example 10 uses a comma-separated sensitivity list in the always block just two lines before the endmodule statement.

```
//-------------------------------------------
// ram1 model - Verilog-2001 @(a, b, c)
// requires ADDR_SIZE & DATA_SIZE parameters
// MEM_DEPTH is automatically sized
//-------------------------------------------
module ram1 (addr, data, en, rw_n);
  parameter ADDR_SIZE = 10;
  parameter DATA_SIZE = 8;
  parameter  MEM_DEPTH = 1<<ADDR_SIZE;
  output [DATA_SIZE-1:0] data;
  input  [ADDR_SIZE-1:0] addr;
  input                  en, rw_n;

  reg    [DATA_SIZE-1:0] mem [0:MEM_DEPTH-1];

  assign data = (rw_n && en) ? mem[addr] : {DATA_SIZE{1'bz}};

  always @(addr, data, rw_n, en)
    if (!rw_n && en) mem[addr] = data;
endmodule
```

Example 10 - Parameterized Verilog ram model with comma-separated sensitivity list

@* combinational sensitivity list
Expected to be synthesizable? Yes.
When? Almost immediately.

The Verilog-2001 Standard refers to the @* operator as the implicit event expression list; however, members of the VSG called the always @* keyword-pair, the combinational logic sensitivity list and that was its primary intended purpose, to be used to model and synthesize combinational logic.

Experienced synthesis engineers are aware of the problems that can occur if combinational always blocks are coded with missing sensitivity list entries. Synthesis tools build combinational logic strictly from the equations inside of an always block but then synthesis tools check the sensitivity list to warn the user of a potential mismatch between pre-synthesis and post-synthesis simulations [4].

The always @* procedural block will eliminate the need to list every single always-block input in the sensitivity list. This enhancement will reduce typing, and reduce design errors. The intent was to reduce effort when coding combinational sensitivity lists and to reduce opportunities for coding errors that could lead to a pre-synthesis and post-synthesis simulation mismatch.

The @* was really intended to be used at the top of an always block, but the VSG chose not to restrict its use to just that location. The VSG could not think of a good reason not to use, nor did the VSG think it was wise to restrict, the @* operator only to the top of the always block. This enhancement was made orthogonal but it should be used with caution and has the potential to be abused.

The Verilog code for a parameterized ram model in Example 11 uses an @* sensitivity list in the always block just two lines before the endmodule statement.

```
//-----------------------------------------
// ram1 model - Verilog-2001
// requires ADDR_SIZE & DATA_SIZE parameters
// MEM_DEPTH is automatically sized
//-----------------------------------------
module ram1 #(parameter  ADDR_SIZE = 10;
              parameter  DATA_SIZE = 8;
              localparam MEM_DEPTH = 1<<ADDR_SIZE)
             (output [DATA_SIZE-1:0] data,
              input  [ADDR_SIZE-1:0] addr,
              input                  en, rw_n);

  reg    [DATA_SIZE-1:0] mem [0:MEM_DEPTH-1];

  //------------------------------------------------
  // Memory read operation
  //------------------------------------------------
  assign data = (rw_n && en) ? mem[addr] : {DATA_SIZE{1'bz}};

  //------------------------------------------------
  // Memory write operation - modeled as a latch-array
  //------------------------------------------------
  always @*
    if (!rw_n && en) mem[addr] <= data;
endmodule
```

Example 11 - Parameterized Verilog ram model with @* combinational sensitivity list

The Verilog-2001 Standard notes that nets and variables which appear on the RHS of assignments, in function and task calls, or case expressions and if expressions shall all be included in the implicit sensitivity list. Missing from the Verilog-2001 Standard is the fact that variables on the LHS of an expression when used as an index range and variables used in case items should also be included in the implicit sensitivity list. In the 3-to-8 decoder with output enable shown in Example 12, the en input and the a-inputs should included in the @* implied sensitivity list.

```
module decoder (
   output reg [7:0] y,
   input      [2:0] a,
   input            en);

   always @* begin
     y = 8'hff;
     y[a] = !en;
   end
endmodule
```

Example 12 - 3-to-8 Decoder model using the @* implicit sensitivity list

Constant functions
Expected to be synthesizable? Yes.
When? This might take some time to implement.

Perhaps the most contentious enhancement to the Verilog-2001 Standard, the enhancement that raised the most debate and that was almost removed from the standard on multiple occasions in the past five years, was the constant function. EDA vendors opposed this enhancement because of the perceived difficulty in efficiently implementing this enhancement, and its potential impact on compile-time performance.

A quote from an EDA vendor who requested that constant functions not be added to Verilog summarizes some of the opposition:

"Constant functions are another example of how a VHDL concept does not map will into Verilog ... The Verilog language is simply too powerful and unrestricted to support such functionality."

The users on the VSG also recognize that constant functions might not only be difficult to implement, but also impact compile times. Despite this potential impact on compile-time performance, users deemed this functionality too important to omit from the Verilog-2001 Standard. Vendors might want to publicize that a design modeled without constant functions will compile faster than designs that include constant functions.

Constant functions are important to IP developers. The objective of the constant function is to permit an IP developer to add local parameters to a module that are calculated from other parameters that could be passed into the module when instantiated.

Constant functions will require vendors to calculate some parameters at compile time, which will require that some parameters not be immediately calculated when read, but that they will be calculated after a function is used to determine the actual value of a parameter.

Consider the example of a simple ROM model. To make a parameterized version of a ROM model, we need to know the number of address bits, number of memory locations and number of data bits. The data bus width should be passed to the model, but only the memory size or number of address bits should be passed to the model. If we are given the number of address bits, we should calculate the memory depth at compile time. If we are given the number of memory locations, we should be able to calculate how many address bits are required at compile time.

In order to make constant functions somewhat more agreeable to EDA vendors, they were defined with significant restrictions including some that do not apply to normal Verilog functions. Significant restrictions that apply to constant functions include:

- Constant functions shall not contain hierarchical references.
- Constant functions are defined and invoked in the same module.
- Constant functions shall ignore system tasks. This permits a regular Verilog function with system tasks such as $display commands to be changed into a constant function without requiring removal of the system tasks.
- Constant functions shall not permit system functions.
- Constant functions shall have no side effects (they shall not make assignments to variables that are defined outside of the constant function).
- If a constant function uses an external parameter within the internal calculations of the function, the external parameter must be declared before the constant function call.
- All variables used in a constant function that are not parameters or functions must be declared locally in the constant function.
- If the constant function uses a parameter that is directly or indirectly modified by a defparam statement, the behavior of the Verilog compiler is undefined. The compiler can return an unknown value or it can issue a syntax error.
- Constant functions cannot be defined inside of a generate statement.
- Constant functions shall not call other constant functions in any context that requires a constant expression.

The VSG anticipated that the typical use of a constant function would be to perform simple calculations to generate local parameters to insure compatibility with passed parameters. The above restrictions insure that constant functions do not cause undue compile-time problems.

Attributes
Expected to be synthesizable? Partially.
When? As soon as the IEEE synthesis committee finishes its work and includes attributes into the synthesis spec.

Verilog-2001 will add a new construct (new to Verilog) called an attribute. The attribute uses (* *) tokens (named "funny braces" by members of the VSG) as shown in Figure 1.

```
(* attribute_name = constant_expression *)
                                        -or-
(* attribute_name *)
```

Figure 1 - Legal attribute definition syntax using (* *)

Attributes were primarily added to the Verilog language enable other tools to use Verilog as an input language and still pass non-Verilog information to those tools. For many years now, vendors have been adding hooks into the Verilog language by way of synthetic comments. The most famous (infamous) example is the deadly[6] synthetic comment:

```
// synopsys full_case parallel_case
```

The biggest problem with the synthetic comment approach is that attaching tool-specific information to a Verilog comment forces those same tools to parse all Verilog comments to see if the comment contains a tool-specific directive.

To assist vendors who use Verilog as an input language, the VSG decided to add attributes to the Verilog language that for the most part will be ignored by Verilog compilers the same as any Verilog comment. The attributes permit third-party vendors to add tool-related information to the source code without impacting simulation and without having to parse every Verilog comment.

Required net declarations
Expected to be synthesizable? N/A.
When? Soon.

Verilog-1995 has an odd and non-orthogonal requirement that all 1-bit nets, driven by a continuous assignment, that are not declared to be a ports, must be declared. It is the only 1-bit net type that must be declared in Verilog. This non-orthogonal restriction is removed in Verilog-2001.

```
module andor1 (y, a, b, c);
   output y;
   input  a, b, c;
   wire   n1; // not required in Verilog-2001

   assign n1 = a & b;
   assign y  = n1 | c;
endmodule
```

Example 13 - Verilog-1995 required net declaration for the LHS of a continuous assignment to an internal net

'default_nettype none
Expected to be synthesizable? N/A.
When? Soon.

In the Verilog-1995 Standard, any undeclared identifier, except for the output of a continuous assignment that drives a non-port net, is by default a 1-bit wire. Verilog never required these 1-bit net declarations and adding the declarations to a model yielded no additional checking to insure that all 1-bit nets were declared.

The Verilog-2001 Standard adds a new option to the 'defult_nettype compiler directive called "none." If the "none" option is selected, all 1-bit nets must be declared.

Whether or not forcing all 1-bit nets to be declared is a good coding practice or not is open to debate. Some engineers believe that all nets should be declared before they are used. Other engineers find that declaring all 1-bit nets can be both time and space-consuming.

Editorial comment: I personally find the practice of declaring all 1-bit nets to be a waste of time, effort and lines of code. VHDL requires all 1-bit nets (signals) to be declared, and on a VHDL ASIC design that I worked on in 1996, while instantiating and connecting the major sub-blocks and I/O pads at the top-level model of an ASIC design, I spent as much time debugging flawed signal declarations as I did debugging real hardware problems. The only declarations that I personally found useful were multi-bit signals (buses), which are also required in Verilog-1995. My signal declarations extended over three pages of code and offered no additional useful information about the design. Nevertheless, one can now inflict similar pain and suffering into a Verilog design using the 'default_nettype none compiler directive.

6.   Array of Instance
Expected to be synthesizable? Yes.
When? Soon.

A noteworthy enhancement to the Verilog language is the Array of Instance that was added to the 1995 IEEE Verilog Standard. This enhancement was implemented by Cadence more than two years ago, but the other simulation vendors and all synthesis vendors were slow to follow.

An array of instance allows an simple one-dimensional linear array of instances to be declared in a single statement.

Most ASIC designers build a top-level module that only permits instantiation of other modules, no RTL code allowed. The RTL code is used in sub-modules but not in the top-level module.

In the top-level module, all of the major sub-blocks are instantiated along with all of the ASIC I/O pads. Consider the task of instantiating the I/O pads for a 32-bit address bus and a 16-bit data bus. Verilog engineers have always been required to make 32 address-pad and 16 data-pad instantiations in the top-level model as shown in Example 14.

```
module top_pads1 (pdata, paddr, pctl1, pctl2, pctl3, pclk);
  inout  [15:0] pdata;                // pad data bus
  input  [31:0] paddr;                // pad addr bus
```

```
input          pctl1, pctl2, pctl3, pclk; // pad signals
wire    [15:0] data;                       // data bus
wire    [31:0] addr;                       // addr bus

main_blk u1 (.data(data), .addr(addr),
        .sig1(ctl1), .sig2(ctl2), .sig3(ctl3), .clk(clk));

IBUF c4 (.O(ctl3), .pI(pctl3));
IBUF c3 (.O(ctl2), .pI(pctl2));
IBUF c2 (.O(ctl1), .pI(pctl1));
IBUF c1 (.O( clk), .pI( pclk));

IBUF i15 (.O(data[15]), .pI(pdata[15]));
IBUF i14 (.O(data[14]), .pI(pdata[14]));
IBUF i13 (.O(data[13]), .pI(pdata[13]));
IBUF i12 (.O(data[12]), .pI(pdata[12]));
IBUF i11 (.O(data[11]), .pI(pdata[11]));
IBUF i10 (.O(data[10]), .pI(pdata[10]));
IBUF i9  (.O(data[ 9]), .pI(pdata[ 9]));
IBUF i8  (.O(data[ 8]), .pI(pdata[ 8]));
IBUF i7  (.O(data[ 7]), .pI(pdata[ 7]));
IBUF i6  (.O(data[ 6]), .pI(pdata[ 6]));
IBUF i5  (.O(data[ 5]), .pI(pdata[ 5]));
IBUF i4  (.O(data[ 4]), .pI(pdata[ 4]));
IBUF i3  (.O(data[ 3]), .pI(pdata[ 3]));
IBUF i2  (.O(data[ 2]), .pI(pdata[ 2]));
IBUF i1  (.O(data[ 1]), .pI(pdata[ 1]));
IBUF i0  (.O(data[ 0]), .pI(pdata[ 0]));

BIDIR b31 (.N2(addr[31]), .pN1(paddr[31]), .WR(wr));
BIDIR b30 (.N2(addr[30]), .pN1(paddr[30]), .WR(wr));
BIDIR b29 (.N2(addr[29]), .pN1(paddr[29]), .WR(wr));
BIDIR b28 (.N2(addr[28]), .pN1(paddr[28]), .WR(wr));
BIDIR b27 (.N2(addr[27]), .pN1(paddr[27]), .WR(wr));
BIDIR b26 (.N2(addr[26]), .pN1(paddr[26]), .WR(wr));
BIDIR b25 (.N2(addr[25]), .pN1(paddr[25]), .WR(wr));
BIDIR b24 (.N2(addr[24]), .pN1(paddr[24]), .WR(wr));
BIDIR b23 (.N2(addr[23]), .pN1(paddr[23]), .WR(wr));
BIDIR b22 (.N2(addr[22]), .pN1(paddr[22]), .WR(wr));
BIDIR b21 (.N2(addr[21]), .pN1(paddr[21]), .WR(wr));
BIDIR b20 (.N2(addr[20]), .pN1(paddr[20]), .WR(wr));
BIDIR b19 (.N2(addr[19]), .pN1(paddr[19]), .WR(wr));
BIDIR b18 (.N2(addr[18]), .pN1(paddr[18]), .WR(wr));
BIDIR b17 (.N2(addr[17]), .pN1(paddr[17]), .WR(wr));
BIDIR b16 (.N2(addr[16]), .pN1(paddr[16]), .WR(wr));
BIDIR b15 (.N2(addr[15]), .pN1(paddr[15]), .WR(wr));
BIDIR b14 (.N2(addr[14]), .pN1(paddr[14]), .WR(wr));
BIDIR b13 (.N2(addr[13]), .pN1(paddr[13]), .WR(wr));
BIDIR b12 (.N2(addr[12]), .pN1(paddr[12]), .WR(wr));
BIDIR b11 (.N2(addr[11]), .pN1(paddr[11]), .WR(wr));
BIDIR b10 (.N2(addr[10]), .pN1(paddr[10]), .WR(wr));
BIDIR b9  (.N2(addr[ 9]), .pN1(paddr[ 9]), .WR(wr));
BIDIR b8  (.N2(addr[ 8]), .pN1(paddr[ 8]), .WR(wr));
BIDIR b7  (.N2(addr[ 7]), .pN1(paddr[ 7]), .WR(wr));
BIDIR b6  (.N2(addr[ 6]), .pN1(paddr[ 6]), .WR(wr));
BIDIR b5  (.N2(addr[ 5]), .pN1(paddr[ 5]), .WR(wr));
BIDIR b4  (.N2(addr[ 4]), .pN1(paddr[ 4]), .WR(wr));
BIDIR b3  (.N2(addr[ 3]), .pN1(paddr[ 3]), .WR(wr));
BIDIR b2  (.N2(addr[ 2]), .pN1(paddr[ 2]), .WR(wr));
BIDIR b1  (.N2(addr[ 1]), .pN1(paddr[ 1]), .WR(wr));
BIDIR b0  (.N2(addr[ 0]), .pN1(paddr[ 0]), .WR(wr));

endmodule
```

Example 14 - Verilog-1995 structural top-level ASIC model with multiple I/O pad instantiations

VHDL engineers have been able to use two generate for-loops to instantiate the same 32 address and 16 data pad models. With Verilog-2001, Verilog engineers can now use similarly simple generate for-loops to instantiate the 32 address and 16 data pads, as shown in Example 15.

```
module top_pads2 (pdata, paddr, pctl1, pctl2, pctl3, pclk);
   inout  [15:0] pdata;                    // pad data bus
   input  [31:0] paddr;                    // pad addr bus
   input         pctl1, pctl2, pctl3, pclk; // pad signals
   wire   [15:0] data;                     // data bus
   wire   [31:0] addr;                     // addr bus

   main_blk u1 (.data(data), .addr(addr),
                .sig1(ctl1), .sig2(ctl2), .sig3(ctl3), .clk(clk));

   genvar i;

   IBUF c4 (.O(ctl3), .pI(pctl3));
   IBUF c3 (.O(ctl2), .pI(pctl2));
   IBUF c2 (.O(ctl1), .pI(pctl1));
   IBUF c1 (.O( clk), .pI( pclk));

   generate for (i=0; i<16; i=i+1) begin: dat
     IBUF i1 (.O(data[i]), .pI(pdata[i]));

   generate for (i=0; i<32; i=i+1) begin: adr
     BIDIR b1 (.N2(addr[i]), .pN1(paddr[i]), .WR(wr));

endmodule
```

> Generated instance names
> dat[0].i1 to dat[15].i1

> Generated instance names
> adr[0].b1 to adr[31].b1

Example 15 - Top-level ASIC model with address and data I/O pads instantiated using a generate statement

For simple contiguous one-dimensional arrays, the array of instance construct is even easier to use and has a more intuitive syntax. Finally, simulation and synthesis vendors are now starting to support the Verilog-1995 Array of Instance construct that makes placement of 32 consecutively named instances possible with an easy instantiation by bus names as ports and applying a range to the instance name as shown in Example 16.

```
module top_pads3 (pdata, paddr, pctl1, pctl2, pctl3, pclk);
   inout  [15:0] pdata;                    // pad data bus
   input  [31:0] paddr;                    // pad addr bus
   input         pctl1, pctl2, pctl3, pclk; // pad signals
   wire   [15:0] data;                     // data bus
   wire   [31:0] addr;                     // addr bus

   main_blk u1 (.data(data), .addr(addr),
                .sig1(ctl1), .sig2(ctl2), .sig3(ctl3), .clk(clk));

   IBUF c4 (.O(ctl3), .pI(pctl3));
   IBUF c3 (.O(ctl2), .pI(pctl2));
   IBUF c2 (.O(ctl1), .pI(pctl1));
   IBUF c1 (.O( clk), .pI( pclk));

   IBUF i[15:0] (.O(data), .pI(pdata));

   BIDIR b[31:0] (.N2(addr), .pN1(paddr), .WR(wr));

endmodule
```

> Arrayed instance
> names i[15] to i[0]

> Arrayed instance
> names b[31] to b[0]

Example 16 - Top-level ASIC model with address and data I/O pads instantiated using arrays of instance

7.   Conclusions

The Verilog-2001 enhancements are coming. These enhancements will increase the efficiency and productivity of Verilog designers.

8.   Honorable Mention

Although the Behavioral Task Force benefited from the expertise and contributions of numerous synthesis experts, a particular honorable mention must go out to Kurt Baty of WSFDB.

Kurt has experience designing some 50 ASICs and has written a significant number of Design Ware models that are used in Synopsys synthesis tools. Kurt complains that he had to write all of the models using VHDL because Verilog lacked a few of the key features that are required to make parameterized models. Kurt's insight into the 1995 Verilog limitations lead to enhancements that will make future IP model creation not only doable, but also easier to do in Verilog than it was in VHDL.

9.   References

[1]   IEEE Standard Hardware Description Language Based on the Verilog Hardware Description
        Language, IEEE Std P1364/D5

[2]   Douglas L. Perry, *VHDL*, McGraw-Hill, Inc., 1994, p. 1.

[3]   IEEE Standard Hardware Description Language Based on the Verilog Hardware Description
        Language, IEEE Computer Society, IEEE Std 1364-1995

[4]   www.chris.spear.net

[5]   Don Mills and Clifford E. Cummings, "RTL Coding Styles That Yield Simulation and Synthesis
        Mismatches," *SNUG'99 (Synopsys Users Group San Jose, CA, 1999) Proceedings*, section-TA2
        (1st paper), March 1999.

[6]   Clifford E. Cummings, "'full_case parallel_case", the Evil Twins of Verilog Synthesis,' *SNUG'99
        Boston (Synopsys Users Group Boston, MA, 1999) Proceedings*, section-FA1 (2nd paper),
        October 1999.

10. Revision 1.2 - What Changed?

The ANSI style ports in previous versions of this paper incorrectly showed semi-colons between port declarations and between the parameter list and the port list. These errors were fixed in this version of the document.

11. Author & Contact Information

Cliff Cummings, President of Sunburst Design, Inc., is an independent EDA consultant and trainer with 20 years of ASIC, FPGA and system design experience and ten years of Verilog, synthesis and methodology training experience.

Mr. Cummings, a member of the IEEE 1364 Verilog Standards Group (VSG) since 1994, chaired the VSG Behavioral Task Force, which was charged with proposing enhancements to the Verilog language. Mr. Cummings is also a member of the IEEE Verilog Synthesis Interoperability Working Group and the Accellera SystemVerilog Standardization Group

Mr. Cummings holds a BSEE from Brigham Young University and an MSEE from Oregon State University.

E-mail Address: cliffc@sunburst-design.com
This paper can be downloaded from the web site: www.sunburst-design.com/papers

(Data accurate as of December 17th, 2001)

Chapter 3

Advanced ASIC Sign-Off Features of IEEE 1076.4-2000 And Standards updates to Verilog and SDF

Steve Wadsworth

Dennis Brophy

AMI Semiconductor, Pocatello, Idaho

Model Technology, Inc

1. INTRODUCTION TO HDL LANGUAGE STANDARDS

In the ASIC industry there is much discussion about design complexity, validation cycle time, tools, and overall design methodology. There are concerns that today's Electronic Design Automation (EDA) tools and standard organizations cannot keep pace with the requirements placed upon them by growing design complexity. This gap is expected to widen even further with each advancement in semiconductor technology that reduces feature size and allows for even larger, faster, and more complex designs. Intellectual Property (IP), large megacells, cores, and a myriad of rapid design methodologies will only continue to put more pressure on these standards and design tools.

In the late 70's and 80's ASIC and tool suppliers created their own defacto standards for the generation and verification of designs. Although each had great ideas, communication between the various tools was either painful or nonexistent. Standards organizations were created to define and standardize languages, interfaces, protocols, etc. thus enabling the user community and tool vendors to communicate together and make great strides in technology. The areas which language standards address is the language constructs, verification, and in some cases the ability to interface with other tools.

1.1 Language construct

Language construct includes the many forms of the language from the most abstract to the low level detail. This is the means in which a user can define the functionality of the IP and then through the use of a tool transform it into other forms until eventually a physical version of the IP can be created.

1.2 Language Verification

Verification requirements to validate the functionality and performance of the designs continue to push the standards. It has long been considered that analog designs are difficult and that developing a digital design simply meant defining logic functions and making sure timing requirements are met. This is no longer the case since signals in deep submicron digital designs are beginning to take on more analog characteristics. It is becoming more important to have a closer link between circuit simulators and other validation processes, especially with designs that are not fully synchronous. As long as designers develop asynchronous circuits and

A. Mignotte et al. (eds.), System on Chip Design Languages, 35–42.

design complexities continues to rise, verification accuracy will continue to be a major focus in the industry. Standards must continue to ensure the languages rise to the task.

1.3   Language Interfaces

Language interfaces allow 3rd party productivity tools to assist in the design and verification process. This allows other tools to interrogate and modify the status of the design by providing direct access to the language database.

This paper addresses the progress made with the three language standards, Verilog, VHDL (VITAL), and SDF (Standard Delay Format) standards. Both authors have been involved with and provided much direction to the furthering of these three standards for the design community. To better appreciate the new enhancements to each of these standards, which will be discussed in detail later in this article, it is important to provide a brief history of each of them.

VERILOG

In the early 80's, an Electronic Design Automation (EDA) company developed Verilog as a design and verification language. In an effort to standardize it's use in the industry, it was later put into the public domain under the direction of Open Verilog International (OVI). In 1995 after several years of work by a group of dedicated users, tool vendors and ASIC Vendors in the industry, IEEE 1364-1995 was born. Since that initial release some of the original group and several others began addressing necessary changes and is in the final balloting stages of releasing IEEE1363-2001. Early in the development of the new standard the chairman of the standards group created three task forces to better focus on each aspect of the language. The Behavioral Task Force addressed all language constructs of the language, the ASIC Task Force addressed all timing and modeling related aspects of the language, and the PLI Task Force addressed all PLI and VPI interfaces issues within the language. They also incorporated all the required changes to the PLI as a result of changes made by the Behavioral and ASIC taskforces. The responsibility of each of these task forces was to address all known deficiencies in the language within their respective focus and bring solutions to the general standards group for review and ratification. The list errata and enhancements to the language came from both outside and inside the standards organization from concerned users.

VHDL first became the IEEE standard IEEE 1076. The language covered well both design documentation and functionality, however, it did not have the accuracy for validating gate level designs. A group was formed to address the accuracy issue and thus the VHDL Initiate Towards ASIC Accuracy (VITAL) extension to the language became the IEEE standard 1076.4 in 1995. Like Verilog there were some anomalies and necessary enhancements that were required for the language keep up with the demands of the technology and thus a group of users, EDA vendors, and ASIC vendors became the team to make the changes that have been ratified in the VITAL 2000 release. Unlike the Verilog standards group, which addressed the various facets of the language, this group only focused on the timing and modeling aspects of the language. VITAL standard was the result of significant contributions from premier ASIC and EDA vendors such as LSI, TI, AMI Semiconductor, Motorola, Cadence, Synopsys, Mentor Graphics, MTI, and GDA technologies over the last 4 years.

In the ASIC design flow the first level of validation is performed using an estimated for the wiring interconnect. Once the actual physical design has been completed the actual wiring related delays are annotated into the design for accurate final verification. Like the early proprietary languages the format for these delay files were not standardized which caused users to perform numerous translations from one form in the design process. SDF provides a means for adding the appropriate signal propagation delay changes of each design elements caused by other elements in the design such as gate and wiring loads. Open Verilog International (OVI) first adopted SDF as a pseudo standard, which were improved to meet the growing requirements. In 1997 an IEEE working group was established to move OVI SDF standard version 3.0 with some enhancements to the IEEE standard 1497. The Verilog and VITAL standards have been enhanced those languages to take advantage of these new features.

The users of the languages were heard and as a result numerous changes were made to all three standards in an effort to address those needs. A brief list of improvements to each of these standards will be addressed in the following text.

2. VERILOG

A noted earlier, The Verilog standards committee was comprised of three task forces to better focus on each of the language issues. Overall, 33 major enhancements were added to the language and numerous errata was corrected.

2.1 BTF ENHANCEMENTS

The Behavioral Task Force added many enhancements to meet the HDL design requirements. Some of the enhancements were already provided in VHDL, which now provides users the ability to select their language of choice without compromise of capability. Some of these enhancements include Configurations, Generate Statements, Constant Functions, Indexed Vector Part Selects, Multi-dimensional Arrays, Array Bit and Part Selects, Signed Arithmetic Extensions, Power Operator, Re-entrant Tasks and Recursive Functions, Comma-separated Sensitivity List, Combinational Logic Sensitivity, Automatic Width Extension Past 32 bits, Default Nets with Continuous Assigns, Disable Default Net, Declarations. Other additions included explicit In-line Parameter Passing, Combined Port/Data Type Declarations, ANSI-style Port Lists, Reg Declaration With Initialization, Enhanced Conditional, Compilation, File and Line Compiler Directives, Attributes, Standard Random Number Generator, Enhanced Invocation Option Tests, Enhanced PLA Modeling, Accurate BND with Subsections. File I/O was enhanced to provide similar to the power to that of the popular "C" language. In an effort to reduce confusion of the term "Register" it was changed To "Variable" in the new standard.

2.2 ATF ENHANCEMENTS

The ASIC Task Force (ATF) focused primarily on increasing the verification accuracy of the language and increased functionality. Negative-Preemptive Pulse Detection was added to compliment positive preemptive glitch detection. New Timing Constraint Checks such as $removal (removal of asynchronous signals), $recrem (recovery/removal of asynchronous signals), $timeskew (unidirectional time based skew check), and $fullskew (bi-directional time based skew check). Negative Timing Constraint capability was added to address complex timing relationships in sequential elements. SDF (IEEE 1497) support was clarified in the language to formalize its already implied use. This includes all SDF constructs including the newly added label construct, which extends the ability to annotate outside the current specparam limitation. Multi-Source Interconnect definitions was added to the language to formalize the way complex interconnect networks are handled during SDF annotation. VCD support was extended to add such capabilities as dump port, strength, time,

2.3 PLI ENHANCEMENTS

The charter of the PLI Task Force was to correct any errata found in 1364-95 and make necessary enhancements to the VPI (PLI 2.0) sections of the LRM. They also implemented all changes to the VPI as a result of changes made by Behavioral and ASIC task forces. Errata for PLI 1.0 (TF and ACC routines) were also addressed. Over 200 errata/enhancements were made to PLI & VPI as a result.

3.   VITAL

As discussed earlier, the main language and behavioral constructs of the VHDL language are covered in the IEEE 1076 LRM standard. The VITAL group addresses the same types of issues as the Verilog ATF group. One main difference between the two languages is that Verilog LRM provides definitions for the behavioral of the simulator in the LRM. In VITAL both the definition and actual working code is provided to the users and developers as a package of routines. Developers are not required to use the supplied package, but are required to provide the same functionality and capability as found in the standard. Some of the enhancements to VITAL 2000 addressed not only enhancements to this package, but also addressed some known anomalies.

All changes to the VITAL 1995 standard came from formal Issue Reports that came from the users. All issue reports were reviewed and those that could be incorporated into the standard were. Unless an anomaly was being correct in the language, all other changes to the language were made to ensure backward compatibility with the existing standard. Some key improvements to the standard was Multi-source interconnect, Improved Negative Timing Constraints (NTC), Skew Timing Checks, Improvements to setup/hold timing checks, and Improvements to glitch handling routines, and corrected anomalies in the Internal Timing Check (ITC) routines. Level 1 compliant skew check procedures are now supported for both inphase and outphase bi-directional skews relationships. The modeler now has the control over how the simulator selects the default path delay in the event none of the path conditions are met. Accurate pulse modeling has been added to provide extra verification accuracy.

3.1   VITAL ASIC Memory Models

Memory modeling was added to VITAL as a consistent way to model memories and provide the increased simulation performance using Level one models like those of other Vital Models. This also provides an easier means for the modeler to define the behavior and timing of the model without using more behavioral constructs. Routines similar to those used for combinational and sequential timing elements were added to the language to support memories. Support for bit/sub-word/word addressability, timing and functional violations, corruption handling, range checks, contention policies, memory initialization and dump via files, negative timing constraints, and SDF backannotation including IORETAIN are all included. There is also support for both scalar and vectored interfaces.

4.   SDF IEEE 1497

The IEEE 1497 standards committee used as it's starting point the OVI SDF 3.0 standard and added to it the proposed labels construct that had been proposed to OVI before the IEEE standards work began. Also, a complete review of the document was performed to ensure compliance with IEEE guidelines and that the standard would meet the needs for the next 5 years of the industry. In the earlier versions of SDF all known propagation and timing check key words were defined in the standard. As time went on new timing requirements were needed that needed to be addressed in the language. The labels construct now provides that capability by allowing the user to define any timing related parameter as a name value pair. These can then be incorporated in any of the other languages that support this standard.

5.   KEY ISSUES COVERED IN DETAIL

To cover all of the issues that are covered in all three standards in detail would take more than the space allotted for all of the papers in this conference. For a complete discussion on all of the issues on these standards, a copy of each LRM Language Reference Manuals (LRM) can be obtained from IEEE. The following provides some more detailed information on a few of the key issues that were common to both Verilog and VITAL.

5.1   Pulse Filtering

Simulators designed for validating deep submicron ASIC devices are continually being upgraded, as new accuracy is required. One accuracy issue becoming more important due to shrinking technologies is pulse filtering. Most simulators, including those compliant with VITAL and Verilog, allow for two different pulse filtering modes: inertial and transport. The first mode, which is better suited to older technologies, is "inertial". This mode filters out all input transitions that are smaller than the gate propagation value. It was assumed that it takes a certain amount of inertia (i.e. the time it takes for the input to propagate to the output) for the input transition to have an effect on the gates output. Any pulses smaller than the propagation delay were filtered out. As technologies have continued to shrink, transport delay mode has become more important. All pulses, no matter how short, are allowed to propagate to the device output and many simulators allow the propagated pulse to contain "X" state to indicate ambiguity in the signal value. This is important because during this region of uncertainty, the actual amplitude and duration of the signal is unclear and depending on the technology can cause the devices to fail. These problems can result in either non-functional silicon or yield problems when these glitches drive direct action signals on sequential elements such as clocks, resets, and sets.

Any time another event is scheduled on a device output before an already scheduled event has a chance to mature, the second event is considered to be preemptive. When the second event is scheduled after the first event, it is a positive preemptive event and when it is scheduled prior to the first event it is a negative preemptive event.

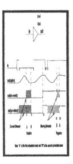

Figure 1

Figure 1 shows the results of narrow glitches being injected into a simple buffer. For this example, all delays are being represented with simple values. The waveform includes the input, SPICE, on-event, and on-detect representations of the output result. VITAL (and the latest Verilog standard) allow for both on-event and on-detect pulse propagation. The first condition is a positive preemptive event since the second event is scheduled to occur after the first. If this signal were driving a clock input of a sequential device and the amplitude and duration met the criteria for minimum clock pulse width, there would be a potential for clocking in new unwanted data into the device. Even SPICE simulations using a 0.8µ technology have indicated that narrow glitches around 80% of the required signal width can in fact cause problems in sequential devices. The problem only gets worse with deep submicron technologies.

The second narrow pulse causes a negative preemptive glitch since the second event is scheduled prior to the first unmatured event, the new event is negative preemptive. Unlike the positive preemptive pulse, which is being caught by VITAL 1995, and Verilog 1995 simulators today, the negative preemptive pulses have been ignored. As shown by the SPICE waveform, both events are real and they are analog, not digital, in nature. The device delays given to the logic simulators ensure that the device output level is at the level to guarantee that it can effect the input of the gates it drives. In reality this output begins affecting it's driving gate much sooner and all pulses must be considered for accurate simulation results.

This example is very simple and probably not as likely to happen as the situation caused on multiple input gates such as NAND, AND, ORs, NORs used to create decoded signal events. In these cases nearly simultaneously switching inputs can cause the outputs to swing in one direction only to have another inputs transition cause it to swing back to its original logic level. In fully synchronous circuits this condition is not a significant problem, but in circuits that contain some asynchronous parts, it can become a real problem.

As mentioned earlier, circuit performance and signal immunity have increased the need to detect all circuit anomalies, especially glitches. Signals within digital circuits are becoming more analog in nature all the time. Slow slew rate of input signals, glitches, interconnect dominance on the total delay, and narrow pulse width requirements for deep submicron sequential elements demand increased design accuracy. Due to the efforts of the Verilog and VITAL standards committees the languages now have full glitch detection capabilities in the new standards.

5.2   Negative Timing Constraints

Sequential devices not only have propagation delays, but certain timing relationships between various primary inputs must be met for stable operation. In some cases, these relationships can become negative, as in the case of hold times. This is the time that the data input must stay in a stable state from the active transition of the clock. Depending on the way the device was built and modeled, this could become a critical relationship to maintain. Since digital simulators by nature do not maintain negative time, it is common practice to move all negative values to zero. Device performance and accuracy requirements have now required that simulators maintain this relationship and make the appropriate adjustments to all the remaining timing relationships.

5.3   Delay Modeling

Delay modeling has evolved over the years in order to accurately reflect signal delays. In older technologies, assumptions such as sharp signal edges, simple linear equations, and lumped wire interconnect were sufficient. With the signals looking more like "analog" sinusoidal waveforms and with the increasing role that interconnect is playing in the overall delay, it is important to have complex modeling equations for the delays.

5.4   Signal Skew

Signal skew has normally been associated with a design's master clocking scheme, but can also include certain scan devices and other complex functions with special clock requirements. For this reason signal skew must be an integral part of the verification process.

Signal skew is the amount of time allowed for one clock signal to be shifted either in or out of phase from another clock edge. If the skew is out of tolerance, complementary devices in a memory structure can either become both on, or both off causing either signal contention at the node or cause it to float. Both cases can cause the circuit to malfunction.

5.5   Interconnect

In older technologies a lumped capacitance for all device receivers on a net was considered sufficient. As technology has shrunk, wiring interconnect has become a significant portion of the overall delay. For deep submicron technologies the time required for a signal to propagate from the signal driver to its receiver is at least as long as the device's internal switching time.

A whole new approach is now required to accurately reflect the part that interconnects plays in the overall delay. One approach being considered by ASIC vendors is called Elmore delay. This delay model takes into account the individual R/C (resistance and capacitance) for each of the wiring segments. Another issue facing verification accuracy is the multiple receiver/driver scenario. This is commonly referred to as the "H" networks since each network in the design can have multiple receivers and drivers connected to a common net. Figure 2 shows the changes to in interconnect handling changes from the 1995 to the 2000 standard. VITAL 95 verses 2000. Taking into account the differences between Verilog and VITAL, the Verilog LRM closely matches the VITAL 2000 standard for "H" network interconnect.

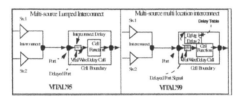

Figure 2

This is common within large clock or bus networks in which each receiver can be driven by multiple sources and the actual device delays and individual interconnect delays are different depending on which driver(s) is/are active. Controlling Interconnect delays also plays an important role in balancing clock trees.

Current Status of the IEEE Standards

IEEE 1497 (SDF) Completed balloting and awaiting Revcom approval.

IEEE 1076.4 (VITAL) Completed Revcom approval September 2000

IEEE 1364 (Verilog) Completed second Ballot January 2001 and plan for a March Revcom release.

6.   CONCLUSION

It is clear that design complexity and process technology are outpacing the available tools. Various design conferences such as DAC and HDLCON have featured much discussion on this issue over the last several years. The design and verification process cannot be compromised no matter how much pressure there is to get it out quickly.

Each new generation of technology will continue to bring with it new unfounded challenges that will likely require new standards to emerge. Close relationships must exist between the standards committees, Silicon Vendors, and Tool Vendors and users will be essential to keep up with the demands placed on this industry. IEEE's policy of requiring standards to be reballoted at least every 5 years, will not be enough to ensure these standards meet the current needs of the industry. Silicon and tool vendors must work closely together with the standards committees to ensure the standards keep pace.

7.   ABOUT THE AUTHORS

Steve Wadsworth has 20 years of industry experience in test, design, EDA tool management, Manager of Library Development, and is currently the Manager of Memory and Library Methodology for AMI

Semiconductor, Inc. in Pocatello Idaho. He is the chair of the ASIC Task Force (sub group under IEEE 1364) which is responsible for all timing aspects of the Verilog language. He is also a member of the VITAL TAG committee (IEEE 1076.4) and the IEEE 1497 standards committee. He has been the only individual involved in all three standards committees for the 2000 revisions of the standards. This helped to ensure the needed capabilities were in both languages such that the users could choose either HDL language without compromise to verification and functional capability.

Dennis Brophy has 21 years experience in the EDA industry. Currently he is the Director of Strategic Business Development at Model Technology Inc. He is the Chairman of Accellera and has been the acting chair of VITAL TAG committee responsible for VITAL 2000 standard.

ANALOG SYSTEM MODELING AND DESIGN

Chapter 4

VHDL-AMS Model of a Synchronous Oscillator including Phase Noise

A. Fakhfakh, N. Milet-Lewis, J-B. Bégueret, H. Lévi

IXL Laboratory - Bordeaux I University. 351 cours de la Libération, 33405 Talence France. fakhfakh@ixl.u-bordeaux.fr

Abstract: Synchronous oscillators are a class of oscillators used in the design of frequency synthesisers due to their good characteristics in term of phase noise and frequency multiplication. A VHDL-AMS synchronous oscillator model has been developed, including phase noise effects. Its performances have been compared to a 2.4 GHz synchronous oscillator implemented on a 0.8 µm BiCMOS technology.

Key words: VHDL-AMS, Behavioural Modelling, Synchronous Oscillator, Phase Noise

1. INTRODUCTION

High performance portable RF communication systems impose great challenges in term of phase noise. Frequency synthesisers are key function blocks for the design of such systems. They allow several channels selection with a single frequency reference. Synchronous oscillators are an alternative way to design low phase noise frequency synthesisers. These circuits are complex to simulate using transistor level simulators; first due to the extensively long runtime required to capture the characteristics and second because simulations can diverge, impeding the adjustment of system parameters. Behavioural modelling technique offers a solution to solve these problems. This technique uses standard modelling languages such as VHDL-AMS.

To study phase noise effects, one problem must be solved. The response of oscillators and frequency synthesisers is simulated in transient domain whereas measurement instruments (spectrum analysers) and RF simulators (SpectreRF, EldoRF [1]) provide noise spectrums which are frequency dependent. Therefore, we need to elaborate a noise modelling technique for transient simulations and to develop relationships between frequency and transient noise characteristics in order to compare behavioural simulations and measurement results.

In this paper, we present a VHDL-AMS model elaborated for a synchronous oscillator. It is simulated with ADVanceMS simulator [2]. Its performances in term of tracking range and phase noise are compared to both transistor level simulations and measurement results.

A. Mignotte et al. (eds.), System on Chip Design Languages, 45–58.

2.   SYNCHRONOUS OSCILLATOR

A synchronous oscillator (SO) is a free running oscillator, which oscillates at its free running frequency without external applied signal. When such an input signal is applied, and if its frequency is near the free running frequency, then the oscillator is locked on the input signal. The SO can also be synchronised on both harmonics and sub-harmonics of the input signal [3] . This characteristic offers a great interest as it is applied to design low phase noise frequency synthesisers. Figure 1 shows an example of SO based frequency synthesiser design.

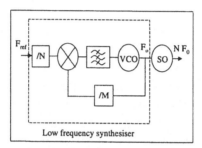

Figure 1. SO based frequency synthesiser

A 2.4 GHz synchronous oscillator has been fully implemented on a 0.8 μm BiCMOS technology. It is able to lock on a sub-harmonic external signal and its locking range is about 40 MHz for 400 MHz injected signal [4] . It consists on a COLPITTS oscillator. Its simplified schematic is shown on figure 2.

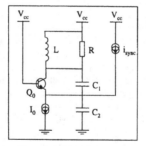

Figure 2. COLPITTS oscillator

Badets [4] [5] have proposed a general theory of oscillator synchronisation. When applied to our COLPITTS circuit, we obtain two expressions given the free running frequency f_0 and the tracking range Δf.

$$f_0 = \frac{1}{2\pi} \sqrt{\frac{1 + \left(\dfrac{L.g_c}{C_2' + C_1}\right)(g_m + g_\pi)}{L\left(C_\mu + \dfrac{C_1.C_2'}{C_1 + C_2'}\right)}} \qquad (1)$$

with $C_2' = C_2 + C_{dg} + C_{db} + C_\pi$

where g_m is the transconductance, g_π the base emitter conductance, g_c the base collector conductance, C_μ, C_π, C_{dg} and C_{db} are respectively the base collector, the base emitter, the drain gate and the drain bulk capacitors.

$$\Delta f = 2\frac{I_n}{V_0}\sqrt{F_b^2 + F_g^2} \qquad (2)$$

where $F_g = \frac{1}{8\pi^2}\frac{1}{f_0}\frac{g_c}{C_\mu(C_2' + C_1) + C_2'C_1}$

and $F_b = \frac{1}{4\pi}\left(\frac{1}{C_1 + C_2'}\right)^2\left[\dfrac{Lg_c(g_m + g_\pi)}{1 + \dfrac{Lg_c(g_m + g_\pi)}{C_1 + C_2'}} + \dfrac{C_1^2}{C_\mu + \dfrac{C_1C_2'}{C_1 + C_2'}}\right]$ F_g and F_b are called compliance factors and V_0

is the voltage amplitude across the load. The synchronisation injected signal I_{sync} is a periodic pulse waveform and I_n represents its nth harmonic amplitude. Fourrier series develop- ment gives the following expression for I_n:

$$I_n = \frac{2I_0}{an^2\pi^2}[1 - \cos(a\,n\,\pi)] \qquad (3)$$

where I_0 is the pulse amplitude, T the signal period and aT the pulse duration.

3. PHASE NOISE AND JITTER

The synchronous oscillator is simulated in the transient domain where the phase noise is expressed by a jitter. It represents the random fluctuations of the output signal frequency due to the noise sources induced in the electrical devices of the circuit. It is illustrated by figure3.

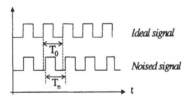

Figure 3. Illustration of the jitter

We find in the literature many definitions to characterise the jitter. The cycle jitter ΔT_c is defined as the rms value of the timing error ΔT_n that is the difference between the mean signal period T_0 and the nth fluctuated period T_n [8] :

$$\Delta T_c = \lim_{N \to \infty}\sqrt{\frac{1}{N}\sum_{n=1}^{N}\Delta T_n^2} \qquad (4)$$

with $\Delta T_n = T_n - T_0$

To compare transient simulation and measurement results, we need to develop relationships between frequency and transient noise characteristics. We have exposed in [7] the basic theory of noise in oscillators and how to convert jitter into phase noise. If we only consider white noise sources, the cycle jitter ΔT_c is related to the single sideband noise spectral density $L(f_m)$ by the following expression [8] [9] :

$$\Delta T_c = \frac{f_m}{f_0^{3/2}} \sqrt{2} \sqrt{L(f_m)} \qquad (5)$$

where f_0 is the mean signal frequency and f_m the offset frequency from f_0.

4. MODELLING METHOD

We have developed a VHDL-AMS model for the COLPITTS oscillator shown on figure 4. It is given in appendix.

The synchronous oscillator is driven by a sinusoidal periodic waveform. A pulse generator block permits to generate the synchronisation current I_{sync}.

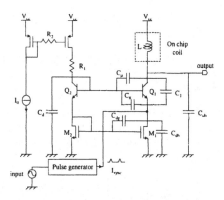

Figure 4. Modelled COLPITTS oscillator

The model is decomposed in three main parts. The first part consists in detecting the input signal frequency.

We calculate in the second part characteristics that will permit to generate the output signal. We start with calculating the oscillator free running frequency and the tracking range. Then, we compute the synchronisation harmonic and the output signal frequency.

We have also modelled the phase noise of the synchronous oscillator that affects the output frequency. We will expose in the following our modelling technique.

In the third part of the model, the output signal is generated.

4.1 Input period capture

The first process of the VHDL-AMS model (see appendix), called *input_period_capture*, determines the input signal period. It detects each input threshold crossing by using the instruction *vin'above (level)*. The difference between two successive threshold crossings gives the input signal period. This approach may be applied for any frequency detection. The input pulsation ω_{in} is then deduced from the input frequency f_{in}.

4.2 Synchronisation harmonic determination

The free running frequency f_0 of the SO is calculated by applying the expression (1) obtained from theory [4] [5] [6] . To determine the synchronisation harmonic, we first calculate the ratio *"y"* between f_0 and the input frequency f_{in}. The synchronisation harmonic range *"n"* is obtained by rounding *"y"* to the nearest integer value by using the function *round*. If the ratio is less then 0.5, we consider *"n"* equal to 1 as shown by the process *sub_harmonic* in the VHDL-AMS model.

4.3 Tracking range calculation

To obtain the tracking range, the amplitude of the synchronisation current is first calculated by applying the expression (3). We then calculate the compliance factors F_g and F_b and we deduce the tracking range given by the expression (2).

4.4 Output frequency determination

Before determining the output signal frequency, we should test if the synchronous oscillator is either synchronised or not.

The interval $[f_{in\text{-}min}, f_{in\text{-}max}]$ corresponds to the input frequency range that synchronises the oscillator. $f_{in\text{-}min}$ and $f_{in\text{-}max}$ are calculated from the two following expressions :

$$f_{in\_min} = \frac{f_0 - 0.5 \, \Delta f}{n} \qquad (6)$$

$$f_{in\_max} = \frac{f_0 + 0.5 \, \Delta f}{n} \qquad (7)$$

The process *synchronisation_test* determines the output signal frequency. If the oscillator is synchronised, it is equal to the input frequency f_{in} multiplied by the synchronisation harmonic n. If not, it is equal to the free running frequency f_0.

4.5 Phase noise modelling technique

The phase noise affects the oscillator output frequency. Our phase noise modelling technique, exposed in [7] ,consists on randomly varying the output period by using a random signal generator.

The process *random_signal_generator* uses the function *uniform* that returns a pseudo-random number x with uniform distribution in the interval [0, 1]. This function is provided by the library *math_real* of ADVanceMS software. The process defines then the quantity *noise* and returns a random number in the interval [-A_{noise}, A_{noise}]. The parameter A_{noise} represents the maximum period perturbation.

There isn't any correlation between the generated numbers, so our random generator can be considered as a white noise source.

Finally, we randomly vary the half of the output period T, by applying the following expression :

$$T_{s\_noised} = 0.5\, T_s\, (1 + noise) \qquad (8)$$

4.6 Phase noise characterisation

To characterise the jitter, we have developed three processes to obtain respectively the cycle jitter, the cycle-to-cycle jitter and the sideband phase noise spectral density.

The process *cycle_jitter* calculates the following quantity :

$$cycle\_jit = \sqrt{\frac{1}{N}\sum_{n=1}^{N}\Delta T_n^2} \qquad (9)$$

When simulating the process with ADVanceMS software, we obtain the following characteristic:

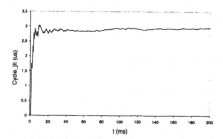

Figure 5. Cycle jitter simulation

The cycle jitter corresponds to the value of the quantity *cycle_jit* after a long simulation runtime. In practice, it is obtained after a hundred of output signal period.

The process *power_density* deduces from the expression (6) the single sideband phase noise $L(f_m)$. The single sideband phase noise spectrum is obtained by varying f_m value.

4.7 Output signal generation

In the last part of the model, we generate the output signal. It consists in a sinusoidal periodic signal which frequency is that calculated in the process *synchronisation_test*.

Processes *input_period_capture* and *sub_ harmonic* are activated at each input threshold crossing whereas processes *synchronisation_ test, random_signal_generator, cycle_jitter* and *power_density* are activated at the beginning of each noised half period.

5. MODEL SIMULATION RESULTS

Figures 6 and 7 depict the oscillator output signal obtained respectively from the transistor level simulation with spectreRF (CADENCE) and the behavioural simulation (ADVanceMS). The behavioural simulation doesn't introduce any settling time for oscillation. The oscillator is not synchronised; we can compare the free running frequency. It is about 2.389 GHz for both transistor level and behavioural simulations.

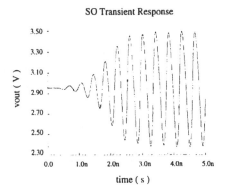

Figure 6. Transistor level simulation with spectreRF

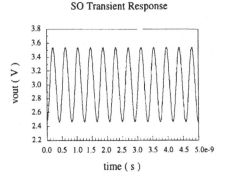

Figure 7. Model simulation with ADVanceMS

5.1 Tracking range simulation

Figure 8 shows the tracking range versus injected current. Two curves are compared : the first one is obtained with SpectreRF simulations and the second is the response of the VHDL-AMS model. We see the good agreement of the two depicted curves, particularly for current value less then 200 μA (injected current for the prototype is about 100μA). To increase accuracy of our behavioural simulation result for high injected current, we should modify the the expression (2) giving the tracking range [10].

For a fixed injected current value, we should do several simulations with SpectreRF before detecting the correspondent tracking range; whereas, we need to do only one simulation with ADVanceMS to obtain the same characteristic. Therefore, the simulation runtime gain is huge.

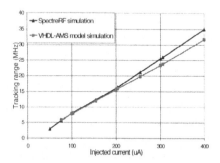

Figure 8. Tracking range simulation results

5.2   Phase noise

Figure 9 shows the single sideband phase noise spectral density obtained after several behavioural simulations. It is compared to both Spectre RF simulation and experimental results. We see a good agreement between the model simulation curve and the two other ones. This result validates our phase noise modelling methodology. However, we have only considered white noise sources when writing the VHDL-AMS model. To increase accuracy of our behavioural simulation results for low frequencies, we should consider the Flicker noise.

SpectreRF needs 157s before getting the phase noise characteristic; ADVanceMS needs only 29s. So the simulation runtime gain is about 5.5.

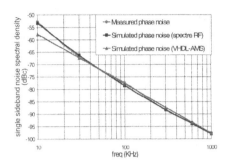

Figure 9. Free running phase noise spectrum

6. CONCLUSION

We have exposed a behavioural model of a synchronous oscillator using the standard language VHDL-AMS. We have detailed our modelling procedure to obtain a reliable model in term of tracking range and phase noise determination. The model performances have been compared to both transistor level simulations and measurement results. Our modelling technique can be adapted for other oscillator designs.

Further works will focus on the introduction of Flicker noise effect in oscillator behavioural models and the development of a behavioural model library for frequency synthesisers based on synchronous oscillator. Our goal will be the optimisation of the phase noise in such systems by using the behavioural simulation.

7. REFERENCES

[1] Reference manual, Cadence, 1997.

[2] ADVance MS reference manual, Mentor Graphics, 2000.

[3] C. Poole, *Subharmonic injection locking phenomena in synchronous oscillators*, Electronics Letters, October 1990, Vol. 26, N°21, pp. 1748-1750.

[4] F. Badets, Y. Deval, J.B. Begueret, A. Spataro, P. Fouillat, *A fully Integrated 3V 2.3 GHz Synchronous oscillator for WLAN application*, IEEE BCTM'99, Minneapolis, USA, September 99.

[5] F. Badets, Y. Deval, J.B. Begueret, A. Spataro, P. Fouillat, *A 2.7V, 2.64 GHz Fully Integrated Synchronous oscillator for WLAN applications*, procceding of the 25th European Solid-State Circuits Conference, Duisburg, Germany, September 99, pp. 210-213.

[6] R. Huntoon and Weiss, *Synchronisation of oscillators*, Proceedings of the I.R.E, December 1947, Vol. 35, pp. 1415-1423.

[7] A. Fakhfakh, N. Milet-Lewis, Y. Deval, H. Lévi, *Study and behavioural simulation of phase noise and jitter in oscillators*, ISCAS'2001, May 2001, Vol. 5, pp. 323-326.

[8] F. Herzel and B. Razavi. A study of oscillator jitter due to supply and substrate noise. *IEEE transactions on circuits and systems- II: analogue and digital signal processing*. Vol. 46, N° 1, january 1999.

[9] M. Takahashi, K. Ogawa and K. S. Kundert. VCO jitter simulation and its comparison with measurement. *Proceeding of the ASP-DAC'99* Asia and South Pacific Design Automation Conference, Vol. 1, p 85-88, 1999.

[10] F. Badets, *Contribution à l'étude de la synchronisation des oscillateurs: intégration des oscillateurs synchrones dans les systèmes radiofréquences en technologie Silicium*, Ph. D. thesis, Bordeaux 1 university, January 2000.

8.   APPENDIX :
VHDL-AMS MODEL

```
library disciplines;
use disciplines.electromagnetic_system.all;
library IEEE;
use IEEE.math_real.all;

----------------------------------------------------

entity synchronous_oscillator is
    generic(vdd : real := 3.0;
    L : real := 3.252e-9;
    c1 : real := 1.7e-12;
    c2 : real := 3.639e-12;
    cu : real := 441.0e-15;
    gm : real := 40.0e-3;
    gpi : real := 5.5e-3;
    gc : real := 6.54e-3;
    io : real := 2.0e-3;
    vo : real := 215.0e-3;
    vs : real := 540.0e-3;
    duration : real := 500.0e-12;
    level : real := 0.0;
    Anoise : real := 0.0013;
    fm : real := 600.0e3);
    port (terminal inp, inm, outp, outm: electrical);
end entity synchronous_oscillator;

----------------------------------------------------

                            -- COLPITTS oscillator --
architecture comp of synchronous_oscillator is
quantity vin across iin through inp to inm;
quantity vout across iout through outp to outm;
quantity wo : real;
quantity fo : real;
quantity Fg : real;
quantity Fb : real;
quantity cw : real;
quantity i : real;
quantity rang : real;
quantity fin_min : real := 4.0e8;
quantity fin_max : real := 4.0e8;
```

```
quantity fin : real := 4.0e8;
quantity win : real;
quantity a : real := 0.2;
quantity ts : real;
quantity ts_noised : real;
quantity fs_noised : real;
quantity counter : real := 0.0;
quantity t : real;
signal n : real := 1.0;
signal y : real := 6.0;
signal period : real := 2.5e-9;
signal t2 : real := 0.0;
signal fs : real := 2.4e9;
signal count : real := 1.0;
signal nois : real := 0.0;
signal jitter : real := 0.0;
signal counter_n1 : real := 2.085e-10;
signal t0 : real := 0.0;
signal vss : real := vdd;
signal M : real := 1.0;
signal sum_DTn2 : real := 0.0;
signal sum : real := 0.0;
signal DTn : real := 0.0;
signal DTn2 : real := 0.0;
signal cycle_jit : real := 0.0;
signal DTn1_n : real := 0.0;
signal cycle_c_jit : real := 0.0;
signal absolute_jit : real := 0.0;
signal square : real := 0.0;
signal Lphi : real := 0.0;


begin
iin == 0.0;
t == now;
counter == t - t0;
```

```
                                    -- Capture of the input signal period --
input_period_capture : process
begin
  wait until vin'above(level) = true;
  if count > 1.0 then
      t2 <= t;
      period <= t - t2;
  else
      t2 <= t;
```

```
    period <= 2.5e-9;
end if;
count <= count +1.0;
end process input_period_capture;
```

-- *calculation of the input pulsation* --

```
fin * period == 1.0;
win == MATH_2_PI * fin;
```

-- *calculation of the free running frequency* --

```
wo==sqrt(((gm+gpi)*(L*gc/(c1+c2))+1.0)*(1.0/L)*
(1.0/(cu+((c1*c2)/(c1+c2)))));
fo == 0.5*wo/MATH_PI;
```

-- *synchronisation harmonic determination* --

```
sub_harmonic : process
begin
wait until vin'above(level) = true;
y <= period * fo;
if y <= 0.5 then n <= 1.0;
else n <= round(y);
end if;
end process sub_harmonic;
```

-- *calculation of the synchronisation current* --

```
  a == duration*fin;
i * (a*n*n*MATH_PI*MATH_PI) == 2.0*io*(1.0-cos(a*n*MATH_PI));
```

-- *tracking range determination* --

-- *compliance factors* --

```
Fg == (1.0/(8.0*MATH_PI*MATH_PI))*(1.0/fo)*
(gc/(cu*(c1+c2)+c1*c2));
Fb == (1.0/(4.0*MATH_PI))*(1.0/((c1+c2)*
(c1+c2)))*(L*gc*(gm+gpi)/((1.0+L*gc*(gm+gpi)/
(c1+c2)))+c1*c1/(cu+c1*c2/(c1+c2)));
```

-- *tracking range* --

```
cw == sqrt(Fg*Fg+Fb*Fb);
rang == 2.0*(i/vo)*cw;
```

-- *output frequency determination* --

```
fin_min * n == (fo-0.5*rang);
fin_max * n == (fo+0.5*rang);
synchronisation_test : process
```

```
begin
  wait until counter'above(ts_noised) = true;
  if fin > fin_min and fin < fin_max then
        fs <= fin * n;
     jitter <= 0.0;
     else  fs <= fo;
     jitter <= nois;
     end if;
end process synchronisation_test;
```

                                    -- output period calculation --
```
ts * fs == 1.0;
```

                                      – phase noise modelling –

                                      -- random signal generation --
```
random_signal_generator : process
  variable seed1 : positive := 19823;
  variable seed2 : positive := 124;
  variable x : real;
begin
  wait until counter'above(ts_noised) = true;
  UNIFORM(seed1, seed2, x);
  nois <= Anoise*2.0*(x - 0.5);
end process random_signal_generator;
```

                                    -- noised half period calculation --
```
ts_noised == 0.5*ts*(1.0+jitter);
```

                                    -- phase noise characterisation --

                                    -- cycle jitter determination --
```
cycle_jitter : process
begin
  wait until counter'above(ts_noised) = true;
  DTn <= counter -  0.5 * ts;
  DTn2 <= DTn**2.0;
  sum_DTn2 <= sum_DTn2 + DTn2;
  cycle_jit <= sqrt(sum_DTn2/M);
  M <= M + 1.0;
     t0 <= t;
end process cycle_jitter ;
```

                                    -- power density calculation --
```
power_density : process
```

```
begin
  wait until counter'above(ts_noised) = true;
  if cycle_jit > 0.0 then
  Lphi<=10.0*log10(cycle_jit*cycle_jit*fs*fs*fs/(2.0*fm*fm));
  else Lphi <= 0.0;
  end if;
    t0 <= t;
end process power_density ;
```

_____

                                            – output signal generation –

```
fs_noised* ts_noised == 0.5;
vout == vdd – vs*cos(2.0*MATH_PI*fs_noised*t);
end architecture comp;
```

Chapter 5

AnalogSL
A C++ - Library for Modeling Analog Power Drivers

Ch. Grimm[1], P. Oehler[2], Ch. Meise[1,2], K. Waldschmidt[1], W. Frey[2]
University of Frankfurt[1], Contintental Teves AG oHG[2]

Key words: Analog behavioral modeling, C++, SystemC

Abstract: A C++ library for the creation of behavioral models for analog power drivers is presented.
The C++ models created with the library can be integrated easily for example in SystemC.
They simulate magnitudes faster than conventional methods for analog or mixed ana-
log/digital simulation.

The underlying method is quite similar to the switch-level simulation for digital circuit simulation. In difference to switch-level simulation, circuits can also contain inductive loads. In
order to increase simulation speed, pre-solved parameterizable differential equations are used.

1. INTRODUCTION

For the validation of complex heterogeneous systems, analog components are simulated together with the whole system for a long period in simulated time. This requires very fast simulation of analog components.

For analog signal processing, transfer functions can describe analog behavior in an abstract way, which can be simulated efficiently. However, the abstract behavioral modeling of power electronics is an open problem. In this domain, the conservative sizes such as current or voltage cannot be omitted, because they are the values, in which we are interested even on system level.

In order to simulate such circuits, we could use a circuit simulator, such as SPICE. Unfortunately, SPICE is magnitudes too slow for the validation of complex systems. A speed up of the simulation is typically achieved by the use of *macro models* in SPICE. With macro models, a speed up of up to 10 can be achieved. More sophisticated simulation tools such as Saber/MAST or VHDL-AMS support the direct formulation of *behavioral models* (e. g. in [HKCG97], [GHWK00]). However, the creation of behavioral models is a time-consuming and error-prone task.

If behavioral models are available, simulation is often still too slow, because
- numerical integration requires the calculation of many discrete time steps and

A. Mignotte et al. (eds.), System on Chip Design Languages, 59–67.
© 2002 *Kluwer Academic Publishers.*

– the coupling of analog and digital simulators leads to a further performance degradation.

For the use of analog models in system simulation or "virtual prototyping", a speedup of some magnitudes is required.

However, for the simulation of power drivers with capacitive and/or inductive load, an approach similar to the switch-level modeling of digital CMOS circuits (e. g. MOSSIM [Bry81], RSIM [Kao92]) could permit the modeling of the most important effects in combination with a very fast simulation. A transistor is thereby modeled as a switch which has an on resistance R_{on} and an off resistance R_{off}. This approach is useful for modeling power drivers, because normally only one component, like a current source, a pull-up or pull-down resistor, a transistor as a switch, bipolar or MOS, pulls a signal node to a fixed voltage level at one   time.

This paper gives an overview of the C++ library AnalogSL. AnalogSL allows us the creation of behavioral models of analog power drivers with inductive and/or capacitive load by simple instantiation and connection of the components of a netlist.

Figure 1 gives an overview of a typical design flow using AnalogSL. C++ prototypes of digital and analog signal processing functions are generated for example by Matlab, MatrixX or are programmed manually, for example with SystemC [SCFD00]. Analog power drivers are usually designed "bottom up". The resulting netlist can be converted to a netlist in AnalogSL/C++. AnalogSL provides classes of components such as resistors, capacitors, coils, transistors. These can be instantiated in a netlist. Furthermore, AnalogSL provides a very fast and efficient algorithm for the simulation of this netlist.

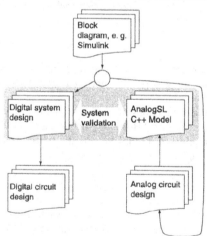

Figure 1. Use of AnalogSL classes in a top-down design flow.

In order to permit fast simulation, we make some requirements, which are typically fulfilled by circuits such as analog power drivers. These requirements allow us to reach the simulation speed required for "system level simulation":

First of all, a load may only be driven by up to one driver at one point in time. The use of different drivers which in parallel drive one load is not supported at the moment.

Second, we only support linear components such as resistors, capacitors and coils in addition to transistors, which are modeled as switches.

2. MODELING AND SIMULATION

The basic idea of modeling and simulation the power drivers can be explained easily by a simple example. *Figure 1* shows a typical example of an integrated analog power driver with an inductive load (L, R_L).

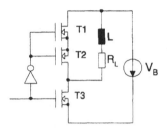

Figure 2. Typical example of a power driver.

In this example, the transistors are either switched on (R_{on}, on-resistance between drain and source) or off (R_{off}, off-resistance between drain an aource). This is typical for many power drivers or for modeling physical effects of digital circuits.

The behavior of the power driver shown in *Figure 2* can be described in two different "modes":

– If the input voltage is higher than the treshold voltage of T3, the transistors T1, T2 are switched "off", and transistor T3 is switched "on". Then, the current through the coil is increasing to a maximum of

with a time-constant

$$\hat{I}_L = U / (R_L + R_{on}(T3))$$
$$\tau = (R_L + R_{on}(T3)) / L$$

– If the input voltage is below the treshold voltage, the transistors T1 and T2 are switched "on", and T3 is switched "off". The current through the coil $I_L(t)$ then goes through these transistors. This permits to keep the energy in the coil for a certain time while the lower transistor is switched off.

The behavior of this simple example can be described in an analytical way by the following equation:

More general, the behavior of analog power drivers is dominated by the path from a

$$I_L(t) = (I_L(t_0) - \hat{I}_L)e^{-t/\tau} + \hat{I}_L$$

power source to the load. More abstract, the behavior is determinated by the path with the lowest resistance between a load and a power source. Together with the load itself, it describes a cycle, in which we find coils or capacitors and resistors together with transistors. In the following, we call this cycle the *dominant cycle* of the network.

In the simple example given above, we find two different dominant cycles, depending on the input state of the circuit. *Figure 3* shows the dominant cycle for the first case.

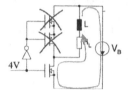

Figure 3. Dominant cycle of the simple example for the first case.

The dominant cycle describing the behavior of the circuit in the second case is shown in *Figure 4*.

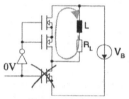

Figure 4. Dominant cycle for the second case.

If transistors are modeled as ideal switches controlled by their gate, we can replace them by resistors with one of the values R_{on} or R_{off}. Then, we get the networks shown in *Figure 5*.

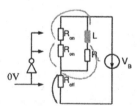

Figure 5. Search for dominant cycles with Dijkstra's algorithm for single-source shortest path problem (here: second case).

In order to find the dominant cycle, we use the Dijkstra algorithm for solving the single source shortest path problem. The result is a cycle, which contains the load and the components (resistors, capacitors, coils, sources) between the pins of the load.

All these components are linear components. The behavior of this cycle is described by a linear differential equation of first or second order, whose solution is well-known (exponential function for first order, two real or complex exponential functions for second order). In the example given above, the current in the cycle can be calculated by a simple differential equation of 1st order. Knowing the current, we can then calculate all voltages. For circuits, which fulfil the requirements made above, the influence of other cycles on the behavior can be neglected.

3.   REALIZATION

To permit efficient creation of behavioral models of drivers from a netlist, we have implemented a C++ class `asl_netlist`. In objects of this class, other objects modeling resistors, capacitors, coils and transistors (classes `asl_r`, `asl_c`, `asl_l`, `asc_mosfet`) can be instantiated. The structure of the netlist can be described by calling methods of these objects.

The idea of the simulation method has been described above. *Figure 6* shows the implemented algorithm in more detail.

Note, that the coupling of the analog behavioral model with discrete-event simulators is very simple, but also very efficient: Only, when an input-value has changed, the method checks, whether the dominant cycles have changed. In this case, it calculates actual internal states and sets up new equations.

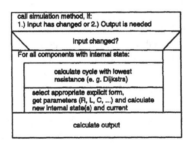

Figure 6. Implemented algorithm for simulation

The coupling of AnalogSL models and discrete models corresponds exactly to the coupling of discrete processes in discrete simulators. An activation of the simulation method in discrete time steps for numerically solving a differential equation is not required. The analog model cannot cause discrete events, e. g. by going above or below a certain value. This forbids in example the modeling of comparators that asynchronously produce discrete events. However, in most circuits, analog values are sampled by an A/D converter or processed synchronously.

4.   CASE STUDY

AnalogSL has been realized and used for the design and validation of a pulse width modulated driver, controlled by a digital PID controller. The system is shown in *Figure 7.*

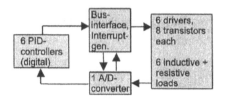

Figure 7. Circuit designed using AnalogSL

The system controls a programmable current through 6 inductive loads of 6 drivers. Note, that the "analog" behavior of the driver is essential for understanding the control loop! The current is measured by one multiplexed A/D converter. 6 PID-controllers calculate a pulse-width that leads to the programmed current. For a validation of the protocol that selects a driver or other source for A/D conversion, a simulation of the whole system over a long time period is essential. Furthermore, the coefficients of the PID-controllers must be optimized also to avoid effects such as the wind-up effect which occurs due to the non-linear discrete behavior.

Using MatrixX or Simulink, only a rather abstract simulation of the system would be possible. Neither the validation of the system controlling the multiplexing of the converter nor the wind-up effects due to limited value range of digital signals can be simulated with these tools in a reasonable way, because these effects are both too dependent on the hardware. For such rather detailed simulations, a description using Verilog on RT-Level and Saber/MAST would be appropriate. *Figure 8* shows the step response of the control loop simulated with Saber/MAST and Verilog.

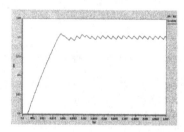

Figure 8. Step response of control loop from co-simulation with SABER and Verilog

However, simulation using SABER is by far too slow. As an alternative, we have used a C++ model of the digital part (PID-controller, bus-interface, etc.) modeled using the in-house-standard AVSL, which is quite similar to SystemC. The analog drivers, each consisting of 8 transistors, and the inductive/resistive load have been modeled using AnalogSL. *Figure 9* shows the step response of the circuit simulated with a C++ model created with AnalogSL.

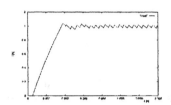

Figure 9. Step response of from co-simulation with AnalogSL and AVSL (both C++)

All relevant effects that could be observed in the SABER simulation, can also be observed in the C++ model.

Table 1, *Table 2* and *Table 3* compare resources required for simulation of the system on different levels of abstraction. Of course, the more abstract models are simulated by far faster. *Table 1* shows the effect of abstraction of the complete model on simulation time.

Table 1. Time needed for mixed-mode simulation using models on different levels of abstraction.

Tool/Level of abstraction	Simulation time
Spice (Transistor-Level)	189360 sec
Saber+Verilog (RT-Level)	1059 sec
C++ (Clock-Cycle, AnalogSL)	5 sec

Although the speedup is evident, it could also result from the use of different abstract models in the digital domain. *Table 2* shows the simulation time required by the analog simulator. Note, that this shows very clear, that the speedup is most notably due to the use of AnalogSL.

Table 2. Time needed for analog simulation.

Tool/Level of abstraction	Simulation time
Saber (Netlist, level 1 transistor models)	975 sec
C++ (AnalogSL)	<< 2 sec

The reason for the speedup becomes clear when we compare the number of time steps needed for simulation of the analog part (*Table 3*): AnalogSL only calculates solutions at the 80 points in time, where the digital simulator either reads or writes to the analog model.

Table 3. Time steps calculated

Tool/Level of abstraction	Simulation time
Spice (Netlist)	6.150.000
Saber (Netlist)	120.000
C++ (AnalogSL)	80

5.   CONCLUSION

The methods described above permit the easy creation of behavioral models of analog drivers. The resulting models can easily be integrated in a discrete simulator, such as SystemC, and simulate magnitudes faster than conventional approaches. Note, that the methods presented support different structures and load models - the structure shown as an example is not the only one supported.

Furthermore it should be mentioned, that in addition to the well-known (solved) differential equations for RC, RL, RLC - loads, it is of course possible to add equations for non-linear loads (e. g. modeling loading/unloading of a capacitor via a (non-linear) CMOS transistor).

In future work, we plan to add methods that warn a user in case of a violation of requirements and a resulting too low precision. Furthermore, we plan to extend the library by methods for simulation of general linear analog networks and/or transfer functions, different A/D converters and some selected non-linear effects.

REFERENCES

[HKCG97] K. Hofmann, J.-M. Karam, B. Courtois, and Manfred Glesner. "Generation of HDL-A-code for nonlinear behavioral models". In: *IEEE/VIUF International Workshop on Behavioral Modeling and Simulation*, pages 9-16. VHDL International, Oct 1997.

[GHWK00] Christoph Grimm, Frank Heuschen, Klaus Waldschmidt, and Stephan Klesy. "Rechnergestützte Erstellung von Modellen zur schnellen Simulation analog/digitaler Architekturen". In: *Architekturentwurf eingebetteter Systeme 2000 (AES 2000)*, FZI Karlsruhe, January 2000.

[Bry81] Randal E. Bryant. "MOSSIM: A Switch-Level Simulator for MOS LSI". In: *Eighteenth Design Automation Conference (DAC 81)*, pages 786-790, Nashville, Tenn., 1981.

[Kao92] Russel Kao. *Piecewise Linear Models for Switch-Level Simulation*. WRL Research Report 92/5, Western Research Laboratory, September 1992.

[SCFD00] Synopsys, Inc., CoWare, Inc, and Frontier Design, Inc. *SystemC User's Guide*. 2000. http://www.systemc.org.

Chapter 6

Modeling Micro-Mechanical Structures for System Simulations
Combining Models of Physical Effects for Describing Complex Electromechanical Devices

Lars M. Voßkämper[1], Rainer Schmid[2] and Georg Pelz[3]

[1] *Dolphin Integration GmbH, Bismarckstr. 142a, D-47057 Duisburg, Germany, dolphin@me-park.com*
[2] *Fraunhofer-Institut IMS, Hansastr.27d, D-80686 München, Germany*
[3] *Infineon Technologies AG, St.-Martin-Str. 76, D-81541 Munich, work was carried out at Gerhard-Mercator-University Duisburg, Germany*

Abstract: In contrast to classical object-oriented electromechanical modelling, i.e. describing plates, suspensions, drives etc. [4], this paper proposes combining models of basic physical effects to object models which in turn can be used for system modelling. This allows freely choosing which effects are to be considered for some simulation. Moreover, the development of new object models is simplified. The paper shows how to model a wide variety of electromechanical devices with a well-defined library of basic effects.

Key words: analytical modelling; electromechanical effects; gyroscope; mixed technology; VHDL-AMS.

1.   INTRODUCTION

Complex mechanical devices can be modelled with the finite element approach, which is also available in circuit simulators [1]. Unfortunately these models are not always suited for system simulation due to their high computing effort.

Less time consuming during simulation and easy to implement in an analogue hardware description language are finite difference or analytical models. Unfortunately, complex devices usually cannot be described with such models.

A possibility to overcome these problems is to model the components of the mechanical device separately and to describe the complete behaviour of the device by combining the models of its components, see [4]. For object-oriented modelling, the devices are dismantled into masses, springs and dampers. For example, an acceleration sensor can be separated into a seismic mass and a spring, which represents the suspension of the mass. In this case, the behaviour of each mass point can be described in the following way:

$$(1) \quad \vec{F} = \ddot{\tilde{M}} \cdot \ddot{\vec{x}} + \tilde{D} \cdot \dot{\vec{x}} + \tilde{k} \cdot \vec{x}$$

with
   $\vec{F}$: vector of forces and moments
   $\tilde{M}$: matrix of effective masses

A. Mignotte et al. (eds.), System on Chip Design Languages, 69–78.

$\underline{\underline{D}}$: matrix of damping coefficients
$\underline{\underline{k}}$: matrix of stiffness coefficients
$\underline{x}$: vector of (angular) displacements

If this equation describes the behaviour of a beam in a suspended system, we have to consider at least two mass points (one point at each beam end). If we want to calculate the behaviour in 3 dimensions, the equation is of dimension 12 (2 points with 3 forces each + 2 points with 2 moments and 1 torsion each). So the simulator has to calculate 12 complex equations only for a single beam, if no further reduction can be made.

The physical effect approach goes one step beyond the object-oriented method. Its basic idea is to model effects which occur in or between electromechanical structures. These basic effect models are combined into object models, e.g. plate, suspension or drive models. For example, one could dissect a comb drive into an inertia effect of the mass, a capacity and an electrostatic attraction effect between the conductive fingers and an air damping effect, see *Figure 2*. The advantage of this kind of modelling is that the designer can decide which effects are necessary and which effects can be neglected. For example, the air damping effect can be neglected if the structure moves in a vacuum. So, one is able to choose the best trade-off between simulation accuracy and speed.

A gyroscope is a good demonstrator for showing the benefit of effect modelling since it is a complex structure and comprises a lot of different effects. This paper investigates the effects occurring in the demonstrator and its implementation in VHDL-AMS. After this, the gyroscope model, constructed out of the modelled effects, is simulated. The simulation is verified by FEM simulations and analytical calculations. At the end, a system simulation is presented, where the gyroscope is connected with a complex readout circuit.

2.   EDA INTEGRATION

We have created a symbol of each effect model for use in a schematic editor. So it becomes possible to model a complex electromechanical device by graphically combining the effects occurring in this device in the schematic editor. Furthermore, it becomes easy to integrate the electromechanical model in an electrical netlist for system simulation purposes.

The schematic editor is able to netlist the whole system, so the user does not have to deal with time intensive and error prone manual work on the hardware description language level.

Each symbol carries a name and has at least one pair of pins; one represents the plus and the other the minus contact, see *Figure 1*. The quantities, which the model expects or supplies at these pins, are written beside each pin. Every pin holds the "through" and "across" variables of one domain.

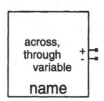

Figure 1. Symbol pattern for models
of electromechanical effects

3. DEMONSTRATOR: GYROSCOPE

The gyroscope in *Figure 3* is a combination of a sensor and an actuator. Two comb drives force an opposite in phase oscillation of two masses in plane direction. The Coriolis effect causes a tilting of the two plates if an angular velocity occurs. The tilting of the masses results in a capacity change between a mass and its bottom electrode. So the angular velocity value can be detected by the capacity difference between the two plates with their bottom electrodes.

Figure 4 displays the schematic of the gyroscope with some basic electrical components. Out of this schematic we can generate the mechanical netlist of the gyroscope, which comprises the basic effect models. Please note that this netlist, respectively the schematic, can be reduced by considering symmetries. To visualize the object models 'comb drive', 'suspension' and 'mass', which are constructed out of the basic effect models, dotted lines surround each object component. An advantage of the basic effect approach is that one is able to model quite different object models out of the same effect components.

The used effect models represented by the symbols in *Figure 4* are described in the following; the names in the brackets indicate the names of the models. Let us begin with the electrostatic attraction effect. A voltage, connected between two conductive plates, induces an attractive force $\vec{F}$:

(2) $\vec{F} = \dfrac{dE}{d\bar{x}}$

with electrical energy E and spatial coordinate vector $\bar{x}$. Solving this equation gives the results for the attraction force in the comb drive (AttracComb) and the attraction force induced by a readout voltage between the masses and its ground electrodes (AttracPlate).

The translational (InertiaTrans) and rotational (InertiaRot) inertia effect of masses calculates to

(3) $F = m \dfrac{d^2}{dt^2} x$

and

(4) $T = J_A \dfrac{d^2}{dt^2} \varphi$

respectively. With force F, mass m, displacement x, torque T, inertia moment J_A relating to turning point A and torsional angle φ.

The equation of Coriolis effect (Coriolis) is

(5) $T = 2m\omega x \dfrac{d}{dt} x$

with angular velocity ω.

The bending effect of beams (BendBeam) can be calculated out of the following differential equation:

$$(6) \ \frac{d^2 w_{(\xi)}}{d\xi^2} = -\frac{M_{(\xi)}}{EI_{(\xi)}}$$

with deflection w, bending moment M, elastic modulus E, moment of inertia I and position ξ.
The next differential equation describes the torsion effect in beams (TorsBeam):

$$(7) \ \frac{d\varphi_{(\xi)}}{d\xi} = \frac{T_{(\xi)}}{GI}$$

with rotational angle φ, torque T, sliding module G, torsional inertia moment I and position ξ.
The capacity effect between two conductive structures influences a current i flowing through the structures:

$$(8) \ i = C_{(\alpha)} \frac{d}{dt} v$$

where the capacity C depends on the displacement x in the case of the comb drive (CapComb) or it depends on the rotational angle φ in the case of two tilting plates (CapPlate).

4.   IMPLEMENTATION

To make the effect models compatible with each other and to provide an easy extension of the model library, we have to carefully define suited ports for connection purposes. *Table 1* shows the used "through" and "across" variables in each domain used by the chosen ports.

In VHDL-AMS we are not restricted to pre-given variable types. Which is on the one hand an advantage because we can implement variable types of non-electrical domains that we want to integrate in the simulation. But on the other hand it means a disadvantage, since the exchange of models of different suppliers becomes aggravated. Because of the lack of an official standard for non-electrical variable types, each supplier chooses his own solution.

Nevertheless, VHDL-AMS provides a comfortable definition possibility of user defined types. *Listing 1* shows an extract of the package "translational_system" to show the implementation of the translational movement variables shown in *Table 1*.

To demonstrate the implementation of the effects, *Listing 2* displays the used VHDL-AMS code of the Coriolis effect, see equation (5). Please note the very easy translation of mathematical models to VHDL-AMS description. So with VHDL-AMS, the modelling task is not an extra charge for the designer, thus contributing to reducing time-to-market.

5.   DEVICE SIMULATION

After implementing the basic effects, the modelling and simulation of the gyroscope with some basic electronic components was carried out. For simulation we used the mixed signal and multi-level simulator SMASH[1]. *Figure 5* displays the simulation results of the schematic in *Figure 4*. The left screenshot shows the applied sinusoidal rotational velocity (omega), the translational displace-

---

[1] Dolphin Integration S.A., Grenoble, France.

ment of one plate due to a driving voltage (vdrive) applying on the comb drives, the tilt angle of one plate and the capacity difference of both plates to their bottom electrodes. This capacity difference is a measure of the applied rotational velocity and can be used in some further readout circuitry.

The time-zoom of the left screenshot of *Figure 5* shows the forces in dependency of the displacement and the torques in dependency of the tilt angle in the gyroscope. One can prove that at every time step the sum of the forces and the sum of the torques is zero in the mechanical system, as we can expect from Newton's laws.

During the simulation of the gyroscope, some more attention has to be paid to possible simulator artefacts. Since the gyroscope is driven at its mechanical resonance frequency to get large displacements with relatively low driving voltage amplitudes, some damping has a strong influence. To reduce simulator intrinsic damping, simulation parameters have to be chosen carefully. Furthermore, the performance of VHDL-AMS simulations depends on the chosen simulation method with its specific solving algorithm.

6.   VERIFICATION

We have compared the simulation results with finite element simulations and analytical equations. In an analytical validation, we have calculated the spring stiffnesses and masses of the gyroscope elements out of their geometrical dimensions and their material properties. With this data we have calculated the first resonance frequencies of the bending mode in drive direction and the torsional mode in detection direction. Comparing the analytical results with finite element modal analysis leads to corresponding resonance frequencies which are also confirmed by the physical effects simulation. *Table 2* compares the calculated resonance frequencies of the two different excitation modes with the solutions of the finite element method and the circuit simulation. It shows a good correspondence between these three runs.

7.   SYSTEM SIMULATION

After modelling, simulating and verifying the gyroscope device, we want to model and simulate a complete electromechanical system (MEMS); this means we connect a complex readout electronic to the gyroscope.

A block diagram with the main functions is shown in *Figure 6* and is described in the following. A driving voltage (vdrive) with a frequency of 3kHz is connected to both comb drives. Additionally two readout voltages (vsine) with a frequency of 500kHz are connected to the plates of the gyroscope. First the output signal of the gyroscope is amplified. After a first band pass filter we have a signal component of 500kHz, which is due to the frequency of the voltage supplies. Furthermore, we have a signal component of 6kHz caused by the translational mass movement and a signal component, which represents the rotational velocity that should be detected.

With the first multiplier we do a frequency shift of 500kHz and after the second band pass filter we receive a signal frequency of 6kHz. To eliminate this frequency proportion we shift again the frequency spectrum. After the low-pass we finally receive the signal component, which represents the rotational velocity that we want to detect.

The components of the readout circuit, as operation amplifiers, resistors and capacitors are modelled like the mechanical components in VHDL-AMS. Thus the micro-electromechanical system was modelled completely in *one* description language, which avoided possible difficulties with the simulation of the MEMS from the beginning. Furthermore, this supports exploring design alternatives on system level.

Figure 7 shows the simulation results if a sinusoidal (left screenshot) rotational velocity is applied to the gyroscope and if the applied rotational velocity is in the form of steps (right screenshot). In both pictures the first line shows the applied rotational velocity, the second line shows the capacity difference between both masses and their bottom electrodes and the last line represents the output voltage of the readout circuit. In the results one can detect well the transient behaviour of the mechanics and electronics.

8.   CONCLUSION AND OUTLOOK

The introduced model of the gyroscope can be easily extended with further effects like the effect of air damping. Moreover, with the same introduced effects, it is possible to model totally different devices like accelerometers or micro mirrors because the basic effects, like bending of beams or inertia effects of masses are the same.

The implementation of the required mathematical equations in the hardware description language VHDL-AMS was simple due to its flexible quantity handling.

The introduced models extend the model library of electrical circuit simulation tools supporting VHDL-AMS with electromechanical effects. So the specific requirements of MEMS regarding mixed domain simulation needs are supported and a system simulation becomes easy.

The introduced model methodology allows the user to model the mechanical part visually like the electronics in a schematic editor. The automated netlisting ability of the schematic editor frees the user from time-intensive and error-prone manual netlisting work.

9.   LITERATURE

[1] J. Bielefeld, G. Pelz and G. Zimmer, "AHDL-Model of a 2D Mechanical Finite-Element usable for Micro-Electro-Mechanical Systems", IEEE/VIUF Workshop on Behavioral Modeling and Simulation (BMAS), Washington D.C., 1997, 177-182.

[2] M. Carmona, S. Marco, J. Sieiro, O. Ruiz, J.M. Gómez-Cama and J. Samitier, "Modelling of microsystems with analog hardware description languages", Sensors and Actuators A 76 (1999)/1-3 32-42

[3] O. Degani, E. Socher, A. Lipson, T. Leitner, D.J. Setter, S. Kaldor and Y. Nemirovsky, "Pull-In Study of an Electrostatic Torsion Micro-actuator", Journal of Microelectromechanical Systems, Vol. 7 (1998), No. 4, 373-378

[4] G.K. Fedder, Q. Jing,, "NODAS 1.3 - Nodal Design of Actuators and Sensors", IEEE/VIUF Workshop on Behavioral Modeling and Simulation (BMAS) 1998

[5] W. Kuehnel, "Modelling of the mechanical behaviour of a differential capacitor acceleration sensor", Sensors and Actuators A 48 (1995) 101-108

[6] R.L. Mullen, M. Mehregany, M.P. Omar, and W.H. Ko, "Theoretical Modeling of Boundary Conditions in Microfabricated Beams", Proceedings of the IEEE - MEMS '91 (1991) 154-159

[7] S.D. Senturia, N. Aluru, and J. White, "Simulating the Behavior of MEMS Devices: Computational Methods and Needs", IEEE Computational Science & Engineering, 4 (1997), 30-43

[8] D. Teegarden, G. Lorenz, and R. Neul, "How to Model and Simulate Microgyroscope Systems", IEEE Spectrum 7 (1998) 66-75

10. APPENDIX

Table 1. Variable types for different domains

type of variable	electrical net- work	rotational move- ment	translational movement
"through"-variable	current i	torque T	force F
"across"-variable	voltage v	angle φ, angular velocity ω	displacement x, velocity v

Table 2. Calculated and simulated resonance frequencies of the gyroscope

method	drive mode	detection mode	higher modes
analytical	5714	5716	-
FEM	5826	5914	> 12k
effect simulation	5745	5760	-

```
PACKAGE translational_system IS
  ATTRIBUTE unit : string;
[...]

-- Length, meter
  SUBTYPE displacement IS REAL
TOLERANCE "default_displacement";
  ATTRIBUTE unit OF displacement :
SUBTYPE IS "m";
-- Velocity, meter/second
    SUBTYPE velocity IS REAL
TOLERANCE "default_velocity";
    ATTRIBUTE unit OF velocity :
SUBTYPE IS "m/s";
-- Force, Newton
  SUBTYPE force IS REAL
    TOLERANCE "default_force";
  ATTRIBUTE unit OF force : SUBTYPE IS
"N";

  NATURE translational IS
    displacement ACROSS
    force THROUGH
    translational_ref REFERENCE;
END PACKAGE translational_system;
```

Listing 1. User defined types in VHDL-AMS

```
USE work.translational_system.all;
USE work.rotational_system.all;

ENTITY Coriolis IS
  GENERIC (width, length, depth, roh:
REAL);
  PORT (TERMINAL
tran_p,tran_n:TRANSLATIONAL;
    TERMINAL rot_p, rot_n: ROTATIONAL;
    TERMINAL rot_om_p, rot_om_n:

ROTATIONAL_OMEGA);
END ENTITY Coriolis;

ARCHITECTURE simple OF Coriolis IS
  QUANTITY pos ACROSS tran_p TO tran_n;
  QUANTITY torque THROUGH rot_p TO rot_n;
  QUANTITY omega ACROSS rot_om_p TO
rot_om_n;
  CONSTANT mass : REAL := width * length *
depth * roh;
BEGIN
  torque == 2.0 * mass * omega * pos *
pos'dot;
END ARCHITECTURE simple;
```

Listing 2. VHDL-AMS implementation of Coriolis effect

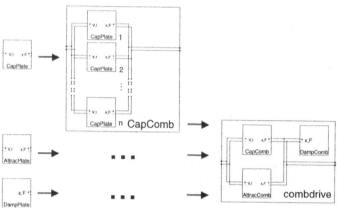

Figure 2. Object modelling of a comb drive with basic effects

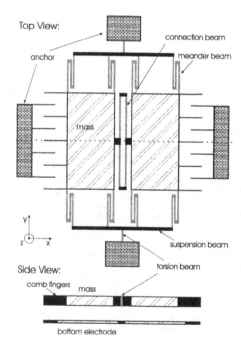

Figure 3. Basic sketch of the gyroscope

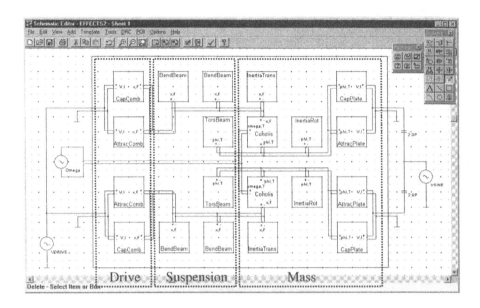

Figure 4. Schematic of the gyroscope with basic test bench

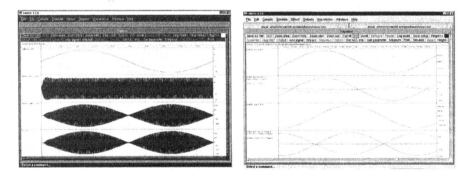

Figure 5. Results of the device simulation:
Left: Displacement (trace 2), tilt angle (3) and capacity (4) in dependence of applied rotational velocity (1)
Right: Displacement (trace 1), forces (2), tilt angle (3) and torques (4) in the gyroscope

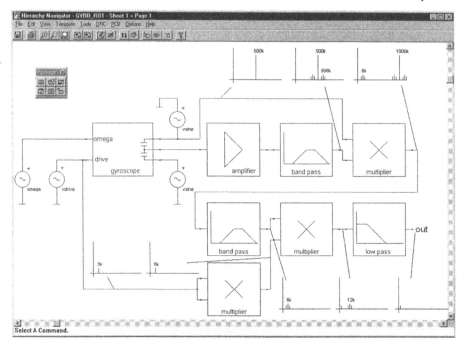

Figure 6. Block diagram of the gyroscope with attached readout electronics.
In order to clarify the mode of operation, the frequency spectra at selected nodes are indicated.

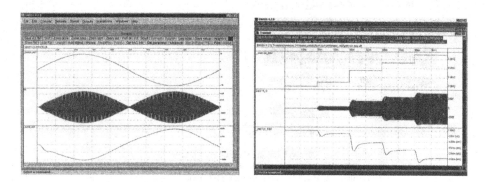

Figure 7. Results of the system simulation:
Both screenshots show applied rotational velocity (trace 1),
capacity difference (2) and output voltage (3) of the system.

Chapter 7

A Comparison of Mixed-Signal Modeling Approaches

Gregory D. Peterson
Electrical and Computer Engineering
The University of Tennessee
Knoxville, TN
(865)-974-6352
gdp@utk.edu

Abstract: Behavioral modeling of analog/mixed signal and mixed-technology designs promises to transform the way in which designs are specified, implemented, and supported in much the same way that hardware description languages such as VHDL and Verilog transformed digital design. Although VHDL-AMS is now an IEEE standard and Verilog-AMS is maturing enough to soon be ready for submission to the IEEE standards process, relatively little research has targeted the best practices for using these languages. To begin to address this issue, this paper compares the relative merits of modeling analog/mixed signal systems with languages such as VHDL, VHDL-AMS, SPICE, and C/C++. We consider modeling issues at different levels of abstraction, top-down and bottom-up design issues, testbench considerations, performance, expressiveness, and productivity. Based on these metrics, we give compare the benefits of analog/mixed-signal modeling languages such as VHDL-AMS.

Key words: mixed-signal modelling, HDLs, behavioural modelling

1.   INTRODUCTION

Behavioral modeling of analog designs promises to be transformed by the use of a standard language to support behavioral and structural representations of analog designs. To improve our ability to design analog and mixed-signal systems, the IEEE and Accellera standards community endeavored to extend existing digitally-oriented hardware description languages. The emerging discipline of behavioral modeling of analog designs as fueled by these emerging analog and mixed-signal design languages may revolutionize analog design and synthesis the way that hardware description languages enabled explosive productivity growth in digital design.

Looking beyond electrical systems, the mixed technology domain supported by analog and mixed-signal hardware description languages will enable dramatic changes in systems design, enabling micro-mechanical, fluidic, optic, and electronic subsystems to be fabricated on the same substrate. Using modeling approaches like the behavioral modeling of analog design, transfer functions from control theoretic applications can be introduced to electronic design automation to create unique mixed technology solutions. Such capabilities to support modeling and design automation will prove to be key enabling technologies for unleashing nanotechnology devices.

A. Mignotte et al. (eds.), System on Chip Design Languages, 79–86.

With the increasing prevalence of SOC design, including applications like telecommunications and cell phones, mixed-signal design is extremely important and a critical enabler of continued systems design productivity [28]. Specific mixed signal applications including such analog components as sensors, ADCs, DACs, and phase locked loops interacting with digital components for signal processing, control, or other applications. By bringing the analog and digital components into the same representation, a single simulation environment is possible.

Digital designs potentially suffer from analog effects, often due to deep submicron design. Gone are the days when a digital designer could ignore the physics of the devices in a circuit. As examples of applying VHDL-AMS within a "digital" design, detailed (currently SPICE) simulations before tapeout can be made much simpler within a single VHDL-AMS framework. Issues regarding timing, parasitics, long wires/transmission line effects, and other physical phenomena within a physical design can be handled with ease by the effective use of VHDL-AMS. Hence, VHDL-AMS can indeed help digital designers, particularly as deep submicron design continues.

This paper compares different modeling languages and levels of abstraction to contrast when one should consider using various modeling approaches and languages, as well as illustrating the types of activities best suited to VHDL-AMS, SPICE, VHDL, or C/C++. Although VHDL-AMS receives most of the focus in this paper on analog/mixed-signal hardware description languages, many of the results should be relevant to Verilog-AMS users as well.

The modeling exercises underlying this particular paper are based on a process control system that was used in an embedded processing environment, a phase-locked loop example, and some filter examples. The modeling effort included abstract behavioral/algorithmic models down to structural models of the constituent devices. A description of the models and their associated source code can be found at http://www.ece.utk.edu/~gdp/mixed-signal.htm.

2.   VHDL FOR ANALOG/ MIXED-SIGNAL DESIGN

VHDL is a widely used hardware description language originally developed by the DoD for digital systems. Since its inception, VHDL (and Verilog) has become a very common digital modeling and design language, particularly for synthesis-based design flows. It was as a result of the 1992 VHDL language revision efforts that the need for a set of analog/mixed-signal extensions was identified.

Despite the fact that VHDL does not elegantly support analog modeling, some have applied VHDL to mixed-signal problems. For example, mixed-signal event-driven simulation using VHDL was applied to I/O pads [3], phase-locked loops [21], operational amplifiers [22], and magnetic recording read channels [24]. For higher fidelity analog modeling of interconnections, Popescu illustrated how VHDL or any other discrete-event simulator can be applied [19]. This approach will also work for VHDL-AMS. Another approach that can be used for analog/mixed-signal modeling in VHDL is to use the foreign attribute or subprogram mechanism as a means to trap out of the language for the analog portions of the circuit.

In all of the above cases, modeling in VHDL (or Verilog) can be accomplished, but is not as natural to the modeler, as efficient with respect to simulation speed, nor as suitable for designer productivity. The researchers above considered the use of VHDL for analog/mixed-signal modeling for several reasons. In addition to being widely used, the VHDL language includes a simulation semantic, supports concurrency, handles different levels of abstraction and design refinement, and avoids language disconnects by supporting different phases of design. Nonetheless, the lack of analog modeling support in the simulation cycle or language constructs and the absence of analog/mixed-signal libraries significantly impairs the applicability of VHDL. Based on these experiences and our application of VHDL to behavioral modeling, we find these digital hardware description languages to be poorly suited to the analog/mixed-signal domain.

When engineers need to model or design analog/mixed-signal systems, VHDL should generally be rejected in favor of VHDL-AMS.

3.   VHDL-AMS FOR ANALOG/ MIXED-SIGNAL DESIGN

Before discussing the applicability of VHDL-AMS to analog/mixed-signal design, we give a brief overview of the language. Because VHDL-AMS extends the base VHDL standard, many of the aspects of VHDL continue in VHDL-AMS. (One design goal of the VHDL-AMS committee was to make VHDL-AMS upwardly compatible with VHDL with valid VHDL models giving the same simulation results in VHDL-AMS [5].)

VHDL-AMS provides the capability to describe the structure of digital, analog, and mixed-signal circuits and systems through the use of the entity, architecture, component, and configuration mechanisms included in VHDL. These mechanisms enable designers to model systems at various levels of abstraction. Support for encapsulation using these mechanisms and packages remains as with VHDL. The VHDL-AMS language is strongly typed, like VHDL, thus providing modeling safety.

The simulation cycle of VHDL-AMS is based on the VHDL simulation cycle, with additions to support the analog solver and the synchronization between the digital and analog domains. VHDL-AMS supports the modeling of continuous time systems by providing the capability to specify a set of characteristic equations describing the system behavior. VHDL-AMS enables modelers to use ordinary differential and algebraic equations (DAEs) to describe the continuous aspects of the behavior of lumped systems. Although the VHDL-AMS standard specifies the classes of characteristic equations which can be described, the specific details of the analog solver used to solve the characteristic equations are not defined.

A *nature* defines values which may be accessed through the attributes of a terminal; each nature corresponds to a different domain such as electrical, thermal, electromagnetic, mechanical, or fluidic. Among the attributes of a nature are the reference terminal of the nature and the across type and through type used to define the types of branch quantities. Natures are similar to types in VHDL.

The analog unknowns in a VHDL-AMS description are called *quantities*. The quantity is a new type of object, similar to signals and variables, but which has its value updated by solving a set of characteristic equations. The characteristic equations are expressed in the form of *simultaneous statements*. A number of predefined attributes exist to support modeling with quantities, including the time derivative, time integral, zero order hold, Laplace transform, and Z-transform.

Another new object in VHDL-AMS, the *terminal*, provides modeling support for the structural composition of systems with conservative semantics. Each declaration of a terminal T includes a subnature indication, which is used in conjunction with the T'reference and T'contribution attributes to give the *across* and *through* quantities respectively from the terminal T to the reference terminal of the simple nature of T. In the case of an electrical nature, the across and through quantities would correspond to the voltage and current values between two terminals.

Because the analog solver depends on numeric methods which are only capable of finding an approximate solution to a problem, *tolerances* are included in VHDL-AMS to specify the ε value used by the solver. Tolerances are specified by an implementation-specific string expression, and the VHDL-AMS standard does not define how a specific tool uses a tolerance string expression.

VHDL simulation is based on the physical type Time. Physical types in VHDL, like Time, are integer-based with constant precision. With an analog solver, a real valued representation is needed to support the analog simulation time. To solve this issue, the new Universal_Time is included in VHDL-AMS for use by the analog solver.

The VHDL-AMS simulation cycle is based on the VHDL simulation cycle, with additional calculations during initialization and the addition of an analog solver solution phase at the beginning of the simulation cycle. Synchronization between the analog solver and the digital simulation kernel is maintained through some additional steps in the simulation cycle.

In order to support the modeling of nonlinearities in a system's behavior, VHDL-AMS includes the *break* statement. A break statement, which may be conditional, is used by a modeler to define the augmentation set, which is the set of characteristic equations for the analog solver to use. Hence, a different set of characteristic equations may be used by the analog solver each time the analog solver is executed.

Analog to digital interactions are supported in VHDL-AMS by digital processes using the values of a quantity or by the use of the 'Above attribute. Digital to analog interactions are possible because digital signal values do not change value during the analog solver execution. VHDL scope and visibility rules and the static semantics of expressions apply for the VHDL-AMS simultaneous statements.

VHDL-AMS supports small-signal frequency and noise modeling and simulation by finding the quiescent point and linearizing the model. The small signal model is constructed by replacing the characteristic equations in the explicit set and in the structural set with their linearized forms. The frequency domain value can then be found. This value is used to help calculate the noise.

VHDL-AMS supports the modeling of both conservative and non-conservative systems. The branch quantities (across and through quantities) between terminals of a particular nature follow conservation of energy laws (such as Kirchoff's current and voltage equations in the case of electrical systems). For a given terminal of a nature, the summation of all through quantities at the node equals zero. Similarly, the summation of all the across quantities in any closed path of the terminals in the system equals zero. To model non-conservative systems, one may describe characteristic equations in simultaneous statements including quantities. Signal flow modeling is a powerful application for non-conservative modeling using VHDL-AMS. The strong typing rules of VHDL-AMS ease the likelihood of making design errors, particularly with respect to mismatches with in and out modes.

Overall, VHDL-AMS builds upon VHDL and is quite consistent with the underlying philosophy of VHDL. The additional constructs provided in VHDL-AMS should be relatively easy for a VHDL user to understand and use.

A very useful application of VHDL-AMS for digital designers is to replace the role of SPICE in checking out detailed timing for library development, custom design, etc. With the aid of SPICE translation tools into VHDL-AMS, designers can use the same test harness and tests as with the digital VHDL model, but with the additional flexibility of having detailed SPICE-like simulation of the parts of the design where the timing may be marginal and requiring more detailed analysis.

Digital designers can exploit the VHDL-AMS modeling capabilities to support the accurate modeling of effects arising from growing device counts and shrinking features due to deep submicron design. For example, VHDL-AMS provides good modeling capabilities to enable designers to take into account transmission line effects for long wires on their chips, electromagnetic coupling between signals, or ground bounce and other ground plane effects.

By using VHDL-AMS to model mixed signal designs, a single language is supported with related simplification for the system specification, integration, and testing. Thus a system may be developed based on an integrated VHDL-AMS mixed-signal specification. The analog and digital designers can complete their designs and use the same testing infrastructure to ensure their designs work separately and when they are integrated. The simulation semantic and concurrency are basic aspects of the VHDL-AMS language. Support for different abstraction levels and design refinement is quite good for VHDL-AMS as well.

There are some difficulties one encounters when using VHDL-AMS. The primary issue facing designers is the immaturity of the language and its associated design environment. To date, few tools supporting the language have become available. The tools that are available do not support the entire language, but instead aim to incrementally add support for language features. The existing tools will improve in quality and performance, but this will require time. Similarly, there is a lack of common modeling libraries that still needs to be addressed by the VHDL-AMS standards committee, the tool vendors, and interested users.

To address the lack of VHDL-AMS simulation tools, researchers developed an environment for modeling in VHDL-AMS, translating the results to Berkeley SPICE3F5, and performing simulations in SPICE [1,4]. This approach may reduce total tool costs for structural analog/mixed-signal modeling, but is not practical for general behavioral modeling tasks.

Because ports mappings in a component instantiation can only be associated with terminals of the same nature and quantities of the same type, in order to mix technologies one must create additional design entities with the necessary behavior to describe the coupling relationships between the different domains. Standard interfaces between modeling domains are needed, and such infrastructure issues are now being addressed by the VHDL-AMS community.

When an entity is declared in VHDL-AMS the number as well as the mode and type of each port is detailed. This requirement comes from the strong typing of the language and helps reduce modeling errors. This constraint can be inconvenient when mixing analog and digital architectures, and when composing or decomposing mixed-signal systems.

The lack of support for frequency modeling and general partial differential equations limits the breadth of potential domains for VHDL-AMS. Potential extensions to VHDL-AMS will provide such capabilities to better support mixed technology modeling and simulation. On balance, VHDL-AMS provides a good modeling capability for the user, but refinements to the language and necessary tool and library infrastructure remain to be completed.

4. VERILOG-AMS FOR ANALOG/MIXED-SIGNAL DESIGN

The Verilog language was originally developed at roughly the same time as VHDL. Since that time, digital design and synthesis using Verilog has become commonplace, with VHDL and Verilog the dominant hardware description languages used for digital design. To provide the capability to model analog and mixed-signal designs, extensions to Verilog were developed, resulting in the Open Verilog International (OVI) approval of the Verilog-A LRM in June of 1996 and the Verilog-AMS LRM in August of 1998 which now supersedes the Verilog-A LRM [15,17,25,26]. Much of the discussion for VHDL-AMS is also applicable to the use of Verilog-AMS.

To address the interfacing issues for VHDL-AMS discussed above, Verilog-AMS supports the notion of connect modules. The use of connect modules for interfacing digital, analog, and mixed-signal Verilog-AMS modules provides a general modeling capability more flexible than with VHDL-AMS, although at the possible cost of interface errors not being identified [11].

Verilog-AMS provides similar modeling capabilities as with VHDL-AMS. The primary difference users will experience comes from the different language design philosophies as illustrated by the use of weak or strong typing.

5. SPICE FOR ANALOG/ MIXED-SIGNAL DESIGN

SPICE (Simulation Program with Integrated Circuit Emphasis) is a general purpose analog circuit simulator developed in the early 1970s. A very wide array of commercial analog simulators are derived from SPICE, and it remains the most widely used analog simulator. SPICE simulates a design by placing the nodal equations describing the circuit elements into a set of matrices. Nonlinear elements are simulated by linearizing the elements at the associated voltage bias. SPICE then uses LU decomposition to solve the system of equations for the circuit. See [14] for more details.

Although SPICE does provide some capabilities for abstraction and refinement via model and subcircuit mechanisms, it is awkward and has limited functionality. Hence, behavioral modeling with SPICE is not easily performed. It is the advent of analog and mixed-signal hardware description languages that has led to the explosion in behavioral modeling. Similarly, interfacing analog and digital subsystems can be done in SPICE, but not as elegantly as with the analog and mixed-signal hardware description languages.

SPICE is typically used for modeling small analog systems or for detailed simulation of extracted netlists associated with portions of digital designs. SPICE remains a good tool for its intended purpose, but does not support the general need for a behavioral modeling and simulation language for analog and mixed-signal systems.

The tremendous infrastructure in existing SPICE tools, users, libraries, and circuit decks guarantees the continued existence of SPICE for the foreseeable future. To cooperate with SPICE and leverage its existing infrastructure, analog and mixed-signal hardware description languages provide a migration path from SPICE to VHDL-AMS or Verilog-AMS.

6.   C/C++ FOR ANALOG/MIXED-SIGNAL DESIGN

Recently, a number of researchers and startup companies have espoused the use of common programming languages as hardware description languages. In particular, C and C++ have enjoyed significant interest as potential systems level design languages due to their popularity with systems and software engineers. Companies such as CynApps and C Level Design propose the use of C++ libraries to provide the concurrency and bit-level operations necessary for use as a hardware description language. Electronic design automation tools are then used to transform the C/C++ representations into a hardware description language for simulation or synthesis.

There are potential benefits for such an approach for analog and mixed-signal applications as well. The popularity and flexibility of the C/C++ languages promise to help with their adaptation for a new behavioral modeling language. The lack of concurrency could be addressed by a suitable set of classes. One could also use a class inheritance or overloading-based approach to support the interactions between digital and analog elements. Barring the development of a complete language design automation infrastructure, a translation from C/C++ into another language would be necessary; an analog/mixed-signal hardware description language or SPICE seem to be the only options. The current lack of widely used C++ libraries to support its use for analog and mixed-signal modeling currently eliminates it from effective use in a top-down, single language development environment.

Since a number of systems engineering tools can output C/C++ or use them as an intermediate language, the widespread use of C/C++ already exists. The use of C/C++ to model behavior may be quite satisfactory from a cost, productivity, and accuracy perspective using customized class libraries. The primary drawback to such an approach is the need for eventual translation into another language, which could introduce errors, and the lack of design automation tools to process such representations. Concrete language proposals, standardized packages and libraries, and a user base are all lacking as well.

Nonetheless, for creating a behavioral model, or executable specification, of a mixed-signal design, C/C++ remains a fast, inexpensive alternative to analog and mixed-signal hardware description languages.

7.   CONCLUSIONS

The emergence of VHDL-AMS and Verilog-AMS provide new capabilities to support the design of analog and mixed-signal systems. These include the capability to perform behavioral modeling, to refine the design to detailed structural components, and to verify the system at each level of abstraction. Both VHDL-AMS and Verilog-AMS provide the language constructs needed to perform this task, but suffer from a lack of tools, libraries, and user base. In contrast, SPICE has a tremendous existing infrastructure and is well suited to detailed, structural circuit models, but does not provide the language capabilities to support behavioral design and design refinement. Similarly, C/C++ have good capabilities to support behavioral modeling, but lack the infrastructure to support a top-down flow within the same language in addition to a lack of standard libraries for mixed-signal design activities. VHDL-AMS will become a critical tool for analog and mixed-signal designers, but tool vendors must provide the ability to leverage the existing SPICE infrastructure as well as the flexibility and expressiveness of C/C++.

8. REFERENCES

[1] Oussama Alali, Jean-Jacque Charlot, and Robert Rascalon, "Berkeley SPICE3F5 associated to VHDL-AMS, a multi-technological simulator," IEEE/VIUF International Workshop on Behavioral Modeling ad Simulation, October 1997.

[2] Robert Baraniecki, Przemyslaw Dabrowski, and Konrad Hejn, "Analog and Mixed-Signal Behavioral Modeling - a Tutorial," IEEE/VIUF International Workshop on Behavioral Modeling ad Simulation, October 1997.

[3] Ernst Bartsch and Martin Schubert, "Mixed Analog-Digital Circuit Modeling Using Event-Driven VHDL," IEEE/VIUF International Workshop on Behavioral Modeling ad Simulation, October 1997.

[4] Jean-Jacques Charlot, Edward Barker, Oussama Alali, and Jean-Francois Charlot, "Color Rendering in a Hazy Environment: Simulation with SPICE3F5/VHDL-AMS," IEEE/VIUF International Workshop on Behavioral Modeling ad Simulation, October 1998.

[5] Ernst Christen and Kenneth Bakalar, "VHDL-A Language Architecture," Version 2.0, IEEE 1076.1 Working Group White Paper, December 28, 1995.

[6] Ernst Christen, Kenneth Bakalar, Allen M. Dewey, and Eduard Moser, "Analog and Mixed-Signal Modeling Using the VHDL-AMS Language," Tutorial, Design Automation Conference, June 1999.

[7] DARPA Composite CAD Program, Home Page http://www.darpa.mil/MTO/CompCAD

[8] Allen Dewey et al, "VHDL-AMS Modeling Considerations and Styles for Composite Systems," Version 1.0.

[9] Robert L. Ewing, John W. Hines, Gregory D. Peterson, and Maya Rubeiz, "VHDL-AMS Design for Flight Control Systems." *1998 IEEE Aerospace Conference.* Snowmass, CO 21-28 March 1998.

[10] Gary K. Fedder, "Mechanical Natures," White Paper for the VHDL-AMS Interoperability Working Group, Version 0.2, November 1998.

[11] Peter Frey and Donald O'Riordan, "Verilog-AMS: Mixed-Signal Simulation and Cross Domain Connect Modules," IEEE/VIUF International Workshop on Behavioral Modeling ad Simulation, October 2000.

[12] IEEE 1076.1 Working Group, "IEEE Standard VHDL Language Reference Manual," IEEE Draft document, April 17, 1998.

[13] Michael Keating and Pierre Bricaud, *Reuse Methodology Manual.* Kluwer Academic Publishers, 1998.

[14] Ron Kielkowski, *Inside SPICE.* 2nd Edition. McGraw Hill Publishers, 1998.

[15] H. Alan Mantooth and Ian E. Getreu, "Analog and Mixed-Signal Behavioral Modeling - a Tutorial," IEEE/VIUF International Workshop on Behavioral Modeling ad Simulation, October 1997.

[16] N. Milet-Lewis, J-J Charlot, T. Zimmer, H. Levi, A. Laflaquiere, "Comparing Four Analog HDL Modelings and Simulations of a Complex System," IEEE/VIUF International Workshop on Behavioral Modeling ad Simulation, October 1999.

[17] OVI Verilog Analog Mixed-Signal Group, Home Page, http://www.eda.org/verilog-ams/.

[18] Georg Pelz, Juergen Bielefeld, Guenter Zimmer, "Modeling of Embedded Software for Automotive Applications," IEEE/VIUF International Workshop on Behavioral Modeling ad Simulation, October 1997.

[19] Gabriel Stefan Popescu, "On Accommodating Particular Analog System Models with VHDL," IEEE/VIUF International Workshop on Behavioral Modeling ad Simulation, October 2000.

[20] Ken G. Ruan, Ernst Christen, Darrell Teegarden, and Qing Chang, "Modeling and Simulation of a Multi-Discipline System Using VHDL-AMS," IEEE/VIUF International Workshop on Behavioral Modeling ad Simulation, October 1999.

[21] Martin Schubert, "Mixed-Signal Event-Driven Simulation of a Phase-Locked Loop," IEEE/VIUF International Workshop on Behavioral Modeling ad Simulation, October 1999.

[22] Martin Schubert, "Operational Amplifier Modeling Using Event-Driven VHDL," IEEE/VIUF International Workshop on Behavioral Modeling ad Simulation, October 1997.

[23] C.-J. Shi and W. Tian, "Simulation and sensitivity of linear analog circuits under parameter variations by robust interval analysis", *ACM Transactions on Design Automation of Electronic Systems*, vol. 4, no. 3, July 1999.

[24]   Robert B. Staszewski and Sami Kiriaki, "Top-Down Simulation Methodology of a 500 MHz Mixed-Signal Magnetic Recording Read Channel Using Standard VHDL," IEEE/VIUF International Workshop on Behavioral Modeling ad Simulation, October 1999.

[25]   Verilog-A Language Reference Manual, Analog Extenstions to Verilog HDL, Version 1.0, June 20, 1996, Open Verilog International.

[26]   Verilog-AMS Language Reference Manual, Analog and Mixed-Signal Extensions to Verilog HDL, Version 1.2, June 15, 1998, Open Verilog International.

[27]   Lars M. Voskamper, Andre Ludecke, Michael Leineweber, and Georg Pelz, "Electromechanical Modeling Beyond VHDL-AMS," IEEE/VIUF International Workshop on Behavioral Modeling ad Simulation, October 1999.

[28]   VSI Alliance, Analog/Mixed-Signal Development Working Group, "Analog/Mixed-Signal VSI Extension," Specification 1 Version 1.0, June 1998.

Chapter 8

A unified IP Design Platform for extremly flexible High Performance RF and AMS Macros using Standard Design Tools

Reimund Wittmann, Dirk Bierbaum, Pasi Ruhanen*, Werner Schardein**, and Mohsen Darianian
*NOKIA Research Center, Bochum, Germany, *NOKIA Networks, Espoo, Finland, and **University of Applied Sciences, Dortmund, Germany*

Abstract: The design of future high-performance System-On-Chip solutions requires productivity acceleration and a significant improvement of RF, analog, mixed-signal, and digital key macro performance. Therefore a very flexible highly automated design approach for full custom mixed-signal circuits has been worked out. It is based on the use of a new textual design language (C-level), which for the first time addresses all design domains from specification to layout and can be used in standard design environments. The design language is capable to introduce parameterizability and process portability to the design. Based on this novel approach a 3.3 V 37.7 Mb/s bidirectional microwave radio cable interface has been designed.

Key words: IP, Design Language, Design Automation, Design Reuse, Mixed-Signal, Design Flow, Layout Generator

1. Introduction

Looking in the direction of the enhanced 3rd and the 4th generation of wireless telecommunication systems a lot of challenges on physical level have to be met beside design reuse. Improvement of performance becomes a key issue. Continuously increasing data rates and bandwidth require new algorithms and new system architectures consisting of key components operating at the limit of technology. The basic problem is how to speed up the innovative design process itself with respect to reusability, how to implement a learning curve and how to overcome physical limitations forced by process technology and reducing supply voltages. Existing design methodologies for digital design are ready to meet the SOC demands on reuse and portability since designs can already be synthesized automatically from a high-level description language down to GDSII-level. For high performance analog and mixed signal macros such a standard cell approach has not yet been applicable.

It has to be considered that the lifetime for analog and mixed/signal macros with frozen GDSII data is very short. For a high number of high performance circuits the achieved performance is a compromise between SOC requirement and process capability. Processes are improved continuously. High effort is required for designing these circuits. If a sophisticated macro had been completed in the target process, a better performance would be possible in an already available new process. Also, the reuse of a macro in the same process is limited, since for other applications some conditions may require changes (e.g. power consumption, clock, and timings).

General design approaches for analog and mixed signal design automation are rare. Automated analog circuit synthesis is still not applicable to complex high performance circuits [1] [2]. Another

A. Mignotte et al. (eds.), System on Chip Design Languages, 87–97.

approach is the development of several synthesis tools, each optimized for a particular class of circuits, e.g. CMOS amplifiers [3]. Good results have been achieved but high effort is required for the development of these tools since special CAD tool functions are also included in the development. One promising approach for building a high speed DAC is reported in [4]. The presented design is retargetable to new process and design parameters within a few days. Limitations can be expected only by applying this approach to mixed/signal applications in general since a flat structure is used and layout operations are limited to stretching and tiling operations. An approach which is more related to the presented one is given in [5]. The method is based completely on ANSI-C. A set of functions have been defined to build graphical objects like polygons, contacts and devices. Layout generation is simply done by writing C-code using this library of functions. So this approach works independently from any other tool, but some interface routines have been provided for data transfer to commercial available EDA-tools.

The design of future high-performance System-On-Chip solutions requires productivity acceleration and a significant improvement of RF, analog, mixed-signal, and digital key macro performance. Therefore a very flexible highly automated design approach for mixed-signal circuits has been developed within the Design-Reuse program of the NOKIA Research Center. It is based on the use of a new defined design language (C-level), which addresses all relevant design domains (RF, Analog, Digital) from specification to layout and can be used in standard design environments. The design language is capable to introduce parameterizablity and process portability to the design.

2.   Symbolic Layout Principle

The chosen design style has high influence on the required design effort. A new design style which is based on the Virtual-Grid Symbolic Layout principle [6], defined for digital full custom designs, allows to design with variable design rules. Since the layout is the most complex part in analog circuit design, it focuses on layout generation. The same object oriented design style can be easily adapted for the generation of schematics and symbols.

The improved virtual-grid design principle considers special requirements coming along with analog circuit development. In opposite to the high regularity of digital CMOS circuits, which use common sized transistors and have a lack of passive components, an analog circuit, that was developed for one application already differs substantially only if some input specifications (e.g. bandwidth, supply voltage) changes. All sizes of active and passive components vary in a wide range (Fig. 1).

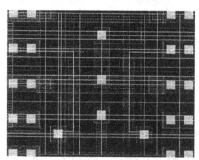

Figure 1. Virtual-Grid for PLL Phase-Comparator (detail)

The grid spacing is not only defined by physical design rules but also on special electrical parameters like e.g. cross-talk, matching of components, current density, required driving capability. All these parameters also have influence on the spacing and sizing of the components in an analog design. Therefore, a flexible grid definition with a variable spacing along the x- and y-axis is required. Since the grid definition is an array of values (2 dimensions) each grid section has to be defined separately. For each grid section a design variable exists. The structured naming scheme which has been defined for the variables containing the technology related data (electrical and physical) guarantees a transparent and concentrated computation of the grid line distances. The end result for the designer is that placement of objectives on the grid can be done without regard to any design rules.

3. IP Design Language Implementation

The proposed analog/mixed-signal IP design description is structured into the master procedure and several sub-procedures responsible for generating the different design views and simulator control (Fig. 2).

```
;File: moduleName

procedure(moduleName_master(parameters)
   let((local_variables)

   ;interactive specification of parameters
   ;computation of parameters
      ; check of plausibility for actual parameter settings

   moduleName_symbol(....)
   moduleName_schematic(....)
   moduleName_layout(....)
   moduleName_testbench(....)
   moduleName_datasheet(....)
   )
)
procedure(moduleName_schematic(....)
   let((local_variables)

   ; virtual grid for schematic
   ; relative placing of components, instances, and terminals
   ; wiring of components, instances, and terminals
   )

procedure(moduleName_layout(....)
   let((local_variables)

   ; virtual grid for layout
   ; automatic generation of subcells used as instances
   ;         measurement          of       actual      geometry      of       used      generated      or
      handcrafted subcells and update of virtual grid
   ; relative placing of components, instances, and terminals
   ; wiring of components, instances, and terminals
   ...)

procedure(moduleName_testbench(....)
   let((local_variables)
   ...)
   ;         actual          sizing        of        components       can         be        based        on
      simulation results
   ;           this           routine         optionally        starts         the        simulator      and
      backannotates simulation results
   )
```

Figure 2. Defined Structure of an AMS IP Generator

The master procedure enables access to the user interface for the setup of the IP generator. The user can choose between the customized interactive setup menus or the setup via an ASCII-file. With the finalized parameter setting the master procedure executes the defined sub-procedures.

Table 1. Selection of Functions for Layout Generation

Functions	Purpose
getContactLayerRadius	returns the radius of a layer of a contact
getLayerProp	returns selected layer properties
path	draws a path for a connection between two points
computeTermCoords	returns the coordinates of a terminal of a used layout instance
createTerm	places a terminal in a specified instance
createInst	places an instance
createNewCell	hierarchical use of generators
createOptCell	hierarchical use of generators with consideration of testbench simulation results
createPolygon	draws a polygon
guardRingPath	draws a guard ring path

A basic set of high level command macros has been defined to reduce the programming effort for the IP generators. Command macros are available for user entry, schematic, layout, simulator control, process data backannotation and datasheet generation. A selection of available layout functions is given in Table 1.

Table 2. Selection of Global Process Variables

Variable	Description
met1_layer	name of Metal1 layer in selected process
con_ndif_met1	name of the N-diffusion/Metal1 contact device
met2_spcmin	value for minimal metal2 spacing
poly_widthmin	value for minimal poly (poly1) width
pwell_ndif_minEnc	value for miminal enclosure for P-well over N-diffusion
mpoly_poly_r	value for poly (poly1) radius inside the metal1/poly contact device
mpdif_m1m2	value for minimal center-center distance between metal1/metal2 and P-diffusion unconnected contact devices
poly_shRes	poly (poly1) sheet resistance [Ohm/square]
poly_poly2_areaCap	area capacity for a poly (poly1)/poly2 capacitor

In the process independent IP design description variables are used instead of absolute values. A structured naming scheme has been defined for the global variables containing the technology related information (Table 2). This naming scheme enables an easy readable and verifiable design description .

4. Influence of Circuit Realisation Concept on Design Effort

The major domains influencing the required design effort for the implementation of the module generators are: circuit topology, hierarchy, degree of automation and required cell performance. Only a detailed analysis of these domains can minimize expenditure. A more regular structure reduces generator complexity since the number of grid lines is reduced. The use of hierarchy also reduces the implementation time with the benefit that basic cells only have to be designed once and can be shared. An important role is played by the target degree of automation. If the target is not to replace but to assist the experienced designer to preserve her/his design knowledge in a reusable manner, the implementation time can be reduced from infinity to a value not much more than required for the traditional handcrafted design style. Similar to the degree of automation also the required cell performance has a nonlinear influence on the implementation time. Especially the demand on a very high layout density increases the design effort due to a very fine grid for the symbolic layout. If a density of about 90 percent compared to an optimized handcrafted layout can be accepted this would save more than 50 percent of implementation time.

A layout example of a high speed output buffer in a 0.35 µm CMOS process is shown in Fig. 3 [7]. The size of the handcrafted design is 0.15mm x 0.125mm and of the generated layout is 0.16mm x 0.135 mm. The defined design methodology considers all these aspects and allows a high level design description with drastically reduced program code complexity for all design views (schematic, HDL-model, layout, datasheet).

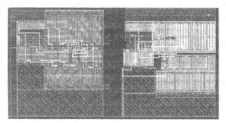

Figure 3. High Speed Buffer: Handcrafted Layout (Left), Generated Layout (Right)

5. Customized Design Environment

The new design approach has been introduced to a state of the art design frame-work with design entry, simulation, verification and backannotation tools (Fig.4) [8].

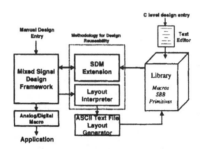

Figure 4. Customized User Interface

An interface has been added to the standard command interface enabling generator programming on higher level. A generator description language has been defined to minimize the effort for implementing the parameterizable designs. The design views schematic, layout, symbol, behavioural model and datasheet are supported in this approach. The renunciation of system level commands in the C-level design entry enables the defined command set to become independent from framework release updates and framework exchange. Only the interface has to be updated in such a case. This means all userdefined software modules are really reusable. Generated designs are fully compatible to handcrafted designs and verification can be handled in same way.

In this new approach there is no need for simulations of schematics since the layout view can be handled as flexibly as a schematic. In addition to the command interface a layout interpreter has been added [9]. This interpreter is able to extract C-level commands from a graphical hierarchical layout database, generating a raw source code block, which can easily be transferred and adapted to some other IP-blocks within this environment. Parameterizabilty such as variable gate length and width, number of input terminals, width of supply lines etc. can be controlled using object properties. Process administration routines decouple design and process related issues.

6.   Design Flow

The defined design methodology is based on the use of the adapted 'Virtual-Grid' principle. Design variables are used instead of values to describe designs in a process independent manner. The use of hierarchy limits complexity and allows shared primitives and simple building blocks (SBBs) for different types of macros. Available process files are used to verify, characterize and optimize the implemented cells. The implemented designs form a portable multi-process library which can be adapted easily to new process and circuit specifications. Since the designs are implemented in a process independent manner, the designer does not require the target process during the generator implementation phase. So, circuit development can be started already before the process selection.

In the first step of the design implementation flow (Fig. 5) all required system level specifications are collected. In analog design it is important that the macro to be developed is not overspecified, which means the increase of requirements without a reason. This would increase design cost exponentially. On the other hand a good yield requires some kind of over-specification in some parameters because of process tolerances. So, the severity of the requirement specifications have high influence on the effort required for the following design tasks.

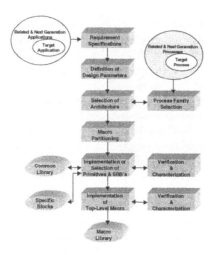

Figure 5. Design Implementation Flow

In addition to the traditional approach, related applications can be considered indirectly by leaving design parameters variable; e.g. for a memory it is useful to have the number of words, the length of word and the aspect ratio variable. For a converter variable resolution and conversion rate guarantee a possible reuse in future applications. The collected requirement specifications and design parameters allow a preselection of suited architectures. Often more than one architecture can be found to meet the requirements and the most regular structures should be preferred in such a case. Architectures which require only standard CMOS processes guarantee highest flexibility for future reuse.

The macros have to be partitioned into Simple Building Blocks (SBBs) and primitives. If other already implemented generators use the same required blocks (e.g. drivers, decoders, amplifiers, ...), they can be re-used for the new macro. The generators are programmed in the defined Generator Description Language (C-level). For using an implemented generator, the target application has to be introduced by fixing the design parameters (Fig. 6).

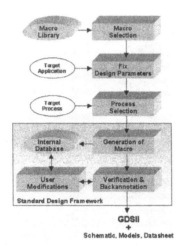

Figure 6. Design Flow based on using Marco Generators

The generators use this information for design partitioning, sizing, and library generation. If possible, simplified models can be used to perform automatic sizing. Since the generation takes place in a standard design framework, the same verification tools which are used for handcrafted design can be involved (DRC, LVS, backannotation of parasitics). The layout can be used directly for simulation. The schematic is left for LVS and documentation purpose only. Optimization and sizing on layout level becomes very easy by changing the setup values before restarting the generator again. The designer is free to make manual changes to the generated designs and also to mix them with additional handcrafted designs. Also handcrafted designs can be accessed from inside a generator at each level of hierarchy without restrictions.

7.   Experimental Results

The presented approach has been verified for several analog, digital, and mixed signal applications in two different design environments. It has been found out that in general every design which can be implemented handcraftedly can be implemented as a parameterizable generator. The following example demonstrates the impact of the new design methodology.

A microwave radio bidirectional cable interface ASIC with a data rate of 37.7 MS/s has been designed completely using parameterizable and process retargetable blocks. The system is able to adapt itself to different cable attenuations without manual tunings and change of settings. It consists of two 10b 85 MS/s DACs, two 8b 50 MS/s ADCs, a 10b 500 kS/s SAR-ADC, 45k gates digital logic and 15 different types of IOs with ESD protection . The measured bit error rate of the entire system is better than 10^{-13} in the specified supply range from 3.0V up to 3.6V and cable attenuation from 0 dB to 12 dB. Fig. 7 shows the microphotograph of the cable interface in a 0.35µm standard CMOS process.

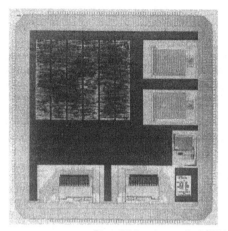

Figure 7. Microphotograph of 37.7 MS/s Cable Interface (5.9mm x 5.9mm)

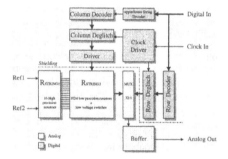

Figure 8. Block diagram of the D/A converter (10 bit)

The used high speed DAC IP (Fig.8) [10][11] is selected here to demonstrate parameterizability and process portability. Inside the cable interface it has been re-used to build the slow successive approximation ADC. The low clock frequency leads to reduced area requirements for this DAC. It is remarkable that the SAR-ADC architecture using the high-speed DAC macro required only 25% of the chip-area of an also available low speed SC-pipelined architecture [12]. A collection of different applications for the DAC IP is given in Table 3.

Table 3. Reuse of DAC IP Block

n (bit)	Clock (MHz)	Process	Application
9	2.2	0.8µ BiCMOS	GSM I/O Port
9	0.1	2µ BCDMOS	Demonstrator for Automotive (-40°C< T < 190°C)
10	85	0.35µm CMOS	Cable Interface
12	0.1	0.35µm CMOS	Transceiver Tuning

12	100	0.25µm BiCMOS	Cable Modem	
13	0.05	0.5 µm BiCMOS	Automotive	Sensor
			Application	

A high speed low power interpolating ADC IP has been developed in about 6 man-month [13]. Variable system level parameters are the resolution, conversion rate, and the code number of interpolation. The resolution can be between 6 and 10 bits. Functionality has been verified up to 100 MHz for a 10 bit converter in a 0.35µm CMOS process. The generation cycle of all design views takes about 15 minutes on a Sun UltraSparc10 machine. Behavioural models enable mixed-mode simulation to reduce simulation time.

A process retargetable standard cell and IO library including ESD protection has been implemented based on the presented design approach [14][15]. A basic brick set forming a standard cell construction set has been defined enabling the designer to define new standard cells without regard to design rules and grid definition. For the cable interface a 0.35 µm library was needed. For library implementation a 0.25 µm CMOS process was used. In total 14 man-days were required to convert a library of 250 cells to a new process (2 days for setup, 7 days for library generation, and 5 days for verification). The characterization and generation of model files is started as fully automated background task.

8.　Conclusion

A unified mixed-signal IP design platform has been introduced. It focuses on flexibility of design and process parameters in analog, digital, and mixed-signal designs within a customized conventional design framework. Special features are the flexible degree of automation and the compability to handcrafted designs. A standard layout editor or the C-level interface can be used for design entry. It was possible to demonstrate strength of the developed methodology on a critical mixed-signal system, a bidirectional cable interface for microwave radio applications. The design effort can be compared to the handcrafted design style but the result is much more flexible. The layout view can be used as flexibly as a schematic and layout parasitics can be considered easily. The reuse of a marco with varying design and process parameters is possible within a few days. The presented approach offers a solution to overcome the design gap problem by substantially increasing the design work efficiency.

9.　References

[1] O. Guerra, E. Roca, F. V. Fernandez, A. Rodriguez-Vazquez, "A hierarchical approach for the symbolic analysis of large analog integrated circuits," Design, Automation and Test in Europe, Conf. and Exh. 2000, Proc., pp. 48-52

[2] Xiang-Dong Tan, C.-J. Richard Shi, "Hierarchical symbolic analysis of analog integrated circuits via dominant decision diagrams," IEEE Trans. on CAD of integrated Circuits and Systems, Vol. 19, No. 4, pp. 401-412, April 2000

[3] H.Y. Koh, C.H. Sequin, and P.R. Gray, "OPASYN: A compiler for CMOS operational amplifiers," IEEE Trans. Computer-Aided Design, Vol. 9, No. 2, pp. 113-125, Feb. 1990

[4] R. Neff, P.R. Gray, A. Sangiovanni-Vincentelli, "A module generator for high-speed CMOS current output digital/analog converters," IEEE JSSC, Vol. 31, No.3, March 1996

[5] W. Schardein, "Ein stand-alone Toolset zur effizienten Entwicklung von Layout-Modulgeneratoren," Analog '99, Entwicklung von Analogschaltungen mit CAE-Methoden, Muenchen, 18./19.02.1999, S.399-406.

[6] N. Weste, K. Eshraghian, "Principles of CMOS VLSI design," 2nd Ed., Eddison Wesley, 1994

[7] U. Lücking, "Prozeßunabhängiger Entwurf eines Buffers in CMOS für schnelle Datenumsetzer", Diplomarbeit, Fachhochschule Dortmund, Juni 1998

[8] R. Wittmann, W. Schardein, D.Bierbaum, M.Darianian, "SOC-driven design methodology for full custom high performance mixed-signal designs," 13th Int. ASIC/SOC Conf. , Proceedings, Washington, pp. 148-152, Sept. 2000

[9] B. Oelkrug, "Entwicklung eines Verfahrens zur automatischen Konvertierung eines nicht parametrisierbaren Hand-Layouts in ein parametrisierbares Design nach dem LIBGEN-Prinzip", Studienarbeit, Universität Dortmund, 1999

[10] R. Wittmann, W. Schardein, B. J. Hosticka, G. Burbach, J. Arndt, "Trimless high precision ratioed resistors in D/A- and A/D converters," *IEEE J. Solid-State Circuits*, vol. 30, no. 8, pp. 935-939, Aug. 1995

[11] R. Wittmann, D.Bierbaum, W.Schardein, E. Matei,"A paramerterizable and process retargetable high speed DAC for digital radio applications," 12th Int. ASIC/SOC Conference, Proceedings, Washington, pp. 404-408, Sept. 1999

[12] Ch. Aslanidis, "Schaltungs- und Layoutgenerator für einen hochauflösenden universellen ADC in CMOS", Diplomarbeit, Ruhr-Universität Bochum, Sept. 1998

[13] A. Bamba, "Entwicklung eines parametrisierbaren schnellen ADU für Entwurfswiederverwendbarkeit bei Prozeßänderung", Diplomarbeit, Ruhr-Universität Bochum, Sep. 1999

[14] H. Bothe, "Einsatz einer parametrisierbaren, prozeßunabhängigen Standardzellen-Bibliothek zur Synthese von CMOS-Digitalschaltungen " , Diplomarbeit, Universität Dortmund, Jan. 1999

[15] A. Herper, "Prozeßinvarianter Entwurf von ESD-Schutzstrukturen für Peripheriezellen in CMOS Prozessen", Diplomarbeit, Fachhochschule Dortmund, Aug. 1999

Chapter 9

Analog Filter Synthesis from VHDL-AMS

Fazrena A. Hamid and Tom J. Kazmierski

Dept. of Electronics and Computer Science, University of Southampton, U.K.

Abstract: An analog synthesis technique for VHDL-AMS behavioral descriptions of very high-frequency filters is described. The technique is based on automatic netlist extraction from VHDL-AMS parse trees. The primary application of this work is automated synthesis of high-frequency filter blocks in analog or mixed-signal ASIC designs. The technique is demonstrated with two practical examples – the first is a second-order, 1 GHz bandpass silicon LC filter, and the second example is a 4th order lowpass Chebyshev filter. Both examples gives an optimized result which are tailored to the specifications.

Key words:

1. INTRODUCTION

Due to the growing importance of mixed-signal ASICs, development of integrated analog and mixed-signal synthesis techniques has become a burning issue. Many modern mixed-signal ASIC designs incorporate analog high-frequency filters design with applications in the highly integrated wireless communications sector. The inclusion of analog circuitry on a chip, which is otherwise digital, is vital for high-performance and high frequency applications. An example of this is the bandpass filtering in a receiver's front-end circuit. A type of filter most suitable for such applications is the active LC filter [1,2,3,4]. LC filters can now be implemented on silicon, mainly because of the recent development in on-chip spiral inductor technologies [5,6]. Silicon inductors with value of several to several dozen nH, with Q more than 6 in the 1-5 GHz frequency range have now become available [1].

We propose to use high-level VHDL-AMS descriptions for synthesis of such filters because filters of this type can exist in a larger, mixed-signal environment and can be described in both time and frequency domain. For example, VHDL-AMS may be used to design and synthesis a single-chip receiver front-end of a communication system employing a bandpass filter. We have developed a technique of automated filter synthesis based on recognizable patterns in VHDL-AMS parse trees. These description patterns can represent time-domain differential equations of a filter or frequency-domain transfer functions.

VHDL-AMS [7,8] is a language with the capabilities of describing mixed-signal circuits in both the frequency and the time domain. Thus, not only the filter can be appropriately modeled, the rest of the communication system can also be modeled, simulated and synthesized from the same description language. Although VHDL-AMS is designed for simulation, it can also be used for synthesis with several restrictions imposed on the description syntax [9]. For its potential, this language is already receiving a significant attention in research; including mixed-signal synthesis. Currently there is VASE (VHDL-AMS Synthesis Environment) [10,11], and NEUSYS [12].

This contribution describes a technique of automated synthesis of analog filters. The synthesis stage is followed by an optimization stage, which chooses a set of parameter values that produces an optimized filter circuit. The

A. Mignotte et al. (eds.), System on Chip Design Languages, 99–109.
© 2002 *Kluwer Academic Publishers.*

input to the synthesizer is a VHDL-AMS description of the filter, from which a successful synthesis will produce a HSPICE netlist of the filter implementation.

We used the classical approach to analog synthesis, which starts from the selection of a circuit and subsequent optimization of the circuit parameters such as the techniques used, for example by OPASYN [13] and OAC [14].

Section 2 describes our method of architectural filter synthesis based on VHDL-AMS parse trees. This is followed by a section describing the parametric optimization illustrated by the example of a second-order 1GHz bandpass filter and a fourth-order lowpass filter.

2. ARCHITECTURAL FILTER SYNTHESIS FROM VHDL-AMS

Figure 1 shows the synthesis process flow from the high-level VHDL-AMS description of a filter to the netlist. The two main blocks are the parser and synthesizer. The synthesizer uses the parse tree generated by the parser for automatic netlist generation.

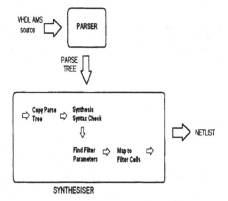

Figure 1. Block diagram of the filter synthesis system.

The procedure starts with the parser performing a VHDL-AMS syntax check, and then generating the parse tree for the synthesizer, which performs a synthesis rule check. If the input description is found to be synthesizable, then a mapping to generic filter cells is done to produce the filter's circuit-level HSPICE netlist.

Filters can be described using VHDL-AMS in two ways: as time-domain models or alternatively as frequency-domain s-transfer functions.

Conventionally, the latter is the most common way to represent a filter to a synthesis system where in VHDL-AMS this is done using the LTF attribute. However, with the intention of having an analog filter integrated with other digital components in a communication system, for example, where the digital part can also be modeled using VHDL-AMS, it may be more practical to describe the filter in its time domain.

However, the two examples in Section 3 will show the two types of modeling analog filters.

2.1 Synthesis syntax check

Both the time and frequency domain models must follow certain syntax restrictions. Firstly, the VHDL-AMS entity declaration can only contain port with quantity declarations as the interface. The quantities for input and output must both be of type real, for example:

```
entity filter is
  port (quantity Vin: real;
        quantity Vout: out real);
end entity filter;
```

Secondly, frequency domain models are described using the LTF attribute. The algorithm used to find the roots of the polynomials requires that the numerator and the denominator coefficients of the transfer function must be arranged in an ascending manner, for example, the transfer function

is written in VHDL-AMS as:

$$H(s) = \frac{a}{1 + bs + cs^2}$$

```
architecture transfer of filter is
  constant num: real_vector:= (a);
  constant den: real_vector:= (1.0,b,c);
begin
    Vout == Vin'LTF(num,den);
end architecture;
```

Filters of any order can be described using this model, keeping in mind only those with the denominator order larger or equal to the numerator order are realizable.

Thirdly, time domain filter models are described using Differential Algebraic Equations in simple simultaneous statements using the DOT attribute, as shown in the example below. The coefficients associated with the output and its first and second derivatives must be static expressions, for example:

```
vin == coeff1*vout'dot'dot + coeff2*vout'dot  + coeff3*vout;
```

Checking the syntax compliance during the initial synthesis stage is done by traversing the parse tree of the architecture body and a search for a simultaneous statement. For an s-domain (frequency-domain) filter model, the program further searches for occurrences of the LTF attribute, and real vectors for the numerator and denominator.

For a time domain model, the program proceeds to search for the pattern shown in Figure 2.

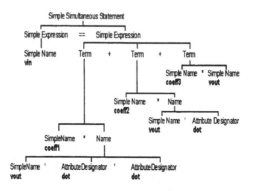

Figure 2. Parse tree for a second-order filter described by
vin == coeff1 *vout'dot'dot + coeff2 *vout'dot + coeff3 *vout

3.   EXAMPLES

We present two examples of automated synthesis of analog filters and their corresponding performance results. One is a 1GHz LC bandpass filter constructed around a Colpitts-type Q-bootstrapping circuit, and the other example is a 4th order Chebyshev filter [20]; a 1GHz filter using nonlinear MOS capacitances and DC currents for accurate frequency and Q-tuning. Both types of filters use positive feedback to reduce the effect of losses at very high frequencies resulting in an improved gain and an improved Q factor [1].

3.1   A second-order LC bandpass filter

As an example, we present the synthesis of a high-frequency Q-enhanced LC bandpass filter. As the filter is intended for implementation on a silicon chip, the on-chip inductor is a spiral inductor. Such inductors have significant losses and, for a bandpass filter, this will result in a very low Q factor. A Q-enhancement method is used to cancel the effect of these losses by introducing a negative resistance. In our implementation we propose a very effective, Colpitts-type LC oscillator for Q-enhancement.

The LC bandpass filter is constructed around a Colpitts oscillator to bootstrap Q as shown in Figure 3. The positive feedback reduces the effect of losses generated by the spiral inductor L1, resulting in an improved Q factor [1].

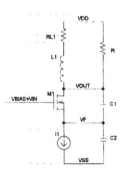

Figure 3. Colpitts circuit producing a Q-enhanced bandpass behaviour at output VOUT

The amount of feedback is controlled by the ratio of capacitors C1 and C2, where the value of both capacitors in series together with inductor L1 determine the frequency of the bandpass filter. The Q factor is determined by the feedback provided by the capacitors C1 and C2, the current flowing into the transistor from current source I1, and the width of the transistor M1.

Inductor L1 is a spiral inductor whose losses are modeled by the series resistor RL1. More accurate models have also been described in literature [15,16]. Although it is possible to construct a higher-value spiral inductor, it is more practical to choose a value of less than 10nH [15]. In the above example the inductor is chosen to be 8nH, and the corresponding loss resistance RL1 is 5 Ω.

The filter's VHDL-AMS time-domain description is shown below:

```
entity filter is
  generic ( Q: real:= 50.0;
            F: real:= 1e9);
  port  (quantity vin: real;
         quantity vout: out real);
end entity filter;


architecture behavioral of filter is
    constant W: real:= 2*3.142*F;
    constant coeff1: real:= Q/W;
    constant coeff2: real:= 1.0;
    constant coeff3: real:= Q*W;
begin
    vin'dot == coeff1*vout'dot'dot +
    coeff2*vout'dot  + coeff3*vout;
end architecture behavioral;
```

Note that in the entity declaration, the user can specify the desired values to be achieved, namely a 1 GHz filter circuit with Q factor of 50.

This filter can be implemented in silicon. The netlist uses 0.35 micrometer CMOS transistor models and is simulated using HSPICE [18].

3.1.1   Optimization

The objective function, in our case, is a Q factor of 50, with the centre frequency of 1 GHz. As explained in the previous section, the circuit parameters that contributed to the Q factor are the capacitor values, the bias current and the transistor width. At the same time, the values of the capacitors and the inductor will determine the frequency of the bandpass response. There is also another optimization constraint - the inductor value - which in order to minimize the losses and parasitic capacitances, should be kept to a minimum [15]. In our experiment, the inductance was kept at a constant value of 8nH.

Although the desired Q factor is 50, the optimization program can also be set to find the maximum Q factor.

The optimizer launches the HSPICE simulator in the optimization loop to evaluate the Q factor at each new set of parameter values. The Q factor of the resulting circuit is obtained from the SPICE AC results file, and the optimizer logs the best set of Q factor that it finds until the optimization loop terminates. The termination condition is either when the value found is closest to specification (in this case 50) or when the default maximum iteration value has been reached. If the goal is to find the best Q factor, the user can specify in the optimization program the number of HSPICE iterations; which may be a large value.

The current optimization strategy uses a random search within the prescribed parameter space but will in the future be expanded to use more sophisticated methods such as the simulated annealing technique [17], to ensure a more reliable result.

3.1.2   Experimental results

Table 1 shows the summary of the optimization result for up to 118 iterations. Iterations beyond the 43rd one did not show a noticeable improvement of the Q factor. Therefore it can be concluded that for this particular Colpitts configuration, the largest Q factor that can be achieved is approximately 217, which the optimizer found at the 43rd iteration and took 74 seconds to find.

Table 1. Summary of optimisation results

CPU Time (s)	No. of iterations	Q Factor
0	0	14.5
5	1	23.3
9	4	31.0
27	11	33.0
49	27	39.4
53	30	48.2
74	43	217.0
209	118	217.1

From simulation, the Q factor of the lossy LC circuit without Q-enhancement at f = 1GHz is 10.2, as shown in Figure 4. This is confirmed by hand calculation; the Q factor of the lossy LC filter without the amplifier circuit at 1 GHz is about 10.1, (where Q = 2 $\pi f L$/RL1 with L=8nH and RL1=5 Ω).

The best result obtained by the optimizer is shown in Figure 5, while Figure 6 shows the result for a bandpass response with Q factor of about 50.

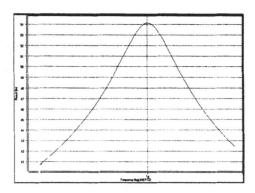

Figure 4. HSPICE simulation result for the lossy LC circuit without Q-enhancement; the graph covers the frequency range from 0.8GHz to 1.2GHz.

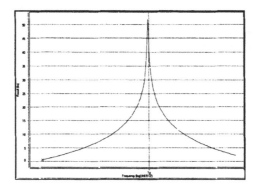

Figure 5. HSPICE simulation result of the filter optimized for the maximum Q factor (Q= 217); the frequency range is 0.8GHz to 1.2GHz.

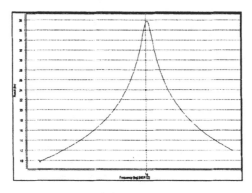

Figure 6. HSPICE simulation result of the filter optimized for the Q factor of 50; the frequency range shown is 0.8GHz to 1.2GHz.

3.2   A fourth-order low pass filter

This example presents the other, perhaps more familiar way of modeling analog filters using VHDL-AMS, that is from their s-domain transfer functions.

The circuit chosen for this example is shown in Figure 7, which is a vertically stacked current-mode biquadratic filter implemented from the regulated cascode configuration [20]. The circuit also includes a Q-tuning circuitry.

A 4th order low pass Chebyshev filter may have the following transfer function:

$$H(s) = \frac{As^2 + Bs + C}{Ds^4 + Es^3 + Fs^2 + Gs + H}$$

This transfer function can be implemented in VHDL-AMS as demonstrated below:

```
entity filter is
   port (quantity Vin: real;
         quantity Vout: out real);
end entity filter;

architecture transfer of filter is
   constant num:real_vector:=(C,B,A);
   constant den:real_vector:=(H,G,F,E,D);
begin
     Vout == Vin'LTF(num,den);
end architecture transfer;
```

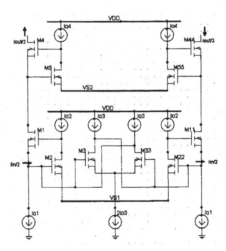

Figure 7. A fourth-order low pass filter

The circuit in Figure 7 as specified in [20] is a 4th order Chebyshev lowpass filter with 1 GHz cutoff frequency and 0.25dB ripple, and is realized by vertically stacking two fully-differential biquad circuits. There is a Q-tuning circuit for the first biquad (the middle part of the lower section of the circuit on Figure 7), and the Q factor may be tuned by varying the bias current in Io3. Frequency tuning can also be achieved by varying current Io1.

It was stated in [20] that the circuit was simulated using 0.35micrometer CMOS technology.

3.2.1 Optimization

The circuit was simulated on HSPICE using the device specifications as in [20]. Although we are also using a 0.35 micrometer CMOS technology, but different transistor models gave a result which was not according to the design specifications.

The parameters to be optimized are all the transistor widths and the bias current Io1.

The optimization strategy for this particular example differs slightly from the previous one in that we attempt to use the built-in optimization feature of HSPICE [18].

3.2.2 Experimental results

Figure 8 shows the HSPICE simulation result of the 4th order lowpass filter using the original circuit parameters as in [20]. It can be seen that the circuit produces a high overshoot of almost 7 dB with a cutoff frequency exceeding 1 GHz.

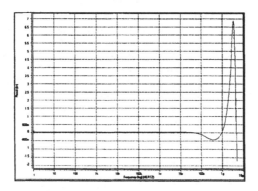

Figure 8. AC characteristic before optimization; using original circuit parameters as in [20].

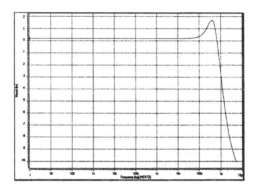

Figure 9. AC characteristic of the optimized circuit.

Therefore the goal here is to obtain a cutoff frequency of 1GHz, and at the same time limiting the overshoot to be lower than 3 dB. The final result is shown in Figure 9.

The time taken for HSPICE to complete the optimization is 31.6 seconds.

4.   CONCLUSION

This contribution presents a novel, VHDL-AMS based technique of architectural synthesis and optimization of high-frequency analog filters. VHDL-AMS provides a simple yet accurate and natural way to represent filters that can potentially be embedded in larger, mixed-signal VHDL-AMS systems. The presence of such filters in a predominantly digital ASIC causes significant delays in the completion of the mixed-signal design, because analog ASIC parts are currently implemented manually. Automated filter synthesis from high-level VHDL-AMS descriptions provides an important step towards a fully integrated, mixed-signal synthesis system, in which both the digital and analog behavior can be described using a single, standard description language.

The successful operation of the synthesizer and optimizer has been demonstrated using the two examples of high frequency analog filters. Further work will concentrate on the improvement of the integrated optimizer and filter standard cell libraries.

The aim of this contribution is to show the two main ways to model analog filters for automated synthesis using VHDL-AMS, and to demonstrate how post-synthesis optimization specifications for filter circuits can be included in the VHDL-AMS description.

5.   REFERENCES

[1] Li, D., Tsividis, Y., "Active LC filters on silicon", Circuits, Devices and Systems, IEE Proceedings, **147**, (1) , Feb. 2000 , pp. 49 –56.
[2] Duncan, R.A., Martin, K., and Sedra, A., "A Q-enhanced active-RLC bandpass filter", IEEE Transactions on Circuits and Systems II, Analog and Digital Signal Processing, 1997, **44**, (5), pp. 341-347.
[3] Gao, W., and Snelgrove, W.M., "A linear integrated LC bandpass filter with Q-enhancement", IEEE Transactions on Circuits and Systems II, Analog and Digital Signal Processing, 1998, **45**, (5), pp. 635-639.
[4] Kuhn, W.B., Yanduru, N.K., and Wyszynski, A.S., "A high dynamic range, digitally tuned, Q-enhanced LC bandpass filter for cellular/PCS receivers", Proceedings of IEEE Radio Frequency Integrated Circuits Symposium, 1998, pp. 261-264.
[5] Kuhn, W.B., Elshabini-Riad, A., and Stephenson, F.W., "Centre-tapped spiral inductors for monolithic bandpass filters", Electronic Letters, 1995, **31**, (8), pp. 625-626.

[6] Burghartz, J. N., Edelstein, D.C., Soyuer, M., Ainspan, H.A. and Jenkins, K.A., "RF circuit design aspects of spiral inductors on silicon", IEEE Journal Solid-State Circuits, 1998, **33**, (12), pp. 2028-2034.

[7] Design Automation Standards Committee of the IEEE Computer Society, "IEEE standard VHDL analog and mixed-signal extensions", IEEE Std 1076.1-1999 , 23 Dec. 1999.

[8] Christen, E., Bakalar, K., "VHDL-AMS - a hardware description language for analog and mixed-signal applications", IEEE Transactions on Circuits and Systems II: Analog and Digital Signal Processing, **46**, (10), Oct. 1999, pp. 1263–1272.

[9] Doboli, A., and Vemuri, R., "The Definition of a VHDL-AMS Subset for Behavioral Synthesis of Analog Systems", 1998 IEEE/VIUF International Workshop on Behavioral Modeling and Simulation (BMAS'98), Oct 1998.

[10] Vemuri, R., Nunez-Aldana, A., Dhanwada, N., Doboli, A., Campisi, P., Ganesan, S. "Analog System Performance Estimation in the VASE", Proc. EETimes Analog And Mixed-Signal Applications Conference, pp. 65-70, July 1998.

[11] Doboli, A., Dhanwada, N., Nunez-Aldana, A., Ganesan, S., Vemuri, R., "Behavioral Synthesis of Analog Systems using Two-Layered Design Space Exploration", Proceedings of the 36th Design Automation Conference, June 1999.

[12] Domenech-Asensi, G., Kazmierski, T.J., "Automated synthesis of high-level VHDL-AMS analog descriptions", *First On Line Symposium For Electronic Engineers*, Sept. 2000, http://techonline.com/osee/.

[13] Koh, H.Y., Sequin, C.H., and Gray, P.R. "OPASYN: A Compiler for CMOS Operational Amplifiers", IEEE Transactions on Computer Aided Design of Integrated Circuits and Systems, **9** (2), Feb. 1990, pp. 113-125.

[14] Onodera, H., Kanbara, H., Tamaru, K., "Operational-amplifier compilation with performance optimization," IEEE J. Solid-State Circuits, vol. 25, Apr. 1990, pp. 466-473.

[15] Lee, T.H., The Design of CMOS Radio-Frequency Integrated Circuit, Cambridge University Press, 1998.

[16] Yue, C. P., Ryu, C., Lau, J., Lee, T. H., Wong, S. S., "A Physical Model for Planar Spiral Inductors on Silicon," *IEDM Proceedings*, December 1996.

[17] Kirkpatrick, S., Gelatt, C.D., and Vecchi, M.P.J., "Optimization by Simulated Annealing," Science, 1983, **220**, (4598), pp. 671-680.

[18] Star-HSPICE Manual, Avant!, Release 2000.2.

[19] Kuhn, W.B., Stephenson, F.W., and Elshabini-Riad, A., "A 200 MHz CMOS Q-Enhanced LC Bandpass Filter", IEEE Journal Solid-State Circuits, 1996, **31**, (8), pp. 1112-1121.

[20] Yodprasit, U., Sirivathanant, K., "A Compact Low-Power Vertical Filter for Very-High-Frequency Applications," The 2001 IEEE International Symposium on Circuits and Systems (ISCAS 2001), Vol. 1, pp. 164 -167, May 2001.

SYSTEM DESIGN EXPERIENCES

Chapter 10

Using GNU Make to Automate the Recompile of VHDL SoC Designs

Michael D. McKinney
Senior Member of the Technical Staff, DLP™ Products, Texas Instruments, Inc., Dallas, Texas

Abstract: In every ASIC design project there comes a time that the design and its component parts must be functionally verified. In today's design environment, the design is usually described in an HDL and the majority of the verification task is accomplished using an HDL simulator. In preparation for the simulations, it is always required that at least some of the design hierarchy be successfully compiled. The first successful compile and the subsequent recompilations of a design expressed in VHDL is the focus of this paper.

This paper details the use of GNU 'make' in controlling and automating the compile of VHDL designs. The paper focuses primarily on using 'make' in a hierarchical manner via a set of makefiles, in order to correctly compile the designs that utilize external, sharable, reusable and independently verified VHDL components. Secondarily the paper focuses on constructing the 'make' programs so that the compiles are done in the most efficient manner possible.

Key words: VHDL, GNU, make, Systems-on-Chip, Design Automation

1.   INTRODUCTION

Many large ASIC designs being created in today's market are called SoC or System-on-Chip devices. They utilize methodologies to partition and encapsulate components. In many cases each of these reusable components is independently verified using it's own verification environment and test cases. Further, these components may be independently synthesized, may have timing and/or layout information extracted, and may have ATPG patterns generated.

While many software tools focus on the verification of these blocks, at some point in time the system itself (ASIC, SoC, board, etc.) will have to be functionally verified. This is typically done with an HDL simulator using a compiled executable image of the design being verified. A key piece of the successful simulation of the design is the successful compilation of all the required HDL files that comprise the design. For many years and for most design teams this process has been implemented with make.

This paper presents three special areas of consideration that are focused on a make-based compilation methodology. The first area for special consideration is that in most design projects the act of compiling the HDL source code is done repeatedly. These repeated compiles should be done in the most efficient manner possible, based on simulator/compiler capability. Addressing the issue of efficiency involves how the makefile itself is constructed.

The second area for special consideration is the use of pre-verified components in an SoC design. This type of component is sometimes called intellectual property (IP), sharable or embeddable. The

A. Mignotte et al. (eds.), System on Chip Design Languages, 113–127.

makefiles or other compile methodologies used when those components were verified should not be abandoned just because the focus has shifted to the system level.

The third and final area for special consideration is the use of make in a team environment. That is, an environment in which team members can develop, simulate and debug individual aspects of the design (even individual VHDL files) without disturbing the workflow of the other team members.

This paper encourages the use of GNU make, and will develop these ideas in order to create a more complete verification flow and methodology.

For the purposes of this paper, the term 'make' refers to the GNU (www.gnu.org) program. This program is an interpreter style of program that reads, parses, interprets and executes the instructions contained in a separate text file. For purposes of this paper the term 'makefile' refers to that separate text file. Its format is very well known and recognizable in the electronic circuit design industry.

2.   WHY CHOOSE 'GNU' MAKE?

GNU make was designed as a clone and as an extension of UNIX™ make. GNU make was chosen for this paper and its use is encouraged largely because of these extensions.

First, for example, GNU make offers conditional execution with the inclusion of 'if' style constructs. This is very helpful in determining (for example) if a makefile is being executed in a block- or system-level environment. Second, GNU make offers built-in functions that can modify text and filenames on the fly. This is helpful in calculating (for example) the local directory name for a targeted file. Third, GNU make offers the ability to use (and create) special 'match-anything' rules. Several of these special rules are pre-defined, and called 'implicit rules'. These special rules (whether built-in, created or modified) are convenient for executing specific commands for **all** targets -- for example the rule for automatic check-out of an RCS file in preparation for compilation.

These reasons together with the fact that GNU make is just as accessible and contains all of the function of UNIX™ make contributed to the choice of GNU make.

Figure 1 displays a functional makefile for a small component. This basic makefile will be modified throughout this paper to illustrate the changes being discussed.

```
# ####################################
# makefile for component therm
# ####################################


#
# define path to the HDL code and object library
#
DESIGN = /design/component_path/therm
LIBRARY = $(DESIGN)/libraries
DESIGN_SRC = $(DESIGN)/hdl
VLIB = $(LIBRARY)/therm_lib


#
# define targets for the individual HDL files
#    (inside compiler object library).
#
```

```
TARG_FILE1 = $(VLIB)/file1/file1.dat
TARG_FILE3 = $(VLIB)/file3/file3.dat
TARG_FILE4 = $(VLIB)/file4/file4.dat
TARG_CFG3 = $(VLIB)/cfg3/cfg3.dat
TARG_CFG1 = $(VLIB)/cfg1/cfg1.dat


#
# define VHDL compile command and options
#  ('therm_lib' is also defined in 'modelsim.ini' file).
#
VCOM = vcom −93 −source −work therm_lib


#
# define the 'whole_library' target.
#   note: no commands.  Only rule triggered is the
#      top-level configuration.
#
whole_library : $(TARG_CFG1)




#
# define the rules for the individual HDL files
#
$(TARG_FILE1) : $(DESIGN_SRC)/file1.vhd \
     $(TARG_CFG3)
  $(VCOM) $(DESIGN_SRC)/file1.vhd

$(TARG_CFG3) : $(DESIGN_SRC)/cfg3.vhd \
     $(TARG_FILE4) \
     $(TARG_FILE3)
  $(VCOM) $(DESIGN_SRC)/cfg3.vhd

$(TARG_FILE3) : $(DESIGN_SRC)/file3.vhd \
     $(TARG_FILE4)
  $(VCOM) $(DESIGN_SRC)/file3.vhd

$(TARG_FILE4) : $(DESIGN_SRC)/file4.vhd
  $(VCOM) $(DESIGN_SRC)/file4.vhd

$(TARG_CFG1) : $(DESIGN_SRC)/cfg1.vhd \
     $(TARG_FILE4) \
     $(TARG_FILE3) \
     $(TARG_CFG3) \
     $(TARG_FILE1)
  $(VCOM) $(DESIGN_SRC)/cfg1.vhd

#
```

```
# define the 'clean' target : no dependencies
#
clean:
  \rm -rf $(VLIB)
  vlib $(VLIB)
```

Figure 1. Basic Makefile

3.   THE ISSUE OF EFFICIENCY

A well constructed make control file (i.e., a makefile) used for compiling VHDL files is guaranteed to execute commands only for the individual files that have been touched or otherwise updated since the last execution of make. Furthermore, this make-controlled compilation is guaranteed to maintain the total executable (and simulatable) image by additionally compiling all of the VHDL files that hierarchically depend on the updated files, in the required order as specified by the VHDL LRM[1]. For design teams that do not utilize make (for example, by compiling using a pre-defined list of HDL files listed in compile order) this is already a massive step forward in the area of efficiency since by using the list all files must be compiled, while with make only the updated ones are compiled. However, a question remains about whether any further steps toward compilation efficiency may be effective by further modifying the makefile. The answer is yes. The following paragraphs will further develop and detail these modifications.

3.1   An efficiency proposal

One modification for efficiency that can occur utilizes more of the capabilities of the simulator system's HDL compiler, and builds those additional capabilities into the makefile. For example, the HDL compiler programs associated with most modern simulator systems allow at least filenames and sometimes command-line options to be placed in a separate file. This separate and uniquely formatted file, sometimes called a 'command file', is then accessed by a compiler command-line option, like '-f <filename>' or '-file <filename>'. The idea here is that even with a long list of HDL files the compiler itself need only be executed once. This is a more efficient process because the license manager needs to process only one request instead of several or hundreds. A makefile can guarantee that a file of this kind is formatted correctly (syntactically) and that the list of HDL source files placed in this file is in the correct hierarchical compile order (bottom-up).

3.2   Implementing the proposal

Changes to a makefile to create the more efficient compile process described in the previous paragraph are straightforward textually, but require some thought logically. Areas of concern are focused on the definition of the targets, the construction of the rules themselves, and the overall order of target execution. The makefile of Figure 1 is used as the reference for the following discussions, and the resulting new makefile is shown in Figure 2.

3.2.1. The target definitions. In Figure 1 the targets for the rules are the actual object files that are touched (updated) by the execution of the HDL compiler, typically inside a compiled library directory tree. However, if it is the purpose of the makefile to create a list of VHDL files to be compiled at some later time (as in this proposal), then at the time a make rule triggers for a particular file the compiler would not be executed and its output files would not be updated as in Figure 1. Therefore, for this new behavior the defined targets must identify some other file that can be updated when a rule is triggered. Make calls these special files "empty targets".

The suggested target for this stage is simply an empty file, updated by 'touch'. Since 'touch' updates the timestamp of a file, this is adequate for make to determine when a rule's commands were last executed. A unique timestamp file is associated with each individual VHDL file.

3.2.2. Rule construction. In the makefile of Figure 1 the 'command' portion of the rules consists of a single call to the HDL compiler together with the associated options and filename to compile. Since in this proposal the makefile is designed to create an external compiler control file, the new rules would contain two commands: a simple 'echo' of a fully qualified filename, redirected into the external file, and 'touch $@', updating the target as explained in the previous section. The '$@' symbol is a special variable within make and refers to the target of the rule currently being triggered. The dependency or prerequisite portion of the rules are not affected by this change in rule structure.

3.2.3. Order of rule execution. Rule execution in a makefile begins with the first rule parsed in the file, but otherwise is dependent on the top-down evaluation of the dependency or prerequisite section of the other rules (if any). In many makefiles the first target therefore is a general one, called "whole_library" or "design" or, more often, simply "all". Typically this first rule will contain only a dependency list, and the dependency list will contain references to only a very few other targets -- in Figure 1 only one dependency target is listed: the top-level configuration file.

Since for this proposal the command portion of the rules no longer execute the HDL compiler directly in favor of appending filenames to an external file, the initially triggered rule must now contain some special dependency rules that 1) create the external file, and 2) execute the simulator compiler when all targets associated with HDL files have completed. These special rules do not exist in Figure 1 and so are inserted into Figure 2, and in this paper are called '.INIT' and '.DONE'. These special targets may be called by any user-selected name.

The .INIT rule creates the external file with 'touch' and proceeds to install into the external file the required set of VHDL compiler options as specified by the compiler being used. All further rules will append file names to this file with 'echo' commands.

The .DONE rule will execute the HDL compiler **IFF** at least one additional rule has triggered, meaning that at least one file name has been entered into the external file. The .DONE rule has to recognize this because it is usually an error to execute the HDL compiler with no filename or list of filenames.

To complete the discussion of the .INIT and .DONE rules, note that the 'if' syntax included in the command sections of these rules is *not* the make-included 'if' constructs notes in a previous section, but rather Bourne shell (sh) syntax. This is a general aspect of make: all commands are executed in a Bourne shell and so must exhibit Bourne syntax.

Now that the desired modifications have been identified and discussed, please refer to Figure 2 for the complete transformation of the makefile in Figure 1.

```
# ####################################
#  makefile for component therm
# ####################################
#
# define path to the HDL code, and object library,
#    and timestamp file directory
#
DESIGN = /design/component_path/therm
LIBRARY = $(DESIGN)/libraries
DESIGN_SRC = $(DESIGN)/hdl
VLIB = $(LIBRARY)/therm_lib
STMP_DIR = $(LIBRARY)/tstamp


#
# define targets for the individual HDL files
#    (now located inside tstamp directory)
#
TARG_FILE1 = $(STMP_DIR)/file1.stamp
TARG_FILE3 = $(STMP_DIR)/file3.stamp
TARG_FILE4 = $(STMP_DIR)/file4.stamp
TARG_CFG3 = $(STMP_DIR)/cfg3.stamp
TARG_CFG1 = $(STMP_DIR)/cfg1.stamp


#
# define VHDL compile command options
#    and touch command for all rules.
#
VOPT = –93\n-source\n–work therm_lib
TCH = touch $@ dovcom


#
# define the 'whole_library' target.
# note: no commands.  First rule triggered is the
#       .INIT rule.
#
whole_library : \
    .INIT \
    $(TARG_CFG1) \
    .DONE


#
# define the .INIT and .DONE rules
#
.INIT :
    @ echo ">> Make for THERM begins."
```

```
    @touch vcom.cmd
        @echo $(VOPT) >> vcom.cmd

.DONE
    @if [-e dovcom] then vcom –f vcom.cmd
    @\rm –f dovcom vcom.cmd
    @echo ">> Make for THERM is complete."

#
# define the rules for the individual HDL files
#
$(TARG_FILE1) : $(DESIGN_SRC)/file1.vhd \
    $(TARG_CFG3)
  echo $(DESIGN_SRC)/file1.vhd >> vcom.cmd
  @$(TCH)

$(TARG_CFG3) : $(DESIGN_SRC)/cfg3.vhd \
    $(TARG_FILE4) \
    $(TARG_FILE3)
  echo $(DESIGN_SRC)/cfg3.vhd >> vcom.cmd
  @$(TCH)

$(TARG_FILE3) : $(DESIGN_SRC)/file3.vhd, \
    $(TARG_FILE4)
  echo $(DESIGN_SRC)/file3.vhd >> vcom.cmd
  @$(TCH)

$(TARG_FILE4) : $(DESIGN_SRC)/file4.vhd
  echo $(DESIGN_SRC)/file4.vhd >> vcom.cmd
  @$(TCH)

$(TARG_CFG1) : $(DESIGN_SRC)/cfg1.vhd \
    $(TARG_FILE4) \
    $(TARG_FILE3) \
    $(TARG_CFG3) \
    $(TARG_FILE1)
  echo $(DESIGN_SRC)/cfg1.vhd >> vcom.cmd
  @$(TCH)

#
# define the 'clean' target : no dependencies
#
clean:
  \rm –rf $(VLIB)
  vlib $(VLIB)
```

Figure 2. Makefile with Efficiency Modifications

4.   USING PRE-VERIFIED COMPONENTS OR IP

In many companies and design teams pre-verified components and/or IP have been purchased or created in-house, but they almost always reside in their own directory spaces and are associated with unique test environments, test cases, and makefiles that are focused on those single components. If there is a makefile designed to compile the VHDL files that comprise a component, and if it is written with reuse aspects in mind, it may be used by the project-level makefile by means of the 'include' directive. An important thing to remember about using the 'include' directive is that each variable, and target definition in the entire set of included makefiles must be uniquely named. If it is not so, make will not parse the makefile correctly, perhaps indicating that there is more than one rule for a particular target. The aspects of reuse and uniqueness include target naming and location of the compiled simulation library directory.

4.1   Variable and Target naming

The target names in a reusable makefile (one focused on IP or pre-designed components) should contain information unique to the object being 'made'. For example, note that in the makefile of Figure 2 the name of the component ("therm") is identified only in comments and in directory specifications. If the target definitions were not modified to contain the component name (or another unique marker for this component), this makefile could not easily be called a "reusable" makefile. Therefore for implementing the reuse aspect in to the makefile of Figure 1 all variables and targets should be modified in this way, including the new targets .INIT and .DONE. In all cases, the simple addition of the component name or other unique marker into the variable and target definitions is sufficient.

4.2   Location of the simulation library

It is assumed that the makefile for a pre-designed component will compile its HDL into a directory tree that is local to that component. When 'included' in a project-level makefile however, the component makefile should compile into a project-level directory. To create this activity automatically with make, Figure 2 needs to be modified to include a conditional statement.

Consider the following conditional statement:

```
ifeq ($(strip $(PROJ_LIB),))
    USERS_LIB = $(LOCAL_DIR)/libraries
else
    USERS_LIB = $(PROJ_DIR)/libraries
end
```

The 'strip' function removes all white space from the contents of the variable $(PROJ_LIB) -- spaces, tabs, etc. The 'ifeq' function then compares the result of 'strip' with the empty variable (the blank space after the comma). The expression returns true if the variable $(PROJ_LIB) was initially undefined (or was defined as white-space only, or did not exist), and false if the variable has some real value after stripping. The variable $(PROJ_LIB) would normally be a project-level makefile variable carried over via an "include" statement, or a shell environment variable.

If the expression returns TRUE (indicating that $(PROJ_LIB) is empty after stripping...), it means that the component makefile has been invoked as a stand-alone file. The local variable $(USERS_LIB) is then set to a value declared in the local makefile, and the make process for the component will compile its VHDL source code into a local directory path. If the expression returns FALSE, it means that the component makefile has been invoked from a project makefile via an 'include' statement. The local variable $(USERS_LIB) is set to the passed-in value, and the make process for the component will compile its VHDL source code into a non-local (or project-level) directory path.

In this way a component-level makefile may be safely invoked as a stand-alone component for block-level simulations or 'included' in a project-level makefile as part of system-level simulations. Figure 3 details the modifications of Figure 2 discussed in this section.

Another very useful way to link top-level and block-level makefiles (although not illustrated in the Figures) is to invoke make recursively. That is, a target for the downstream makefile is constructed, and triggered by the "all" or "library" target discussed earlier. The command section of the makefile rule would appear something like the following:

```
$(MAKE) -f $(PATH)/<make_file_name>
```

$(MAKE) is a built-in variable that automatically refers to the make program in a user's environment. The GNU make documentation[2] indicates that users should always use this variable when recursive calls to make are desired.

Unlike the 'include' directive, the downstream makefiles for this technique need not name their variables uniquely. This is because only the environment variables and any variables from the calling makefile that have been intentionally 'exported' will be understood by the downstream makefile. This technique is well suited for very large SoC designs that contain a large number of (possibly auto-generated) block and top-level makefiles.

```
# #####################################
# makefile for component therm
# #####################################
#
# define path to the HDL code
#
THERM_DES = /design/component_path/therm
THERM_SRC = $(THERM_DES)/hdl

#
# define USERS_LIB based on PROJ_LIB,
#    possibly sent in from a project makefile
#
ifeq ($(strip $(PROJ_LIB)),) then
    USERS_LIB = $(THERM_DES)/libraries
```

```
else
    USERS_LIB = $(PROJ_DIR)/libraries
end

#
# define component object lib and tstamp dir,
#    based on just-defined USERS_LIB
#
THERM_LIB = $(USERS_LIB)/therm_lib
THERM_TSP = $(USERS_LIB)/tstamp

#
# define targets for the individual HDL files
#   (now defined in timestamp directory)
#
THERM_FILE1 = $(THERM_TSP)/file1.stamp
THERM_FILE3 = $(THERM_TSP)/file3.stamp
THERM_FILE4 = $(THERM_TSP)/file4.stamp
THERM_CFG3 = $(THERM_TSP)/cfg3.stamp
THERM_CFG1 = $(THERM_TSP)/cfg1.stamp

#
# define VHDL compile command options, and
#   touch command for all rules.
#
THERM_OPT = -93\n–source\n–work therm_lib
THERM_TCH = touch $@ dotherm

#
# define the 'therm_library' target.
#
therm_library : \
    .THERM_INIT \
    $(THERM_CFG1) \
    .THERM_DONE


#
# define the .INIT and .DONE rules
#
.THERM_INIT :
    @echo ">> Make for THERM begins."
    @touch therm.cmd
    @echo $(THERM_OPT) >> therm.cmd

.THERM_DONE
    @if [-e dotherm] then vcom –f therm.cmd
    @\rm –f dotherm therm.cmd
```

```
    @echo ">> Make for THERM is complete."

#
# define the rules for the individual HDL files
#
$(THERM_FILE1) : $(THERM_SRC)/file1.vhd \
        $(THERM_CFG3)
    echo $(THERM_SRC)/file1.vhd >> therm.cmd
    @$(THERM_TCH)


$(THERM_CFG3) : $(THERM_SRC)/cfg3.vhd \
        $(THERM_FILE4) \
        $(THERM_FILE3)
    echo $(THERM_SRC)/cfg3.vhd >> therm.cmd
    @$(THERM_TCH)


$(THERM_FILE3) : $(THERM_SRC)/file3.vhd \
        $(THERM_FILE4)
    echo $(THERM_SRC)/file3.vhd >> therm.cmd
    @$(THERM_TCH)


$(THERM_FILE4) : $(THERM_SRC)/file4.vhd
    echo $(THERM_SRC)/file4.vhd >> therm.cmd
    @$(THERM_TCH)

$(THERM_CFG1) : $(THERM_SRC)/cfg1.vhd \
        $(THERM_FILE4) \
        $(THERM_FILE3) \
        $(THERM_CFG3) \
        $(THERM_FILE1)
    echo $(THERM_SRC)/cfg1.vhd >> therm.cmd
    @$(THERM_TCH)

#
# define the 'clean' target : no dependencies
#
clean:
    \rm -rf $(THERM_LIB)
    vlib $(THERM_LIB)
```

Figure 3. Makefile with IP Modifications

5.   MAKE IN THE TEAM ENVIRONMENT

In a typical team-oriented design and verification environment the various individual members must be able to effectively develop and test their assigned sections of the HDL design without disturbing the workflow of their teammates. A well-formed environment will have an aspect of commonality as well as an aspect of isolation.

The common aspect of a team-oriented work environment are that all team members have access to and may utilize the very same HDL files, shell or automation scripts, pattern generators, etc., that comprise the design. Having this common access means that (for example) all team members can utilize a common automation or script interface and/or that a compilation of the HDL design and test environment source code files will obtain identical results when simulated.

The aspect of isolation in a team-oriented work environment is that the compiled simulation image and simulation results obtained by each individual team member will not be overwritten or destroyed by any other team member. This also means that individual users can modify parts of the design (sometimes even the same part of the design, but modified in different ways), re-compile and re-simulate and still obtain completely isolated and safe results – although the simulations would be expected to produce different behaviors during simulation. Make fits into this environment in a very straightforward way.

Implementing the isolation aspect of team-oriented environment in a project could mean that each team member is provided with a directory space keyed (for example) to that person's workstation login name. In the UNIX™ OS, this would be the contents of the built-in shell variable $user.

Figure 4 is a representation of a project-level makefile that uses the 'include' directive to execute IP or pre-designed external component makefiles (like the makefile shown in Figure 3). This project-level makefile would typically reside in a common directory tree and would be universally visible and accessible to all members of the project design team. It would typically be invoked while logged into a $user's directory space.

```
# #####################################
# makefile for project hammer
# #####################################
#
# define path to all included IP components
#
THERM = /design/component_path/therm
USBR = /design/component_path/usbr
PDASH = /design/component_path/pdash
MEMC = /design/component_path/memc


#
# Define the path to the users environment
# $Users_dir is an environment variable that describes
#      the path to a protected space specifically for a
#      single design team member, identified by the
#      UNIX built-in shell variable $user.
#
PROJ_LIB = $(Users_dir)
```

```
#
# define path to project top
#
HAMMER = /design/project_path/hammer


#
# define the 'project' target. Note, no commands.
#    dependencies are the 'library' targets in
#    each component makefile.
#  Each target will be triggered in the order
#    they are listed here.
#  If any target make fails, this makefile also
#    fails, and no following targets are trig-
#    gered, including .PROJ_HAMMER_DONE.
#
project_hammer : \
   .PROJ_HAMMER_INIT \
   therm_library \
   usbr_library \
   pdash_library \
   memc_library \
   hammer_library \
   hammer_tb_library \
   .PROJ_HAMMER_DONE


#
# define .PROJ_HAMMER_INIT and
# .PROJ_HAMMER_DONE rules
#    (commands only)
#
.PROJ_HAMMER_INIT :
    @echo "===================="
    @echo " Begin Make for HAMMER"
    @echo "===================="


.PROJ_HAMMER_DONE :
    @echo "===================="
    @echo " Make for HAMMER is complete"
    @echo "===================="


#
# include necessary component makefiles.
#   May be included in any order.
#
# If any included component makefile re-declares
#    an already declared target, the last one read
#    will take effect. This could also mean that there
```

```
#    may be two rules defined for a single defined
#    target, which is a fatal error in GNU make.
#
# Invoking this file with that kind of problem will
#    produce an initialization error, and none of the
#    targets will ever trigger. In fact, the 'all' target
#    in this file is not triggered because actual execution
#    of this make cannot occur unless all included files
#    come in syntactically clean.
#
include $(HAMMER)/makes/Makefile_hammer
include $(MEMC)/makes/Makefile_memc
include $(HAMMER)/makes/Makefile_hammer_tb
include $(USBR)/makes/Makefile_usbr
include $(THERM)/make/Makefile_therm
include $(PDASH)/makes/Makefile_pdash
```

Figure 4. Project Level Makefile

The very first variable used in the project-level makefile of Figure 4 is called '$Users_dir'. If this was a normal environment variable that contained the qualified path to a $user directory (and assuming each team member is working within his or her on shell environment) then this variable would be different for each team member.

This very simple usage of a team-member-oriented environment variable in the makefile will allow the automatic construction of a qualified path to a simulator object library that is unique for each user. By using this technique each team member creates and uses an object library for the design that is completely isolated from those of other team members, and therefore is completely safe. Individuals may make any design modifications they need to make without disturbing their colleagues, because the compile and simulation of those changes is directed to and comes from directories local to user.

6.   CONCLUSION

This paper has shown how a GNU makefile can be used in a team-oriented SoC style of design and verification flow. The goals of the paper were to identify areas of compilation efficiency, and to show how using make in this way helps to strike just the correct balance of commonality and isolation that will result in a higher performing design and verification team. This higher performance level should in its turn produce circuit designs that are more robust (more strongly verified) within the same or possibly shorter schedules. Easily understood modifications that the readers may utilize in their own design processes were presented.

One final note is appropriate. This paper has presented ideas that create faster and more secure compiles of HDL design code. However, the entire discussion has assumed that the makefile was already present and that its rule set contained all the required hierarchical dependencies. Unfortunately, in many (especially new) designs, the hierarchy is not completely known or understood. The initial creation of the makefile in this situation is not an easy task.

Typically, the initial creation of the makefile for a design is a trial and error process, and usually consumes significant time and effort, especially so if the design is large. Reducing the time and effort in this single area would be greatly appreciated by the design community, and is open to many innovative ideas. Whether it is commercial stand-alone software, an additional button in a GUI-oriented project management package, or even available (but locally constructed) Perl scripts – some tool that can extract the hierarchy from the HDL code and create the makefile from scratch is sorely needed.

Finally, let it be known that other methods can be added to the information supplied in this paper to create even faster or more efficient compiles. For one example, it is possible to work with the makefile in order to compile all sub-components in parallel UNIX™ processes. Or for another example, it may be that invoking a makefile with a large number of included component makefiles (as suggested by this paper) would actually be slower than the individual invocation of the component makefiles, either manually or by letting the makefile itself invoke make recursively (noted earlier).

There is a great deal more power present in GNU make than the techniques that have been presented here. For example, GNU make can be asked to search a list of directories for the filename(s) listed in the dependency list of any rule. Do this by using the 'VPATH' or 'vpath' directives. In addition, GNU make allows users to create macros inside variables. That is, a variable is defined using one or more of the built-in functions. This macro may then be used like any other function. This type of function, for example, may be used in rules to detect whether a filename is present in a list of filenames, and to execute command 'A' or command 'B' accordingly. By using these built-in functions, GNU make could be written to support, for example, more than one simulator or compiler (perhaps for code coverage or synthesis). More may be learned and utilized by studying the manuals available on the GNU web site[2,3].

It is fervently hoped that this paper has caused some spark of creativity for this area of ASIC design methodology, or at the very least some sharing of information that may result in more robust ASIC designs.

7. REFERENCES

[1] ANSI/IEEE Standard VHDL Language Reference Manual, IEEE Std 1076-1993. IEEE Press, New York, NY, 1993.

[2] Stallman, Richard M. and McGrath, Roland (April 2000). *GNU Make, a Program for Directing Recompilation.* Retrieved from: http://www.gnu.org/manual/make-3.79.1/html_mono/make.html

[3] MacKensie, David, Eggert, Paul and Stallman, Richard (November 1994). *Comparing and Merging Files.* Retrieved from: http://www.gnu.org/manual/diffutils-2.7/html_mono/diff.html

Chapter 11

Wild Blue Yonder: Experiences in Designing an FPGA with State Machines for a Modern Fighter Jet, Using VHDL and DesignBook

Brian L Snyder
Brian L Snyder

Abstract: This paper describes the author's experience using the VHDL language and the productivity enhancement tool DesignBook in an FPGA design consisting of a state machine-based DSP I/O controller for the air data computers in a modern Air Force fighter jet. The computers are based on a digital signal processor, which has little in the way of general purpose I/O. The design implemented a memory-mapped I/O controller for the control of DSP peripherals including external program memory, non-volatile storage, temperature and pressure sensing modules, communication transceivers, and DSP boot memory.

The design was implemented in an Actel A42MX series FPGA. The design implemented many state loops for the control of all the DSP peripherals. The state diagrams were input using the state diagram editor in DesignBook and tied together in a hierarchical fashion using the block diagram editor. Other hierarchical blocks were generated, interconnected, and simulated until the complete FPGA design was entered and verified.

1. INTRODUCTION

The air data computers on one of the Air Force's newest fighter jets convert raw pressure data from its pitot probe and static port into a variety of information for the aircraft's main computer, such as basic altitude and airspeed, among other flight data parameters. The computers are based on a digital signal processor (DSP) as opposed to a microprocessor or microcontroller. The choice of a DSP over these other solutions had one drawback: a very limited number of general I/O ports with which to control the various DSP peripherals such as boot memory, non-volatile diagnostic memory, pressure and temperature sensors, and an external programming port.

The solution to this problem was to implement a memory-mapped I/O controller in an FPGA. This FPGA would intercept memory reads and writes from the DSP, decode them, and if a mapped command is recognized, execute a state-control loop to issue the required control signals and timing to the requested peripheral.

The design was developed in the VHDL language using a productivity-enhancement tool called DesignBook from Escalade Corporation. This company has since been purchased by Mentor Graphics and the best capabilities of DesignBook have been added into Mentor's Renoir tool, which is similar in many respects to DesignBook. This tool has many productivity-enhancement capabilities, including graphical entry of block diagrams, state diagrams and flowcharts; a program

129

A. Mignotte et al. (eds.), System on Chip Design Languages, 129–137.
© 2002 *Kluwer Academic Publishers.*

manager to organize the design hierarchy; automatic generation of VHDL code from graphically entered designs; and tight coupling to simulation and synthesis tools.

This tool allowed the author to design, simulate and synthesize the FPGA within a single design environment. In addition, it greatly reduced the time required to document the design due to the ability to export graphical diagrams to a Microsoft Word document.

2.   DESIGN PROCESS

Most programmable logic designs follow a reasonably standard process, from early design definition through coding, simulation, implementation and finally, documentation. This design was no different, though the coding step is a bit different than earlier designs because of the capabilities of the tools used. The flowchart in Figure 1 shows the general process flow used to develop this FPGA:

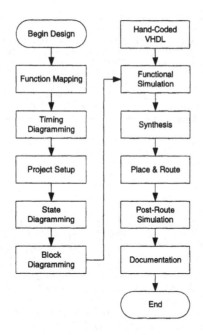

Figure 1

FPGA Design Process Flow

Note that the step labeled "hand-coded VHDL" is shown not in the main design flow, rather as more of an auxiliary process. This is due to the capability of the DesignBook tool in automatically generating code for many different functions, in effect making hand coding a minor step in the overall design process, used mainly when automatic code generation would be more difficult to implement than hand-coded VHDL.

This paper will discuss each step in this flow and give details on what activities occurred within that step, and will note how the tools used enhanced the process.

2.1 Function Mapping

The majority of the peripherals on the processor board utilize a serial data bus to communicate with the DSP. Most of them use the SPI protocol, which requires a clock, data line, and a chip enable. To begin the design, the various peripheral control functions that the FPGA would implement were mapped to addresses within the DSP's external address space. Many functions were required, such as pressure sensor read and write, diagnostic memory read and write, temperature sensor read, MIL-STD-1553B bus read and write (separate functions for registers and RAM), watchdog reset, and pitot probe heater control.

In most cases a mapped function, when decoded, would execute a single state loop. For example, a DSP write to address 0xA042 would trigger the execution of the state loop that controlled reading data from the pressure sensor module. Other functions merely toggled the state of a discrete control signal. For instance, to turn on the pitot probe heater, the DSP would perform a write to address 0xE001. The heater signal would activate and remain active until the DSP performed a read from address 0xE001.

2.2 Timing Diagramming

As stated previously, the functions the FPGA was to perform were made up predominantly of very specific timing sequences for the control of DSP peripherals. Detailed timing diagrams of each sequence made the creation of the state diagrams and simulation testbenches much easier to do. Once all functions were identified, timing diagrams were generated for each one. The timing diagrams showed all relevant control and data signals, beginning with the DSP write cycle which triggered the execution of each function.

Once the signals involved in each sequence were charted, control states were added to the timing diagram wherever peripheral control signals needed to change states. In this way, it could be determined how many states would be required to implement the control sequence, and how many clock cycles each state had to remain active.

Timing diagrams were generated using SynaptiCAD Timing Diagrammer Pro.

2.3 Project Setup

After all required functions had been identified and timing diagrams were completed, the implementation could begin. The FPGA design was set up in a DesignBook project. A working directory was created with a structure as follows:

– FPGA_Top
–   VHDL_Source_Code
–   Simulation
–   Testbenches
–   Input
–   Output

–   Synthesis
–   Place & Route

The DesignBook project manager kept track of the design hierarchy from top down in a format much like the Windows Explorer. Each module in the hierarchy was identified by an icon as to what it consisted of, i.e., VHDL source, state diagram, block diagram, simulation testbench, etc. This made it very easy to see at a glance what type of object the file contained.

The project manager was also used to keep track of other design-related files, such as timing diagrams, reports or any other documents. Any file related to the design could be brought into the project and stored in the design folder. An icon was automatically assigned to the object in the program manager window. Internally, DesignBook kept a pointer to the location where the file actually resided, so files from many different locations could be grouped together under the DesignBook project. To access any one of them, double clicking on it would call up the application in which the document had been developed, like Microsoft Word, Notepad, etc.

Design hierarchy was automatically reflected in the project manager window. Whenever a new module was added, if the software recognized it as being instantiated in another part of the design, the project manager window would be automatically updated to accurately reflect the hierarchy by placing the icon and title of the module indented under its parent module.

2.4   State Diagramming

After the project was set up, the state diagrams were generated using the DesignBook state diagram editor. A wizard assisted in setting up the state loop parameters, such as active clock edge, decoding style (i.e., one-hot, etc.), input and output signal names, reset polarity, number of states expected and default state names. Once the wizard had all required information the state diagram editor itself was displayed. The wizard created the number of states specified and placed them on the diagram automatically. Additional states could be included by clicking an icon in the toolbar to enter "add state" mode and then clicking once in the diagram to add each state bubble. Transitions between states could be added in the same manner.

For each state in the diagram, output signals could be assigned that would be activated when that particular state was active. To assign output signals to a given state, all one had to do was double-click on the state to bring up a dialog box. Within the dialog box any number of output signals could be assigned to the state, along with the logic level at which each should be set while that particular state was active. Default logic levels could be specified for each output signal. This would be the level of each output signal when its controlling state was inactive. The software automatically placed the output signals and their logic level in that state on the diagram underneath the state bubbles in which they were assigned.

Each state itself within a diagram could be configured in a number of ways. Most of the states in this design consisted of three types: states that were active for a single clock cycle, states that transition based upon the logic level of a given input signal, and wait states. The single clock cycle states were used whenever a particular signal (or signals) needed to pulse active for only one clock cycle. The second state type was used for signals that needed to remain active until another signal or expression became true. The third type, wait states, could be programmed to wait for a particular number of clock cycles to pass before either going to the next state unconditionally, or wait for an input expression to become true after the wait period timed out. These types of states were identified with an octagonal boundary around the state bubble, indicating that the loop stopped there for some period of time. The number of clock cycles it waited would be listed within the bubble, so it could be easily seen by looking at the diagram how long the state was active.

State transitions between state bubbles were added by choosing the transition-editing mode with a toolbar button, then clicking once on the source state bubble and again on the destination state bubble. Whenever a transition was added to the diagram a wizard dialog box popped up asking for information. The condition or conditions under which a transition was made to the next state was entered in a text box within the wizard dialog box. Any valid VHDL expression was accepted. The DesignBook tool had many helps for entering an expression quickly. There were buttons to click for AND, NOT, OR, and other VHDL operators. Clicking one of them inserted the operator in the expression at the cursor position. In addition, all signals in the state loop context were listed in a drop-down box. Again, selecting one inserted it into the expression at the cursor position. In this way an expression could be entered very quickly without having to type a single character. Clicking OK in the wizard added the transition graphic to the diagram. The arrow could be stretched and moved in any manner to make the diagram more readable. The transition expression was attached to the arrow, so moving the arrow also moved the transition expression. The expression could be moved anywhere on the diagram to make it more readable. Figure 2 shows an example of a completed state diagram from DesignBook. All the features just described can be seen on the diagram:

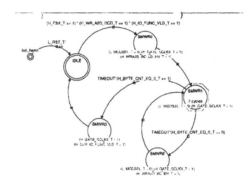

Figure 2
State Diagram Example

Once the state diagram was completed, the DesignBook software automatically created VHDL code that implemented it. The code was implemented in a behavioral style, though the author found it somewhat hard to follow. DesignBook created some processes that defined meaningless signal names like "loc1" and "loc2" and performed some logic on them, then these signals were used in the sensitivity lists of the processes that defined the state output and next-state transitions. However, the state outputs themselves and the conditions for transition to the next state were well documented by DesignBook. The source could be viewed at any time during the creation of the diagram.

2.5   Block Diagramming

DesignBook's block diagramming tool was extremely powerful. The I/O controller design made use of these more than any other feature because it was very quick and easy to generate a lot of logic in a short time with the tool. Block diagrams could be generated top-down or bottom up, but this design made use of the bottom-up methodology. This was to take advantage of the fact that any signal in a block diagram could be defined as a block I/O terminal, and it would automatically be added to the block's entity description. The entity description was used to create the block symbol when the block was placed as a component in a higher level block.

Blocks were color-coded so it was readily apparent what the box represented. Block diagram components would be a green-filled box, state diagrams would be a yellow box, hand-written VHDL code would be white, ModuleWare functions (discussed later) would be blue, etc.

When blocks that interfaced to each other were defined, they were added as components to higher-level block diagrams and interconnected graphically, much like a schematic. Connections between blocks were automatically routed in the diagram, but could be overridden by the designer to make the diagram more readable. Any or all terminals on a block could be specified as module input/output terminals by a simple mouse-click. In this way a block diagram could be very quickly put together.

Again, once the diagram was completed, VHDL code representing the block diagram structure was automatically created. Code for block diagrams was generated in a structural style, as opposed to a behavioral style. For small to medium sized FPGA designs, this is not a problem. Larger designs may encounter some increases in simulation time due to the fact that behavioral code generally simulates faster than structural code.

Figure 3 shows an example block diagram from the I/O controller design:

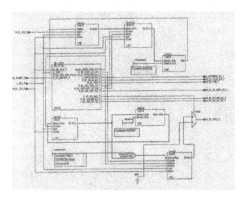

Figure 3
Block Diagram Example

Pre-Created Modules

Some modules in the I/O controller design were created by using the Actel ACTGen tool, which is a piece of software for Actel FPGA's that helps generate logic modules, such as counters, wide registers, adders, wide multiplexers, and the like. The I/O controller contained many such modules. Most were 8, 16, 24, or 32-bit registers and multiplexers or counters of various widths and styles. The menu-driven tool solicited user input to configure a certain type of module. For instance, to create a counter, a dialog box was opened and the width and type of counter was specified (i.e., ripple, carry-look-ahead, etc.), the direction (up, down, or up/down) was chosen, and the active clock edge was defined. The tool then generated the module. Structural VHDL code was generated for synthesis, as well as a behavioral representation of the module for simulation purposes.

In addition to modules created by ACTGen, DesignBook contained a similar module-creation feature called ModuleWare. This was a similar type of tool, but it was more comprehensive and more generic than ACTGen. Registers, counters, adders, multiplexers and the like could be generated, but it went further by including basic logic gates, constants and clock manipulation functions. The difference is that ModuleWare does not create a structural representation of the logic like ACTGen. Rather, it creates behavioral VHDL code that is synthesized with the rest of the logic. For some types of modules this may lead to less than optimal logic. The I/O controller design used it to implement registers, adders, multiplexers, and the clock divider module. The blocks in Figure 3 are made almost entirely of these types of modules.

2.6   Functional Simulation

Once state diagram entry, block diagram entry or hand written sections of code had generated all functions within the FPGA, it was compiled and prepared for functional simulation. Compilation was very fast due to another of DesignBook's features. In any of the entry tools, whether it be the state diagramming tool, block diagramming tool, or any of the others, DesignBook ran a syntax checker for everything entered. Signal names were checked for consistency, expressions were checked for proper syntax, illegal or ambiguous state transitions were flagged, among others. The few errors remaining were quickly corrected and the FPGA design was ready to simulate.

Here DesignBook helped yet again. DesignBook had a feature that allowed the designer to automatically create a simulation testbench containing the module to simulate. All that remained for the designer to do was to define code to stimulate the design and check for errors. For this, DesignBook had another feature in which a waveform editor was invoked where simulation input signals could be described by drawing a waveform for each input. Using this tool, complex stimuli could be generated rather quickly. The author briefly tried this tool, but found the user interface to be somewhat confusing. In the end, this feature was not used due to schedule constraints that did not allow time to study and understand how to use it more effectively.

All testbenches were managed under the DesignBook project manager. To run one, all one had to do was highlight it and click a toolbar button. DesignBook was tightly coupled to Mentor Graphics' ModelSim VHDL simulator, and automatically created the script necessary to call ModelSim, compile the module in the simulation library, load the testbench, and run the simulation.

Each time a simulation was run, DesignBook would create a new directory for the design being simulated and copy all necessary files into it. In this way, revisions could be more easily tracked, though at the expense of disk space. DesignBook allowed the designer to choose to overwrite any particular revision with a subsequent one if it was not desirable to save the files.

DesignBook allowed the designer to run simulations in batch or interactive mode. On this design, interactive mode was used for all debugging.

2.7   Synthesis

The I/O controller design was synthesized using Synplicity's Synplify tool. DesignBook is tightly coupled to synthesis as well as simulation, and Synplify could be configured and automatically called up from within DesignBook. As with simulation, a new directory in which to copy source files was created each time synthesis was run.

2.8   Place & Route

After the design was successfully simulated and synthesized, Actel's Designer tool was used to place and route the FPGA, run static timing analysis, and generate the chip-programming file.

2.9   Post-Route Simulation

After synthesis, post-route simulation was run to verify that the actual gate-implementation matched the functional behavior simulated earlier. Past experience has shown this to be a vital step in the design process, since a circuit that simulates correctly with time-unit delay may not work properly when actual routed delays are added to the design. This step is greatly simplified if the functional simulation testbenches are written in a self-checking style by adding VHDL "ASSERT" statements at various places to verify that signals are correct at the proper time. In this way, the same testbenches can be used for functional and post-route simulation, with the only modification being the test module instantiated in the testbench.

2.10   Documentation

After the design was verified, the task of documentation had to be done. This task was made much easier by DesignBook because the documentation was virtually done already. All the module block diagrams, state diagrams, and timing diagrams were imported into a Word document. A written description of the theory of operation of the chip was added to the document to go along with the diagrams. A table of interface pins was added, a table containing the memory-mapped functions was included, the contents and operation of all FPGA registers was documented, and project files and directories were noted.

In addition, a binder was put together containing the above plus all the VHDL code, either hand-written or automatically generated by DesignBook. This binder turned out to be extremely useful when debugging the system in the lab. The timing diagrams were compared with captured logic analyzer traces and verified to match.

2.11   Bug Escapes

As carefully as any design is developed, bugs inevitably make it through the cracks. This design was no exception. Two bugs made it through to silicon.

The first was merely an oversight. One of the state diagrams had a loop duplicated, but an output signal that should have been deleted from one of the loops after it was copied was not deleted. As a result, a control signal was issued when it should not have been, resulting in a very confused DSP. This problem was easily found and fixed.

The second was not so easy. The FPGA contained logic to control bootload of the DSP from serial EEPROM. An address register in the FPGA told the EEPROM from where to read data to send to the DSP. At one point the address did not increment correctly. A logic analyzer was attached to the serial data pin on the EEPROM and the address was picked out of the serial data stream. It was indeed incrementing incorrectly.

The address register and the adder that incremented it were both implemented with modules created by ModuleWare, so both were theoretically logically correct, and had, in fact, worked correctly in simulation. What, then, could the problem be?

Actel has a design debug tool called Silicon Explorer that allows the designer to look at internal FPGA logic in real time. Using this tool, it was discovered that the clock to the address register was getting to one of the register bits just before the enable edge, causing a missed transition. The design used edge sensitive registers, which should be able to drive each other without minimum timing problems. Why was this register misbehaving?

The answer was in the fact that a clock divider, which reduced the frequency of the input clock by a factor of six, had created the clock driving this register. The mistake was that this generated clock did not utilize the internal clock drive tree in the FPGA, therefore the clock skew was much greater than it would otherwise have been. This skew caused the enable flip-flop to clock late, and one address bit, due to routing delays, received the clock before the enable, resulting in a missed transition. This bug was corrected, and the design then worked properly in-system.

That's all well and good, but why didn't simulation catch this? The answer is that a thorough job of post-route simulation was not run, due to project schedule constraints. As a result, this bug slipped through.

3.   CONCLUSIONS

Some of the lessons learned throughout the development of this design are as follows:

1) When generating clocks other than the main input clock, use the internal clock routing tree to obtain low skew. This is especially important when the derived clock drives lots of gates.

2) Don't let schedule constraints restrict simulation time. In this case, a few days spent simulating would have saved three weeks of debug by multiple engineers plus a chip update. As is usually the case, it is cheaper and faster to do the job right than to do it over.

3) Tools like DesignBook, or its successor Renoir, will undoubtedly save time in development. The automation inherent in these tools cuts weeks off the development time. The larger the design the more time is potentially saved.

Chapter 12

Analysis of Modelling and Simulation Capabilities in SystemC and Ocapi using a Video Filter Design

Benny Thörnberg and Mattias O'Nils

Mid Sweden University, Dept. of Information Technology and Media, Sweden
Phone: +46 60 148600, E-mail:{bentho\mattias}@ite.mh.se

Abstract: Several system specification languages are emerging from C and C++. This development is driven by the large competence that exists for these languages. The programming language itself lacks many of the necessary constructs one requires from a specification language. Therefore, specification languages based on C/C++ are often a superset of the programming language. Where all the necessary constructs for system specification is added to the language. This paper evaluates and compares SystemC and Ocapi, which both are specification methods based on C++. The analysis is done as a case study with focus on the modelling and simulation effectiveness for video systems. The system we have selected is a spatio-temporal video filter. This video filter is characterised by high computational complexity, by high requirements on memory size and memory bandwidth.

Key words: SystemC, Ocapi, video filter, noise reduction, memory modelling, simulation performance

1. INTRODUCTION

During the years several system design languages have emerged from both C and C++. For example HardwareC [3] and C^x [2] that are used in the Vulcan and COSYMA system synthesis environments, respectively. HardwareC supports a subset of C with parallel processes and the possibility to describe timing constraints. C^x is a superset of C with constructs to describe channels that are based on send and receive primitives. A language based on C that also capture structural hierarchy and interface refinement is SpecC [5]. SpecC is developed to support an IP centric design flow with the possibilities to

encapsulate IP-components. Common for these approaches is that they are based on compilers and mainly developed for automatic system synthesis. That is, the system is automatically synthesised to an implementation from a behavioural level description. An alternative approach is to have system design languages that can be used throughout the whole design flow from system description to hardware and software optimisation.

In the CoWare design environment [4], the system description is composed of heterogeneous communicating processes that are specified in a superset of C. This description language can also

A. Mignotte et al. (eds.), System on Chip Design Languages, 139–149.
© 2002 *Kluwer Academic Publishers.*

capture all design transformations down to both hardware and software implementation. To support hardware design refinement, the language encapsulates hardware description languages like VHDL and RTC [4]. CoWare and Synopsys have developed CoWare-C into SystemC [1]. SystemC is a system description language captured in C++ classes. SystemC has capabilities to handle communicating processes, fixed points number representation, interface refinement, and hardware description. The Ocapi approach [8] is similar to SystemC. The big difference is that both the simulation and the synthesis methods are integrated in the C++ classes. Additionally, Ocapi is mostly targeting data flow descriptions with no support for structural hierarchy.

For video and image processing systems, a major task in design process is the analysis and implementation of the memory handling. For these systems, the ability to capture memory and memory hierarchy are very important features of a system design language. This paper presents an analysis of the memory handling capability of two approaches to C++ based system design languages, i.e. SystemC and Ocapi, see *Figure 1*. We selected SystemC and Ocapi since we believe that system specification languages captured with C++ class libraries enable efficient additive research in specification methods for embedded systems.

The analysis is done through a case study of modelling, design refinement and simulation of a spatio-temporal video filter [6][7]. The filter design is a three-dimensional filter that uses information from both the spatial and temporal planes. This requires considerably amount of memory for storing all the frames used in the filter. It also requires the introduction of a memory hierarchy to lower the memory transfer rate.

Next section outlines the behaviour of the video filter. Section 3 describes how the filter is modelled in SystemC and Ocapi. Finally we present results from comparing the specification and simulation effectiveness of the two approaches.

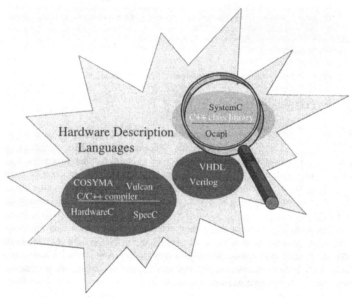

Figure 1. Hardware description languages.

2. FILTER DESCRIPTION

The task of the noise reduction algorithm can be divided into two main sub-tasks:
1. To detect a part of the image and determine whether this is a part of a moving image, that is called local scene-change detection.
2. To filter out noise with local scene-change taken into account.

A block diagram of the filter is depicted in *Figure 6*. The notation and definition used in the algorithm description are: A frame *F(n)*,

$$F(n) = \{R(n), G(n), B(n)\}$$

is a matrix of RGB-values (colour components) in the n:th frame.
A pixel *P(i, j, n)*,

$$P(i, j, n) = \{R(i, j, n), G(i, j, n), B(i, j, n)\} \in F(n)$$

is an element in *F(n)* with the spatial position *(i, j)*. A slice,

$$S(i_0, j_0, n_0) \subset F(n_0)$$

positioned at *(i₀, j₀)* in the *n*:th frame includes the pixel $p_0(i_0, j_0, n)$ and a portion of the *n*:th frame that surrounds the pixel p_0. A tube,

$$T(i_0, j_0, n) = \{S(i_0, j_0, n) \mid (n_0 - d) \le n \le (n_0 + d)\}$$

is a set of slices with same *(i, j)* but located in consecutive frames, where the number of frames is defined as,

$$2 \cdot d + 1$$

The centre frame is surrounded by *d* frames in time. For our case study *d* is set to 3.

2.1 Algorithm

This section outlines the behaviour of the filter algorithm. The first step of the algorithm is to calculate the average luminance for each slice in a tube $\overline{Y}(n)$, see *Figure 5*.

Using the average luminance for a slice and the blue colour component between two in time adjacent pixels, the differences between these two pixels are calculated. If either of the differences is higher than a certain threshold level (T_y and T_b), a scene change is indicated in a vector, $I(n, n-1)$.

From the scene change vector *I*, the length, δ_0, from a scene change to the centre pixel determine the length used by the median filter. The luminance from the centre pixel in a tube and the median filter width, δ_0, are the inputs to the median filter.

The filter output is selected from the centre pixel's original RGB-values in frame number ñ.

Figure 3 and *Figure 4* show two examples of filtered output frames, using a sequence of seven frames, with the centre frame shown in *Figure 2*. The input sequence shows a ball moving from left to right. Additionally, the input sequence is contaminated with 5% impulse noise.

Figure 2. Input frame with 5% impulse noise.

Figure 3 shows the corresponding output frame as the parameters T_y and T_b are both set to 30. In *Figure 4* T_y and T_b are set to 15 and 13. This filter algorithm obviously reduces the amount of noise but to the cost of some distortion exposed on moving objects. The trade of between noise and distortion is done by combining different values of T_y and T_b .

Figure 3. Noise reduced output frame.

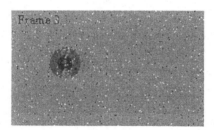

Figure 4. *Less* noise reduced output frame.

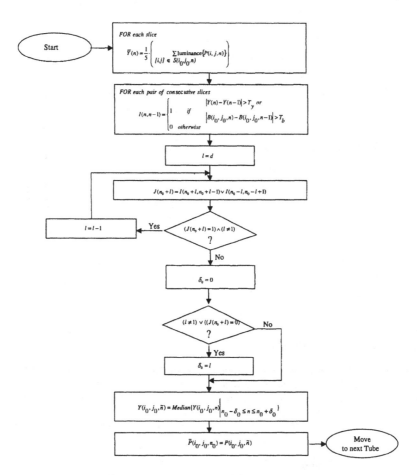

Figure 5. Flow diagram describing the filter algorithm processing one tube.

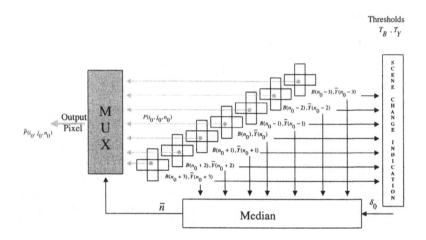

Figure 6. Block diagram for the spatio-temporal video filter.

3.   VIDEO FILTER MODELS

Two models at different abstraction levels have been developed in both Ocapi and SystemC. During simulation, both models are fed with a raw video stream in a 24-bit RGB format. The input stream is stored in a frame memory that stores seven frames. The filter processes the data in the frame memory and produces an output video stream with the same format as the input stream. A frame synchronisation signal triggers the algorithm whenever a new frame is fed into the memory, see *Figure 7*.

3.1   High-level model

A high-level model written in SystemC and Ocapi is derived from a Matlab description of the video filter. The high-level model is modelled using two blocks: (1) a frame memory controller and (2) a block capturing the filter algorithm, see *Figure 7*.

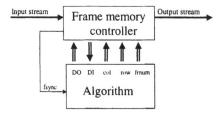

Figure 7. High level video filter model.

This high-level model is parameterised according to *Table 1*. The values of the two parameters: Number of rows and Number of columns are taken from the input video stream format and initialised at run-time. The values of No of frames, Chrominance threshold and Luminance threshold are selected at compile time in order to fulfil the desired noise reduction.

Table 1. Filter parameters.

PARAMETER	TIME AT INITIALIZATION
No of rows	Run time
No of columns	Run time
No of frames	Compile time
Chrominance threshold	Compile time
Luminance threshold	Compile time

The high-level model is used as the reference model for lower abstraction levels and it is used to evaluate different design properties, e.g. memory bandwidth and fixed-point precision. Analysis of the memory bandwidth to the external frame memory [7] shows that the design requires a memory hierarchy to decrease the number of memory accesses. The memory hierarchy is implemented as an on-chip cache memory, depicted in *Figure 8*.

3.2 RTL model

An RTL-model, *Figure 8*, is derived from the high-level model and captured both in Ocapi and SystemC.

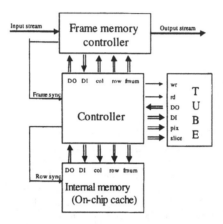

Figure 8. RTL video filter model.

Four blocks are used to model the filter at the register transfer level: (1) the frame memory controller, (2) on-chip cache memory, (3) the Tube, a set of spatio-temporal pixels with local scene change detection and an attached median filter, and (4) the Controller, a state machine providing a sliding window functionality [7] often used in image processing. The window is moving over the image area according to the pattern shown in *Figure 9*. This pattern is modelled in order to reduce the size of the on-chip cache memory. The relationship, cache memory size versus external memory bandwidth, has been analysed by Oelmann et al.[7]. This analysis could be verified during simulation by adding memory access counters to blocks (1) and (2).

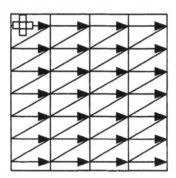

Figure 9. Sliding window moving pattern.

4.   COMPARISON

This section presents the results from the comparison between Ocapi (ver. 0.87) and SystemC (ver. 1.02) using the video filter design as test case. The comparison was made on a Pentium III (800MHz) computer running Windows 2000.

Generally, Ocapi is suitable for modelling data flow oriented designs at RT-level whereas SystemC supports a top-down methodology that takes a design all the way from an executable specification to an RTL-description. SystemC has support for hierarchical descriptions and ways to separate communication from behaviour. SystemC has also support for modelling resolved signals and bus communication. None of these features are supported in Ocapi.

One important feature of a system description language is that it should conceptualise the modelled system with minimum effort. Ideally, there should be a 1-to-1 mapping of the conceptual model and the language. To capture the video filter design one needs to describe the memory hierarchy, the filter algorithm composed of control and the data flow, and reuse of IP-components. None of these two languages have explicit constructs for modelling memory hierarchy. However, SystemC facilitates the modelling of memory hierarchy by supporting structural hierarchy. The support for structural hierarchy in SystemC also enables modelling IP-reuse, i.e. instantiation of both external and on-chip memory in the video filter design. Additionally, the explicit modelling of resolved signals in SystemC also facilitates the description of interfaces to IP components. Modelling the filter algorithm at the system level is well supported by both approaches since they are both based on C++. However at RT-level, SystemC models the control behaviour in a more efficient way than Ocapi. Due to the fact that control statements can only be implemented with state-machines in Ocapi. The number of source code lines reflects to some extent the modelling efficiency. As seen in *Table 2*, the number of lines for SystemC is only 60% of the Ocapi code.

Memory handling is an important issue when modelling and simulating video systems. We have compared the storage space needed for one 24 bits RGB valued pixel during simulation. Ocapi occupies 120 bytes and SystemC 16 bytes. These numbers applies for the class libraries fixed-point data types. Hence, the video filter requires storage of seven 576x705 pixel. This results in 325 Mb for the Ocapi model and 43 Mb for the SystemC model. The RAM-module in Ocapi even failed to initialise due to some run-time error above a frame size of 100 x 200.

The simulation scheduler in Ocapi is based on a signal flow graph model. That is, for all input signals, one token has to be consumed and for all output signals, one token has to be produced. Simulation firing rules has to be written by the designer for each module. SystemC on the other hand is based on a real-time kernel giving the designer the possibility to write process definitions with wait-statements and sensitivity lists. The SystemC simulation performance is very dependent on the modelling style. As seen in *Table 2*, the use of resolved signals causes a more than 20 times degradation of the simulation performance. When it comes to synthesis of the RTL-description the methods differ significantly. RTL-descriptions in Ocapi are object oriented data flow and control graphs that transforms itself into a text based data flow and control graph, which is then translated into VHDL by external tools. In addition, VHDL-based glue cells that connects modules together are directly generated by Ocapi. For SystemC, this is handled in a more traditional way with compiler-based synthesis tools like CoCentric tools from Synopsys [9].

5.   CONCLUSIONS

In this paper, we have compared the modelling and simulation performance of Ocapi and SystemC for a video filter design. One should consider that in the presented comparison we have used an old version of Ocapi, the newer and extended version handles control flow better than the tested version.

The comparison shows that it is easier to conceptualise memory hierarchy and IP reuse in SystemC than in Ocapi. During simulation of the video filter, we saw big difference in memory usage for the two approaches. In Ocapi, the bit-vector data type is implemented using a fixed-point data type. During simulation, the fixed-point data type in Ocapi is implemented using floating-point data. As seen in *Table 2*, this leads to extensive memory usage. Simulation time in SystemC can be 6 times slower than for Ocapi. However, by changing modelling style, the simulation time

Table 2. Comparison of the modelling and simulation capabilities for the video filter.

PARAMETER	OCAPI	SYSTEMC
Simulation scheduler	Linear execution	Real time kernel
Models needed for simulation	Design, test bench and parts of the simulator	Design and test bench
Resolved signals for memory interface	No (implicit)	Yes
Supports hierarchical design	No	Yes
Memory usage for 576 x 705 sized frames (PAL) [Mb]	325	43
Simulation performance, RTL-model for a 120x200 frame [sec./frame]	95	515 (1 sc_thread, 7 sc_methods, resolved signals used) 22 (1 sc_thread, 7 sc_methods) 22 (8 sc_threads)
Lines of code	4160	2670

decreases and turns SystemC four times faster than Ocapi. Based on the results from the compared parameters within this case study, the main conclusion is that SystemC is more suitable system design language for video systems than Ocapi.

REFERENCES

1. SystemC User's Guide, Version 1.1, http://www.systemc.org
2. R. Ernst, Th. Benner, Communication, *Constraints and User Directives in COSYMA*, Technical Report CY-94-2, Institut für DV-Anlagen, Technische Universität Braunschweig, June 1994.
3. G. De Micheli, D. C. Ku, F. Mailhot, T Truong, "The OLYMPUS Synthesis System for Digital Design", *IEEE Design & Test of Computers*, Vol. 7, No. 5, pp. 37-53, 1990.
4. Bolsens, H. J. De Man, B. Lin, K. van Rompaey, S. Vercauteren, D. Verkest, "Hardware/Software Co-Design of Digital Telecommunication Systems", *Proceedings of the IEEE*, Vol. 85, No. 3, pp. 391-418, 1997.
5. J. Zhu, R. Dömer, D. D. Gajski, "Syntax and Semantics of the SpecC Language", *Proceedings of the Synthesis and System Integration of Mixed Technologies*, December 1997.
6. *DVTNR-Method and Device for Noise Reduction*, LIMT Technology AB, Granted patent.

7. B. Oelmann, H. Norell, R. Andersson, Y. Xu, "Design of Real-Time Signal Processing ASIC for Noise Reduction in Moving Video Images", *Proceeding of IEEE Norchip Conference*, pp.228-33, 1999.
8. S. Vernalde, P. Schaumont, I. Bolsens, "An Object Oriented Programming Approach for Hardware Design", *Proceedings of IEEE Computer Society Workshop on VLSI*, Orlando, April 1999.
9. Cocentric tool suite, Synopsys Inc., http::://www.synopsys.com

Chapter 13

The Guidelines and JPEG Encoder Study Case of System Level Architecture Exploration Using the SpecC Methodology

Lukai Cai
University of California, Irvine

Mike Olivarez
Advanced System Architectures, Motorola

Dan Gajski
University of California, Irvine

Abstract: *To implement chip design on satisfactory target architecture, more architecture exploration should be done at higher levels of abstraction, in the earliest design stages. Using the SpecC language, architecture exploration can be processed easily and smoothly. A SpecC methodology of system level architecture exploration is introduced within this paper to illustrate this process. The design of a JPEG encoder is used as an example to illustrate the system level architecture exploration methodology.*

Keywords: *SpecC, system level architecture exploration, JPEG encoder*

1.   INTRODUCTION

During SoC design process, the work of mapping the functionality into target architecture, called *architecture exploration*, is one of the main problems that the SoC designers are facing. In the RTL level models which contain timing and/or pin information of target architectures, performing architectural exploration is too cumbersome to satisfy the time to market requirement. Therefore, a more abstract architecture model is required by the industry to implement fast architecture exploration.

In the SpecC language [1], an architecture model which contains abstract computation and abstract communication is well defined. This model is called architecture model of SpecC. Using this architecture model, designers can implement architecture exploration easily and efficiently. Many different target architectures can be explored in system level. Furthermore, the result of architecture exploration at the system level can be smoothly and consistently changed to an RTL level model, by using the SpecC Methodology.

In this paper, the system level architecture exploration methodology is introduced as part of the SpecC methodology. Unlike the existing SpecC methodology, which mainly concentrates on refining specification model into architecture model and further refining architecture model to communication model [1], system level architecture exploration concentrates on exploring the implementation from one target architecture to another target architecture, at the architecture level of abstraction. This methodology allows the designers to compare implementations on different target architectures and to improve the current implementation by changing some parts of target architecture. As an example of this, a JPEG encoder is used to illustrate this process.

A. Mignotte et al. (eds.), System on Chip Design Languages, 151–161.

The illustration used is organised as follows. Section 2 summarises the existing SpecC methodology described in [1]. In section 3, a description of the JPEG encoder algorithm, which is used for our tests, is given. In section 4, a JPEG encoder model has been architecturally explored and the guidelines of system level architecture exploration are introduced. Sections 5 and 6 outline the system level architecture exploration methodology. Finally, in section 7, conclusions are described.

2.   SPECC METHODOLOGY

2.1   SpecC Methodology

The SpecC methodology is a design methodology to implement design from pure specification into full implementation [1]. It defines four levels of modeling, from the most abstract level to the most detailed level. The first level of abstraction is the *specification model*, which represents pure specification. The second model, which is the *architecture model*, represents the implementation on target architectures with the abstraction of computation and communication specifications. The *communication model*, which is the third in the hierarchy, represents the implementation on target architectures with the abstraction of computation and detailed communication model. The fourth or *implementation model* contains the synthesizable RTL model for hardware implementation and pure C model for software implementation.

Besides the four models, the SpecC methodology also defines the method of refining between these models. *Specification model* is refined into *architecture model* by implementing architecture synthesis. *Architecture model* is refined into *communication model* by implementing communication synthesis. Finally, *communication model* is refined into *implementation model* by implementing hardware synthesis, software development, and interface synthesis.

2.2   SpecC Language

The SpecC methodology is a system level design language. SpecC is a super-set of C, which extends ANSI-C to support hardware design. Besides defining different models of different abstract levels, as mentioned in 2.1, SpecC clearly separates communication and computation. Therefore, IP (Intellectual Property) reuse is well supported. Furthermore, SpecC contains features required for system-level design, including behavioural hierarchy, structural hierarchy, concurrency, synchronisation, exception handling, timing, state transitions, and composite data types.

2.3   Advantages of SpecC as the Specification of System Level Architecture Exploration

The system level architecture exploration utilises the *architecture model* of SpecC for modeling. The main advantages of using SpecC for system level architecture exploration are:

1. SpecC is the super-set of C, therefore, C language programmers can program in SpecC language without tedious training.
2. SpecC supports hardware modeling as well as software modeling, which makes it appropriate for HW/SW co-design modeling and SoC design modeling. Becasuse SpecC is a homogeneous language, co-simulation of HW/SW is not required.

3. *Architecture model* of SpecC methodology contains abstract computation and communication. The communication and computation are completely separate. Therefore, it is straightforward when an *architecture model* is modified to an another one, based on modifications of the target architecture, allocation decisions, and scheduling decisions.
4. *Architecture model* can be simulated. It also contains timing information. In *architecture model* of SpecC language, *wait* and *waitfor* statements represent abstract time. Therefore, execution time can be evaluated and different *architecture models* can be compared for timing performance.
5. SpecC methodology not only defines *architecture model*, but it also supports other models at different abstract levels. Moreover, SpecC methodology provides the ability of modeling refinement. Thus, the system level architecture exploration can be embedded into a complete SpecC SoC design flow: the input of architecture exploration can be directly generated from the architecture synthesis phase. On the other hand, the output of system level architecture exploration can be further refined by the communication synthesis phase.

3. JPEG ENCODER

JPEG is an image compression standard. It is designed for compressing either full-color or grey-scale images of natural scenes [3]. Figure 1 shows the block diagram of the DCT based encoder for a grey scale image. It consists of four blocks: the image fragmentation block, the DCT block, the quantization block and the entropy coding block.

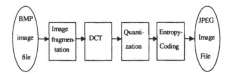

Figure 1. Block Diagram of the JPEG Encoder

4. JPEG EXAMPLE

4.1 Architecture Components and Working Environment

In the JPEG encoder example, a DSP56600 processor with maximum clock frequency of 60MHz (which is called SW in this paper) and an ASIC to be designed (which is called HW in this paper) are chosen as architecture components, from the view of easy implementation. The estimation times of JPEG's four leaf nodes on SW, are derived from reference [4], which is shown in table 1.

Table 1. Estimated Execution Time for Leaf Nodes on SW for Each 8×8 Pixel Block

Handle-data T(HD)	DCT T(DCT_S)	Quantization T(QZ)	Huffman T(HF)
142µs	745µs	93µs	162µs

Since the DCT block consumes most of the execution time, it is a good candidate to be executed in HW. In our example, When the DCT block is executed in selected HW, the execution time is 650µs (named $T(DCT\_H)$), for 8×8 pixel block. Besides the time estimation for computation, time estimation for communication is also needed. Communication overhead between SW and HW is assumed as one pixel per SW cycle. For an 8×8 pixel block, the overhead is 1µs. Finally, the testbench and timing constraint of the system is provided: a bitmap (bmp) file which includes 180 8×8 pixel blocks, is used as input of the testbench, and the expected timing constraint is assumed to be 90ms. To count the overall JPEG encoder execution time, a time simulator, which is also written in the SpecC language, is added to the simulation environment.

4.2 Component Separation Exploration

4.2.1 Pure SW Architecture Model

We assume at the beginning, the four basic blocks are run in SW sequentially, as shown in Figure 2. The four leaf nodes encapsulated within the *SW behavior* are HandleData block (which implements image fragmentation), DCT block, Quantization block, and HuffmanEncode block(which implements entropy coding). There are also four variables in *SW behavior*: *eobmp* is the integer, which indicates the end of the input file, hdata, ddata and qdata are immediate variables between blocks. It should be noted that the model does not involve execution related to input and output files. A reference of this part of JPEG design can be found in [5].

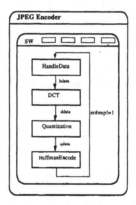

Figure 2. Pure_SW Target Architecture Model for JPEG Encoder

The execution time of the JPEG encoder in pure SW model can be estimated as follows: For each 8×8 byte block, T(block) = T(HD) + T(DCT_S) + T(QZ) + T(HF) = 142 + 745 + 93 + 162 = 1142 (µs). For the testbench which includes 180 blocks, T(total) = Num(block) × T(block) = 180 × 1142 / 1000 = 205.56 (ms).

Among four blocks, it is DCT block that consumes most of execution time, which is 745µs × 180 = 134ms. Therefore, DCT block is the candidate block for reducing execution time in the next step.

4.2.2 Component Separation Exploration Process

To reduce the DCT's execution time, a target architecture, which consists of HW and SW, is explored. The DCT is separated from other parts of code and executed in HW while the remaining parts are executed in SW. This modification process is accomplished by *component separation,* which is defined as the movement of a function block from one component to a new component. Modification process follows the brief guidelines of *component separation*:

1. Create the new component within the top level behaviour.
2. Move the separated function block from the existing component(s) to new component(s).
3. Add channels between the previously existing component(s) and newly created component(s).
4. Add necessary exit condition(s) for the created component.

The guidelines described here are brief. The detailed guidelines of system level architecture explorations are described in [6].

4.2.3 SW_HW_Sequential Model

The resulting architecture model is called SW_HW_Sequential model, as shown in Figure 3. The communications between the blocks are implemented using the channels' synchronisation functions. Since the SW and HW parts cannot be executed until the other part finishes its execution, SW and HW are executed sequentially, although they are parallel in the architecture view. The execution time can be estimated as follows: For each 8×8 pixel block, T(block) = T(HD) + T(DCT_H) + T(QZ) + T(HF) + 2 × T(comm) = 142 + 650 + 93 + 162 + 2 × 1 = 1049 (µs). For the testbench which includes 180 blocks, T(total) = Num(block) × T(block) = 180 × 1049 / 1000 = 188.82 (ms). The estimation result is the same as time simulator's result.

Compared with 205.56ms in the pure SW model, the execution time decreases to 188.82ms, giving an 8.1% throughput increase.

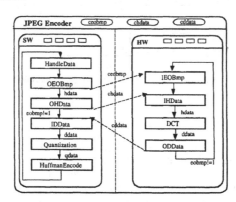

Figure 3. SW_HW_Sequential Target Architecture Model for JPEG Encoder

4.3   Parallel execution exploration

To reduce the execution time further, the SW should be rescheduled to make SW and HW run in parallel. It is possible because they can execute the different 8×8 pixel blocks at the same time. This process is implemented by *parallel execution* exploration.

4.3.1 Parallel Execution Exploration Process

The *parallel execution* exploration process is defined as the scheduling of two or more components in the system, which communicate with each other and execute in parallel. The guidelines shown here can solve the easy case of parallel execution exploration. In this case, one component (called *child component*) is the *sub-function* of another component (called *parent component*). The guidelines of parallel execution exploration that have been created are as follows:

1. Group blocks into four visual blocks (S_1 to S_4) in the parent component.
2. Add control variable for each visual block.
3. Add exit condition for each visual block
4. Rearrange four visual blocks.
5. Change exit condition of the *parent component*'s outer loop.
6. Add an idle visual block in the *parent component*.

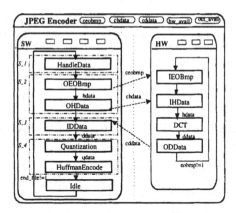

Figure 4. SW_HW_Parallel Target Architecture Model for JPEG Encoder

4.3.2 SW_HW_Parallel Model

After the parallel execution exploration, a SW_HW_Parallel model is developed as shown in Figure 4. The time simulator shows the execution time is 117.94ms. Compared with 188.82ms in SW_HW_Sequential model, it gives 37.5% throughput increase. For each 8×8 pixel block, T(block) = T(total) / Num(block) = 117.94 × 1000 / 180 = 655 (μs).

It should be noted that during the exploration process some overhead computations are added. Since the execution time of the system level leaf node is much larger than added overhead time, the added overhead time can be ignored.

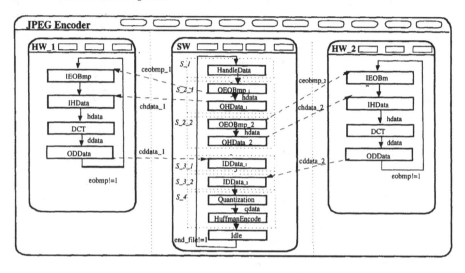

Figure 5. SW_2HW_Parallel Target Architecture Model for JPEG Encoder

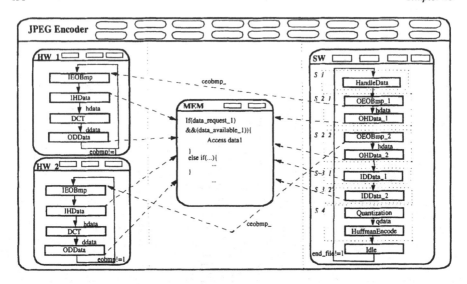

Figure 6. SW_2HW_Parallel_Mem Target Architecture Model for JPEG Encoder

4.4   Architecture Pipeline Exploration

4.4.1 Architecture Pipeline Exploration Process

For each 8×8 pixel block, the execution time of function blocks in SW without *waiting* is: T(SW) = T(HD) + T(QZ) + T(HF) + 2 × T(comm) = 399µs < T(block) = 655µs. The execution time of function block in HW without *waiting* is: T(HW) = T(DCT_H) + 2 × T(comm) = 652µs ≈ T(block) = 655µs. Since execution time of HW is the bottleneck compared with SH, in order to reduce T(block), the execution time of HW should be reduced.

To reduce the execution time of HW, two HW components should be executed concurrently, processing different pixel blocks. In this case, the target architecture that consists of two HWs and one SW running in parallel is explored by *architecture pipeline* exploration.

Architecture pipeline exploration is defined as the changes in the target architecture model by doubling some component(s) to make them run in parallel on different blocks of data, thus, improving the performance of the system. In this section, the component being doubled, is called *doubled component*. The component communicating with *doubled component* is called *communicated component*. The *architecture pipeline* exploration guidelines are shown as follows:

1. Double the *doubled component* and related channels.
2. Make changes in *communicated components* for communication to *doubled components*.

4.4.2 SW_2HW_Parallel Model

After *architecture pipeline* exploration, the SW_2HW_Parallel model is developed as shown in Figure 5, the time simulator shows the execution time is 72.33ms. Compared with 117.94ms in the SW_HW_Parallel model, it gives a 38.7% throughout increase. For each 8×8 byte block, T(block) = T(total) / Num(block) = 72.33 × 1000 / 180 = 402 (μs). This result can satisfy the timing constraint requirement.

4.5 Shared Global Memory Exploration

In some cases, a shared memory is needed for communication. Therefore, the JPEG encoder will change to a shared global memory communication model by *shared global memory* exploration.

4.5.1 Shared Global Memory Exploration Process

To change the communication mechanism between blocks from message passing to a shared global memory, *shared global memory* exploration is needed. In our JPEG encoder example, the data that communicate between HW and SW, which include 8×8 pixel block inputs and 8×8 pixel block outputs of the DCT, will be written/read through a global memory. The brief guidelines of *shared global memory* exploration are described as follows:

1. Create MEM component in the top level.
2. Use MEM channels to update old Channels.
3. Design read and write operations in MEM component.

4.5.2 SW_2HW_Mem Model

After the *shared global memory* exploration, the SW_2HW_Mem model is developed as shown in Figure 6. The time simulator shows the execution time is 72.69ms, compared with 72.33ms in SW_2HW_Parallel model. The difference between two models' execution time is very little, but comes from memory channels. For each 8×8 pixel block, T(block) = T(total) / Num(block) = 72.69 × 1000 / 180 = 404 (μs). This result will also satisfy the timing constraints.

5. SYSTEM LEVEL ARCHITECTURE EXPLORATION PROCESS

In short, four main types of sub-operations of system level architecture exploration: component separation, parallel execution, architecture pipeline, and shared global memory exploration are utilised in JPEG encoder example, as shown in the following steps:

1. Initially, Pure_SW model is generated on reference processor (SW).
2. Component Separation exploration is performed on the Pure_SW model to find the bottlenecks in the SW so hardware accelerators can be added.
3. SW_HW_Sequential model is generated to test whether adding a HW (for DCT) executed sequentially with SW (for HD, QZ, and HF) lowers the execution time.

4. Parallel Execution exploration is performed on SW_HW_Sequential model to test the time reduction when HW(for DCT) is run in parallel with SW(for HD, QZ, and HF), instead of sequential execution.

5. SW_HW_Parallel model is generated to test whether the system requirement can be met by Parallel Execution exploration.

6. SW_HW_Parallel model is changed using Architecture Pipeline exploration, to see the time reduction when the architecture is pipelined in respect to hardware and software.

7. SW_2HW_Parallel model testing allows the testing of a pipelined architecture when using multiple components.

8. SW_2HW_Parallel model then adds Shared Global Memory exploration to model the system that contains global memory. Although one configuration is used, various memory configurations can be created at this time.

9. SW_2HW Shared Memory Parallel model is tested to ensure that the requirements are met.

After architecture exploration, the estimation time of JPEG encoder is decreased from 205.56ms of Pure SW model to 72.69ms of SW_2HW_Mem model. It gives a 64% throughout increase.

6.   SYSTEM LEVEL ARCHITECTURE EXPLORATION

As shown in section 4, system level architecture exploration is the methodology to change the implementation from one target architecture to another target architecture, at the architecture model of SpecC methodology [1].

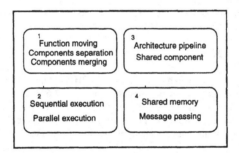

Figure 7. System Level Architecture Exploration Operation Types

The system level architecture exploration methodology includes four types of basic operations shown in Figure 7. Besides the four system level architecture exploration operations mentioned in section 4, *components merging, shared component, sequential execution* and *message-passing* operations are the reverse operations of *components separation, architecture pipeline, parallel execution* and *shared memory* operations, respectively. The *function moving* operation is the operation to move one function block from one component into another component within the target architecture, which is very similar to components separation operation.

The guideline of reverse operations can be implemented in two methods. The first method is to design the guideline for each operation independently. The second method is to use the existing four operations of exploration described in section 4. The second method can be accomplished since the four operations introduced in section 4 changes from a simple situation to a complex situation. While the reverse operations changes from the complex situation to simple situation, the changes from the simple situation to the complex one are more difficult to implement. Furthermore, since the initial specification is sequentially executed in one component, the path of system level architecture exploration operations can be traced. It is easy to go back to the previous step that contains the needed simple situation. In the second method, system level architecture exploration is then restarted using the four operations mentioned in section 4 to continue its exploration from the previous step. Therefore, the second method can be implemented more easily.

Using the guidelines of system level architecture exploration operations, the automatic tools can be implemented.

7. CONCLUSIONS

This paper introduces a new methodology, system level architecture exploration methodology.

With the SpecC language, the process of system level architecture exploration is simple and fast. This is because the communication and computation are completely separate in the architecture model of SpecC. Furthermore, both communication and computation are specified in the abstract level.

This illustration uses a JPEG encoder as an example to show the process of system level architecture exploration. The system level architecture exploration contains nine operations. The brief guidelines for four main operations are given. These guidelines show that system level architecture exploration can be implemented easily with manual modification. To implement these modifications more easily, automated tools can be designed for system level architecture exploration.

References:
[1] [GZDGZ] D. Gajski, J. Zhu, R. Domer, A. Gerstlauer, S. Zhao, *SpecC: Specification Language and Methodology*, Kluwer Academic Publishers, March, 2000
[2] [GZDH] A. Gerstlauer, S. Zhao, D. Gajski, A. Horak, *Design of a GSM Vocoder using SpecC Methodology*, University of California, Irvine, Technical Report ICS-99-xx, February 1999.
[3] [DCT] V. Bhaskaran, K. Konstantinides, *Image and Video Compression Standards*, Second Edition, Kluwer Academic Publisher, 1997
[4] [CPCG] L. Cai, J. Peng, C. Chang, A. Gerstlauer, H. Li, A. Selka, C. Siska, L. Sun, S. Zhao, D. Gajski, *Design of a JPEG Encoding System*, University of California, Irvine, Technical Report ICS-99-xx, September 1999.
[5] [YDLG] H. Yin, H. Du, T. Lee, D. Gajski, *Design of a JPEG Encoder using SpecC Methodology*. University of California, Irvine, Technical Report ICS-00-xx, July 2000
[6] [COG] L. Cai, M. Olivarez, D. Gajski, *System Level Architecture Exploration using the SpecC Methodology*, Irvine Technical Report ICS-00-xx, Sep 2000

Chapter 14

Provision and Integration of EDA Web-Services Using WSDL-based Markup

Heinz-Josef Eikerling, Wolfgang Thronicke, Siegfried Bublitz
Siemens Business Services C-LAB, Fürstenallee 11, D-33 102 Paderborn, Germany

Abstract: This paper studies the integration of resources (e.g., tools used in electronic design automation) into environments used to implement collaborative engineering workflows. Major attention is paid to the consideration of resources that are available through the web. Requirements that are implemented in the integration approach comprise the support of concepts for re-use and the web standards. The latter is achieved by employing the Web Service Description Language (WSDL), an upcoming XML-based format for mark-up of services residing in the web.

Key words: web services, workflow management, electronic design automation, tool integration, XML, WSDL, TES

1. INTRODUCTION

Engineering practice nowadays is significantly influenced by the rapid development of Internet related technologies. Mobile and decentralised working enable site-spanning teamwork and demand techniques for collaborative engineering ([Ap99], [GaPo99], [PaFo99]). The assembling of distributed workflows particularly in the EDA domain with its complex engineering design, modelling, and verification tasks is still rather challenging.

Here, techniques for resource integration are of focal interest. A resource (human, hardware equipment, software service) is an entity that is active for a certain time during a working procedure to achieve a certain (sub-)result. Whereas formerly [SvB93] the integration of tools in a rather centralised environment was stressed, this paper emphasizes on the integration of (software) services that are widely dispersed and exposed through web interfaces. This imposes new requirements, e.g. to cope with secured environments and intellectual property (IP) protection.

We propose an integration mechanism based on the XML founded Web Service Description Language (WSDL) which characterises services by meta information and retrieves this information through a universal directory interface, thus enabling the re-use of integrations and permitting to encompass secured environments. The application of the technology is shown with a simple example, shortcomings and limitations are detailed in the final section.

A. Mignotte et al. (eds.), *System on Chip Design Languages,* 163–172.

2.   RELATED WORK

Web services can be regarded as *loosely coupled re-usable SW components* which can be accessed by other applications through Internet protocols. On the behavioural side a web service acts like a server in the Internet that delivers functionality instead of documents as common web-servers do.

Concepts for deploying a web based design and simulation service were for instance formerly suggested by National Semiconductors. An approach utilising Java for providing EDA tools like synthesis systems was presented in [LaKh97, LaBr00]. These concepts are rather limited and could only be used in special scenarios like integrating PDM or ERP systems. The concepts native, not standardised nature makes it difficult to even retrieve the interfaces of the integrated resources. For the EDA domain, this particular aspect was formerly tackled by CFI's TES standard [CFI TES] which is not widely used. From today's view the descriptive power of TES for tools is still impressive. However, the standard did not address deployment and the network infrastructure for locating the tools.

In larger businesses the notion of computer supported (business) processes has gained increasing importance in the last years. Workflow management systems (WFMs) control complex processes from a higher level of abstraction [WfMC]. Workflows should also be recognized as integrable entities in the sense of a very powerful and sophisticated tool.

Yet, only little effort has been spent on a consistent, standardised and coherent approach for the integration of resources through web services, which is the emphasis of this paper.

3.   REQUIREMENTS FOR RESOURCE INTEGRATION

3.1   Integrable Resource Types

The resources to be integrated can be classified into three major groups:
1. *Human resources*: for collaborative engineering this means essentially supporting engineers concerning the distribution of work and awareness of the overall state of the workflow.
2. *Physical or hardware resources* consist of special and general purpose computing equipment like printers and PCs. They should be seamlessly integrable into the workflow.
3. *Software resources*: software interfaces to tools or services permitting access to lower level (hardware drivers) or higher level (database access) software components.

The coordination of these resources is done by a workflow system. Thus, appropriate language interfaces (C, C++, Java, Perl, ...) for implementing the resource access are needed.

3.2   Modularity, Extensibility and Scalability

Managing the change and customisation of integrated resources is necessary to catch up with changing technologies and to extend the automated processes to new requirements. Ideally, the employed integration technology itself has to turn into an adaptive service that can assimilate the functionality in a structured way, finally leading to a modular / hierarchical, thus scalable integration methodology.

3.3 Mechanisms for Distribution and Deployment

Integration descriptions shall be shareable among different platforms, e.g. as an inherited feature of integration. A practical way to do this is by means of a web server, i.e. integration services are deployed to a web server. Deployed services must also be self-explaining, e.g. via meta-information on the integrated resources.

3.4 Internet Capability, Dissemination and Use

Integration must handle resources located on Internet hosts accessible via standard Internet protocols like plain TCP/IP, HTTP or SMTP.

Support for the integration concept in general purpose applications like design frameworks or workflow management systems and dedicated applications design tools (e.g., as plug-ins) is required. The user is not forced to use a web browser. Consequently a new family of web-clients will evolve unlike a web-browser but centred around the exploitation of available resources deployed in the Internet.

4. SERVICE-INTEGRATION THROUGH WSDL

4.1 Application Scenario

The following application example will serve as a means to illustrate the concept. It consists of a service for modelling an electronic system. A customer completes a web form by specifying the characteristics of the system. The contents of this form is turned into a workflow description by the web server through CGI scripting. This workflow may encompass tool invocations (e.g., analogue/digital simulator) and service calls (e.g., customer billing). Moreover, human interaction (e.g., call to expert consultancy) might be involved. Notice, that these resources may be located on different hosts in the server's intra- or extranet.

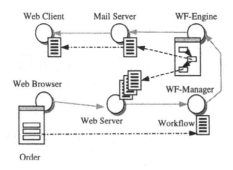

Figure 1. Example scenario: modelling service.

On the server side, the so called workflow manager (a process responsible for creating and managing workflow instances) loads the description into an engine process which in turn executes the workflow and controls the (remote) tool invocation and issues a user notification once the entire job has been completed (see figure 1).

The above straight-forward solution suffers mainly from the unavailability of meta-information on the service interfaces which makes it difficult to retrieve the service. Moreover, relocation of the service implementation is delicate. In order to achieve this, we will describe how to use meta-information for simplifying the integration of services into workflows and how to interface complete workflows in an integration task.

4.2   WSDL, UDDI and Engineering Services

The Web Services Description Language (WSDL) is an XML format for describing network services by identifying the services (and their operations) and providing format definitions for requesting them through a remote call. Actually, a WSDL document realizes an IDL (interface definition language) contract between servers and clients which is extended by the actual deployment and access specifications. A service of this type listens for messages which conform to the Simple Object Access Protocol (SOAP). SOAP is the logical protocol for communication between web services. Function access is usually established in a remote procedure call alike way, i.e., client and server exchange a properly formatted Simple Object Access Protocol (SOAP) request and response object.

For publishing and retrieving services, a generic registry mechanism - the Universal Discovery, Description, and Integration (UDDI) - is provided. A UDDI registry constitutes different sets of information:

– *White pages*: name, address and other business contact information for the service provider.
– *Yellow pages*: business classification according to existing (non-electronic) standards like NAICS or UNSPSC.
– *Green pages*: technical information about the (web) services provided by a given business.

An application queries the UDDI server in order to locate the web service needed. The sevice's details are revealed by the WSDL document that is reference by the UDDI service. Then the requesting application can connect to the web service.

4.3   Service Request Processing

Service processing is technically achieved by using *toolkits* which supply the functionality to create, send and receive SOAP messages. This section explains the communication mechanism of the Java SOAP toolkit. It has to be noted that using one special toolkit for the implementation of a web service does not constrain the implementation paradigm chosen for the client, since SOAP messages contain all references to decode data portably between different platforms and programming paradigms.

Once a service is discovered by an UDDI lookup, the service can be called through the use of the method that are defined in the service interface. The sequence of SOAP formatted requests is as follows:

1. A client (written in Java, Perl,...) addresses the web service by its URL. Usually the service can be either implemented based on scripting (Perl, Python, VBS,...) or Java Servlet/Java Server page or as native C++/C code. A request can be a remote procedure call or the transmission of an arbitrary XML document , e.g. the transmission of an object. The mapping of the request to a specific service implementation is done through tagging the request type and forwarding it to the so called

RPC router. For identifying the service itself the *URN* (Uniform Resource Name) of e.g. the servlet implementing the web service has to be known in advance.

2. The client (based on a web browser or using the SOAP API) submits URL, URN and the original request which contains all parameters of the interface to the API and waits for the results. The SOAP API uses an XML component to generate a SOAP request object. This is an XML encoding of the original request. It may contain additional information, e.g., how to generate the to be replied object. This requires both client and server side to understand the XML schemas describing this objects.

3. The generated request is transmitted via a TCP/IP connection to the server. Interestingly, the request object can be mapped to different kinds of transport, i.e., HTTP or SMTP, which makes SOAP available to rather secured environments (see figure 2). HTTP can be seen as a kind of a standard for the physical protocol. Since web servers are based on this protocol it is quite straightforward to extend them to serve web services over HTTP as well.

4. The server receives the SOAP request, detects the type of the request (i.e., HTTP GET for accessing a static HTML document) and handles it over to its SOAP component which decodes it and passes this to the RPC router servlet which selects the intended servlet implementation and calls it with the initial request parameters.

5. The result takes the reverse way back, being encoded into a SOAP response instead of a SOAP request object.

6. The client finally receives the decoded result or an error message.

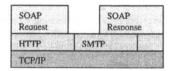

Figure 2. SOAP formatted request/response object.

The overall processing of a SOAP request is shown in figure 3.

The above described technology can be used to turn the introductory application scenario into a widely available web service that can be easily integrated with a workflow system.

5.   IMPLEMENTATION

5.1   Architecture

For implementing the overall functionality the ASTAI(R) system [AST] has been used. This environment is a sophisticated integration platform in heterogeneous networks supporting site-spanning and platform-independent workflows. ASTAI(R) is an open platform with defined interfaces to plug new services and protocols into it. This extensibility is the key feature to easily integrate the access to web services into workflows. The components of the resulting application are shown in figure 4. Workflow encapsulation and access to web services is implemented in a specific WSDL bridge.

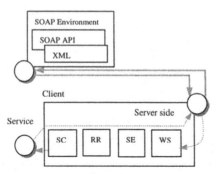

Figure 3. Processing of a SOAP service request. On the server side, the request passes the Web Server (WS), the SOAP
Environment (SE), the RPC Router (RR), and the Servlet Container (SC).

ASTAI(R) comprises a convenient way for implementing this bridge by providing a broadcasting
bus which is also used for the communication and orchestration of the services inside ASTAI(R).
Most importantly, there are tool launchers for controlling the initiation and execution of tools used
within a workflow.

The tool launchers can be deployed to different types of nodes within the network; they are
triggered by events delivered through the central broadcasting server, i.e., the tool launchers listen for
requests regarding the execution of a certain tool and pick up those requests that can be served by the
host which runs the tool launcher. The broadcaster follows CFI's ITC [CFI ITC] standard.

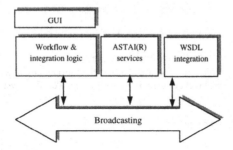

Figure 4. Integration of WSDL infra-structure with the ASTAI(R) workflow system.

Additionally, there are services for logging events deployed over the communication bus and a
generic CORBA bridge permitting to involve business objects (BOs) for workflow creation. Multi-
user mode is implemented through the provision of sessions enabling the coupling of workflows
operated by different users in a collaborative fashion; sessions are registered in and retrieved through
a central repository that is built on top of a CORBA compliant naming service. In ASTAI(R) a lean
workflow-management (workflow manager) component maintains workflows built from the
integrated tools and other resources. Workflows can be arranged using a graphical workflow-editor.

5.2 Service Implementation

Just to give an impression, the overall structure of the simulation service in WSDL syntax is shown below.

```
<?xml version="1.0" ?>
<definitions name="astair"
 targetNamespace="http://www.../simulate.wsdl"
 xmlns:tns="http://www.../simulate.wsdl"
...
    <message name="simulateRequest">
         ...
    </message>
         ...
    <portType name="astairPortType">
      ...
    </portType>
    <binding name="astairbinding"
      type="tns:astairPortType">
      ...
    </binding>
    <service name="astairService">        ...
    </service>
</definitions>
```

First of all, a name space for all subsequent declarations is defined. This eases the hierarchical definition of web services and the re-use of already existing type definitions. Subsequently, the messages accepted and issued by the service are described.

```
<message name="simulateRequest">
  <part name="name" type="xsd:string"/>
  <part name="modelname" type="xsd:string"/>
  <part name="modeltype" type="xsd:string"/>
  <part name="p1value" type="xsd:string"/>
  <part name="p2value" type="xsd:string"/>
  <part name="p3value" type="xsd:string"/>
  <part name="custemail" type="xsd:string"/>
</message>
<message name="simulateResponse">
  <part name="result" type="xsd:string"/>
</message>
```

Now, the port types are defined (the service consists of one input and one output port, the messages acknowledged at the input and sent via the output port are also defined).

```
<portType name="astairPortType">
 <operation name="simulate">
  <input message="tns:simulateRequest"/>
  <output message="tns:simulateResponse"/>
 </operation>
</portType>
```

Next, the previously defined messages are bound to the ports and the name and the location of the service in terms of a URL are specified. Furthermore, the transport mechanism is defined.

```
<binding name="astairbinding"
 type="tns:astairPortType">
 <soap:binding style="rpc"
```

```
transport="http"/>
<operation name="simulate">
<soap:operation
soapAction="http..simulate.wsdl#simulate"/>
 <input>
  <soap:body  use="encoded"
   namespace="http://www..../simulate.wsdl"
   encodingStyle="http://schemas...."/>
 </input>
 <output>
  <soap:body  use="encoded"
   namespace="http://www..../simulate.wsdl"
   encodingStyle="http://schemas...."/>
 </output>
 </operation>
</binding>
<service name="astairService">
 <port name="astairPort"
  binding="tns:astairbinding">
  <soap:address location="http://www...."/>
  </port>
</service>
```

This WSDL description facilitates the client site access and the initiation of the modelling workflow through the browser. A similar document can be gained for the overall response (notification service) after the workflow has been terminated. Having done this, the service can be deployed. The revised scenario resulting out of this mapping can be seen in figure 5.

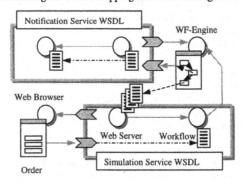

Figure 5. Modified scenario with service definitions.

5.3   Service Binding and Retrieval

Once the simulation service has been registered, it can be retrieved using the UDDI registry. As shown in the initial example scenario, the application issues a notification once the entire process has been finalised. This is done by automatically preparing a reply form, connecting to the mail server and sending the completed form that contains the URL of the documents containing the requested modelling data. The corresponding service can be implemented by creating a corresponding WSDL description as well. However, since this service is only used internally (thus not exposed for access by end-users) this description is not registered with the UDDI directory.

6. EVALUATION

In order to evaluate the viability of the concept, we compare the WSDL based integration methodology with TES approach which by default is offered by the ASTAI(R) system.

6.1 Tool-Integration with TES

One result of the CAD-FRAME Initiative (CFI) has been the specification of a descriptive format to capture the features of a tool. This *tool encapsulation specification (TES)* supplies the building part for an integration approach. Each TES-file contains various information about tool-invocation, data-dependencies, and command line structure. Moreover, it allows the context-sensitive specification of the tool behavior[1] and the transformation of input arguments and return values using LISP-like expressions.

The integration platform ASTAI(R) features a TES-based integration mechanism: An extended TES specification defines the location and hosts of an available tool or service with required and optional data dependencies. This information is used by ASTAI(R)'s lean distributed multi-server integration layer to distribute and start jobs, provide and transfer data and evaluate results.

6.2 Comparison: TES vs. WSDL

Concerning the resource integration, TES is suitable for managing integrated tools even in complex situations where some input or output processing is required, but it has never gained a high degree of usage as tool integration standard Additionally, there is virtually no support for web service integration and the web-based exchange/re-use of already integrated units since such technologies were not known when TES was defined.

However, there are also benefits of using TES when compared to WSDL. Most notably for the ASTAI(R) system, TES can be completely embedded into the extension language that comes with ASTAI(R). Hence, there is rather little overhead for parsing and interpreting TES tool descriptions. On the other hand, processing WSDL descriptions can be quite demanding from the computational point of view especially when Java is used. Moreover, requesting a WSDL service implementation requires to use SOAP as the transport mechanism for the messages that have to be exchanged. As a result, the transmission and processing (which also requires to parse XML message envelopes) of a request takes much longer than would be required by a transport mechanism which utilizes a binary format like CORBA/IIOP: CORBA/IIOP is used by ASTAI(R)'s broadcaster for internal communication.

As a result of all this, TES appears to be a suitable mechanism for internal messaging inside the integration system whereas WSDL provides a standard for integrating dispersed and external web resources.

---

[1] Tool-behaviour means the I/O characteristics, describing which data is needed and which data can be produced when running the application.

6.3   Conclusion

WSDL provides a means for the web based integration of software resources thus enabling the set-up of highly distributed engineering environments. No aspects of re-usability, extensibility and versioning can be handled by TES so that native support for WSDL is an essential value-added for the integration logic of workflow systems.

Finally, the XML approach is also viable for accessing services from and out of secured environments. There is no support for similar concepts within TES.

7.   SUMMARY AND FUTURE WORK

We have described how to make XML-based mark-up available to an engineering workflow system in order to facilitate web-based collaboration. The integrable (web-) resources were described in WSDL and registered with and retrieved by a central UDDI directory. WSDL was shown to be superior to TES.

The lack of standards for providing interfaces is a major obstacle for establishing collaborative engineering, but WSDL seems to be widely accepted. Future work will focus on checking the applicableness of this approach in really distributed settings for a completely web-based system design as described in [Ra00].

8.   REFERENCES

[Ap99]   Appelt, W. (1999) *WWW Based Collaboration with the BSCW System.* In Proceedings of SOFSEM'99, Springer Lecture Notes in Computer Science 1725, p.66-78; November 26 - December 4, Milovy (Czech Republic).

[AST] ASTAI(R) web pages, *http://www.c-lab.de/astair.*

[CFI TES] CFI; Tool Encapsulation Specification; Version 1.0.0, CAD Framework Initiative Inc., 1992, Austin, USA

[CFI ITC] CFI; Inter-Tool Communication Programming Interface; CFI document no. dis-92-S-3, CAD Framework Initiative Inc., 1992, Austin, USA

[GaPo99] Gammack, J., and Poon, S. (1999) *Communication Media for Supporting Engineering.* In Proceedings of the 32nd Annual Hawaii International Conference on System Sciences, Maui, HI, 1999.

[LaKh97] Lavana H., Khetawat A., Brglez F., Kozminski K.: Executable Workflows: A Paradigm for Collaborative Design on the Internet, 34th Design Automation Conference, 9-13 June 1997, CA, US.

[LaBr00] H. Lavana, F. Brglez, R. Reese, G. Konduri, and A Chandrakasan. OpenDesign: An Open User-Configurable Project Environment for Collaborative Design and Execution on the Internet. IEEE Intl. Conference on Computer Design, 2000.

[OMG-WMF2000] Object Management Group. *Workflow Management Facility Specification V 1.2.* Edition April 2000. http://cgi.omg.org/cgi-bin/doc?formal/00-05-02.pdf

[PaFo99] Patrikalis, N.M., Fortier, P.J., Ioannidis, Y.E., Nikolaou, C.N., Robinson, A.R., Rossignac, J.R., and Abrams, S. (1999) *Distributed Information and Computation in Scientific and Engineering Environments.* In D-LIB Magazine, Vol. 5, No. 4, April 1999, ISSN 1082-9873.

[Ra00] Ramming F.: Web-based System Design with Components Off The Shelf (COTS), Forum on Design Languages, Tuebingen, Sept. 2000.

[SvB93] D. Schefström and G. van den Broek (Editors). *Tool Integration - Environments and Frameworks.* Wiley & Sons. 1993. ISBN 0-471-93554-9.

[WfMC] The Workflow Management Coalition. *http://www.wfmc.org.* 2001

[WfMC-Mime] The Workflow Management Coalition. *Workflow Standard - Interoperability Internet e-mail MIME Binding.* Document Number WFMC-TC-1018. 2000.

[WFMC-XML] The Workflow Management Coalition. *Workflow Standard - Interoperability Wf-XML Binding.* Document Number WFMC-TC-1023. Version 1.0. 2000.

SYSTEM VERIFICATION

Chapter 15

A Mixed C/Verilog Dual-Platform Simulator

David A. Burgoon
Edward W. Powell
John A. Sundragon Waitz
Hewlett-Packard Company

Abstract: One of the strengths of Hewlett-Packard's Technical Solutions Lab has been its ability to efficiently develop
workstation graphics subsystems by minimizing serial dependencies in the development process. Central to
achieving this was the use of C-language functional models of the subsystem ASICs in a flexible, mixed-
level, mixed-language simulation environment. Although the first generation of this simulation
environment, known as "NGLE," has been used successfully for a number of years, that experience has also
revealed several important opportunities for improvement. In this paper, we describe the next generation of
this environment, called the Graphics Product Simulator (GPS), and the improvements it brings. These
include support for threaded C-language modeling, an improved method of mixing C-language and Verilog
models, dual platform (Windows NT and Unix) support, and improved system-level modeling facilities.

1.   INTRODUCTION

Several years ago, Hewlett-Packard's Workstation Systems Lab embarked on a program to reduce product development cycle times through top-down concurrent engineering. The verification environment that resulted from that effort, known as "NGLE," has been described [1][2]. Although NGLE has been used successfully for a number of years, that experience has also revealed several important opportunities for improvement. In this paper, we describe the next generation of this environment, called the Graphics Product Simulator (GPS), and the improvements it brings. We begin with a review of concurrent engineering for graphics subsystem design, as pioneered by NGLE. We then discuss the motivation for GPS, our next generation mixed-language verification environment. We then give an overview of GPS and its components. Next, we discuss how the flexible multi-platform nature of GPS allows us to work with a number of simulation configurations. We conclude with some results and observations about future opportunities for GPS.

In order to appreciate our motivation for developing GPS, it helps to understand the system context for the graphics subsystems in our workstation products.

Application programs running on the CPU access the dedicated graphics hardware via the API (e.g. OpenGL) and driver software layers supplied with the operating system (HP-UX or Windows NT). These accesses are converted by the core electronics center (CEC) into reads and writes on the peripheral bus (e.g. PCI or AGP) connecting the graphics hardware. The driver can also interact with the graphics hardware through other channels, i.e. interrupts and DMA. This presents a hardware/software co-design problem: we must verify that the graphics driver interacts correctly with

. Mignotte et al. (eds.), System on Chip Design Languages, 175–186.

the graphics hardware. Note, however, that the software in this co-design is not *embedded* in the hardware under development; rather, it *drives* the hardware.

The NGLE environment tackles this co-design problem by providing a way for the software driver team to test their work against a relevant functional model of the hardware. The hardware team produces a complete C-language behavioral model of the graphics hardware, and verifies the model using tests written in C that draw pictures. The software team then uses this model to validate the driver by writing tests that exercise the driver and hardware naturally through the API and driver under development. Thus, once a reasonably well validated C-language model is available, the software and hardware teams can proceed fairly independently of one another, concurrently progressively refining their respective designs with very little dependence on one another.

To enable concurrency within the hardware teams, NGLE provides a means for models written in either C or Verilog and at various levels of abstraction (behavioral, RTL, and gate-level) to be mixed together in a whole-subsystem model. This fosters concurrency within the hardware teams because it allows for a full-subsystem simulation to be retained even if the blocks are at disparate stages of progress in their refinement from behavioral to gates.

Another advantage of the NGLE mixed C/Verilog approach is that graphics subsystem integration is early and continuous. A complete model of the graphics hardware is brought together with the driver software very early in the design cycle so that hardware/software and block-to-block misunderstanding can be identified early. This full-subsystem model is kept together throughout the entire project, with more detail added as the project progresses via a process of top-down progressive refinement.

2.   MOTIVATION

NGLE has been successfully used for nearly ten years. However, during that time several opportunities for improvement have surfaced. Over this period we found ourselves demanding more of NGLE, adding incremental functionality in a patchwork fashion in order to try to meet our growing expectations. The end result was a bloated implementation that was hard to use and maintain. Even with these incremental patches, there were problems with software verification, hardware and system modeling, and test development that led us to create the next generation NGLE environment, namely, GPS.

There were two main software verification problems. First, due to the nature of the NGLE implementation, separate compilations of the C-language behavioral hardware model were required for the hardware and software teams. This led to configuration management and consistency problems. The other main problem, again due to NGLE implementation idiosyncrasies, was that the driver had to be instrumented for use in simulation with the hardware model. This meant that we were not actually verifying the driver code shipped to customers. Sometimes the differences between the modified and real code were painfully significant.

One problem related to hardware modeling was the cost of developing and maintaining the interfaces between C and Verilog. "PLI shells" written in Verilog and corresponding modules written in C were often difficult to write. Too often, simulation errors were due to defects in these modules. These interfaces lacked a simple, consistent method for linking the C world with the Verilog world. Another deficiency of the hardware model was that the C-language parts were implemented with a single thread of execution. In the early days of NGLE, this was acceptable, as the cascade of function calls during the execution of the C model fit well with the pipelined nature of computer graphics hardware. However, as the hardware grew more sophisticated over the years, the need to model the threaded nature of that hardware in C became readily apparent.

There were also enhancements needed in the area of system modeling. Perhaps the most significant grew out of our desire to pursue the Windows NT workstation market. In this pursuit, our co-design situation became more difficult: we needed to provide a way for Windows NT API and driver layers to be verified against a hardware model developed by engineers whose design environment was rooted in HP-UX. This meant that we needed to facilitate dual-platform C-language modeling, and also provide for the case where the project team did not want to go through the extra effort of developing its C-language model for both HP-UX and Windows NT. In the case of driver verification against a mixed C/Verilog model, we needed to provide a way for a test program running on Windows NT to drive a C/Verilog simulator running on HP-UX.

Other system-related areas for improvement included better support for simulating interrupts and DMA. In NGLE, these were often very difficult to model, and were therefore sometimes omitted. Similarly, graphics-related firmware was often not properly addressed in the graphics subsystem verification plan.

There were also areas for improvement in the cost of developing and maintaining verification tests. The lack of a complete and stable test utility library gave rise to unnecessary rework when leveraging tests from one project to the next, or when leveraging them for real-hardware bring-up, manufacturing test, and field diagnostics.

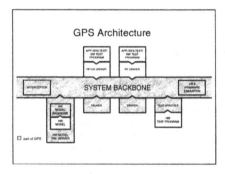

Figure 1.

3.   OVERVIEW OF GPS ARCHITECTURE

The overall GPS architecture (shown in Figure 1) is fundamentally a client-server design, which allows a client (test program or tool) to run on the same or different machine than the simulation server. This section describes most of the major components of the architecture in some detail.

*   The *Hardware Model Simulation Server* is the center of any simulation system. It encapsulates the models and the simulation system (whether exclusively a set of threaded C models, a set of Verilog models, or a mixture) and provides dispatcher/scheduler functionality to connect the simulation to the rest of the world. The server creates all resources that represent the simulated hardware, and also describes the simulated hardware configuration so that clients can interact appropriately with it. Inside the simulation server, the Hardware Model Backbone provides the infrastructure for creating and intermixing models of various types.

In situations where the clients are accessing real hardware instead of a simulation, the simulation server is replaced with a simple *database server* that provides the same configuration information for clients that the simulation server would have furnished.

- The *System Backbone* includes the basic client-server message protocol and the transport mechanisms used to send and receive messages. It also includes a unique mechanism called the *Interceptor* that allows clients to access the simulation as a virtual hardware device, just as they would access real hardware. Provision is also made for emulation of supporting OS functionality and device firmware that is not yet available.

  A *Client API* that can also be considered part of the system backbone supports low-level access to the message protocol.

- The *Viewer* is a tool client that allows real or simulated frame buffers to be visualized in a way that supports verification and problem solving.

- The *Talker* is another lightweight tool client that supports simple command-line interactions with the state of a simulation or of a real hardware device.

- Hardware design teams create *Hardware Test Programs*, which make use of the *Test Utilities* libraries. For graphics device testing, the Test Utilities comprise hardware resource management, an OpenGL-like driver for high-level tests, and register read/write support for low-level tests.

- Software development teams create their product *Drivers*. They also develop *Software Test Programs* and run real *Applications* on those drivers.

4.   SYSTEM BACKBONE

4.1   Client-server message protocol

As in all client-server systems, GPS defines a set of messages that embody the interactions between the server and the clients. There are several groups of messages:

- Messages that manage opening, closing, and synchronizing connections. This includes determination of byte-ordering requirements (which are the responsibility of the server, in order to allow clients to operate "naturally").

- Messages that emulate transactions on the bus or other instruction/data path that provide stimuli to the simulation and responses to the host system. These resemble PCI and AGP bus transactions, and include DMA cycles and interrupts.

- Messages that access simulated resources via fast paths that do not go through the simulation models. These are called "backdoor" accesses and are explained in more detail below. Such messages include reading or writing a block in a simulated frame buffer.

- Messages that access simple databases maintained by the server. For example, messages that set or retrieve symbols in a configuration symbol table are part of this group

In our current implementation, messages are usually passed via Berkeley-style sockets, though an optimization has been implemented to allow certain accesses to occur via shared memory when the client and server are local to the same machine.

Given the availability of the message protocol and supporting libraries, how do clients interact with the server? The next several sections discuss the available routes for interactions, as shown in Figure 2.

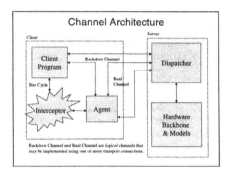

Figure 2.

4.2   Real channel and the interceptor

The most authentic way for a client to interact with a simulation server would be for it to execute real device driver code, right down to the individual register reads and writes. The most common way to implement this has been to make all reads and writes via macro or procedure calls, which can then (depending on a compile-time or runtime mode) convert each load or store into a transaction with the simulation instead of with real hardware. However, this introduces a degree of non-realism into the code, in that the same binary would probably not be shipped as a product. Instead, it would be recompiled to eliminate the overhead of the modal switch and simulation support.

One of the objectives of GPS is to allow graphics driver code in its final form to be run against simulated hardware. (The degree to which this can actually be done depends on the fidelity of the simulation and of the message protocol.) To support this goal, HP has developed proprietary mechanisms to trap actual load and store instructions at the kernel level, and relay them to the simulation. This is accomplished by the use of a kernel-level driver called the *Interceptor* and a user-level daemon program called the *Agent*. The Agent receives trapped loads and stores from the Interceptor and converts them to GPS message protocol. It also receives synchronous (read reply) and asynchronous (DMA load and store, interrupt) messages from the simulation and relays them to the kernel driver, which accesses client process memory and state. The resulting effect is that the client can execute real, shipped code and rely on the Interceptor to make the simulation appear to be the target graphics device. We call this mode of operation the "real channel."

4.3   Backdoor channel

In testing that driver code is correct, or that some simulated blocks are operating as intended, it is not always necessary or practical for the results to be verified via further simulation. For example, when testing the rendering engine, it would be very slow to always inquire the contents of the simulated "frame buffer" into which the simulated graphics device is rendering by actually modeling the frame buffer read operations. By implementing the frame buffer RAM model as a simple memory array in the server, it is possible to provide "shortcut" accesses that do not require simulation. Other parts of the simulated resources can also be implemented (or at least shadowed) in memory to support other such "backdoor channel" accesses. GPS provides messages to support backdoor frame buffer block reads, writes, and clears, since these are all operations that are slow to simulate and yet often not the objective of a particular simulation/test.

The server not only encapsulates the simulation, but also provides some simple database functionality such as a configuration symbol table and a catalog of frame buffer allocations. The advantages of keeping all this information in the server are that it is central (available to and consistent among all clients) and it is persistent (it is available even after the client that created the information has terminated).

A client can connect directly to the server and operate entirely in the backdoor channel. If it needs to use a mixture of real-channel and backdoor-channel accesses, the client can still connect directly to the server for the backdoor messages; or, for convenience and better message ordering, it can connect to the Agent, which will relay backdoor messages to and from the server intermixed with the converted real accesses. When interacting with real hardware, a client usually connects directly to the database server, since the Interceptor and Agent are not active in that configuration.

4.4   OS and firmware emulation

In developing drivers for new devices, it is sometimes necessary to rely on operating system (kernel) features that do not yet exist; that is, the kernel support for new features is being developed in parallel with the hardware and other software. Similarly, the drivers may depend on initializations that would normally be performed on the device by code and data contained in an initialization ROM.

In order to provide as realistic a development environment as possible for drivers, provision has been made for behavioral emulation of kernel features, and emulation or actual execution of ROM code that is still under development. These types of emulations could either be built into the Agent, or they could be performed by a separate special client that can use the real channel just as the driver-testing client does. In order to emulate kernel functions, it is necessary to link the test client with a special library that intercepts the system calls of interest and relays them to the special emulation client. Linking with this intercept library does not require changes in the actual driver code.

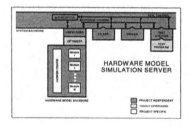

Figure 3.

5.   HARDWARE MODEL SIMULATION SERVER

The simulation server in GPS provides a framework in which to develop models in C or Verilog, without needing to expend much effort to support the client/server architecture. The context for the simulation server within the GPS environment is shown in Figure 3. There are four main architectural elements to note in the server design:

- The *Dispatcher* includes the message transport mechanisms and the action routines to support all expected message types. Messages destined to become stimuli for the actual simulation are sorted onto several task queues. When the model representing the bus interface withdraws a transaction from one of its input buffers, a task scheduler automatically transfers another task into the input buffer from the highest-priority queue that contains any tasks. Similarly, values written by the models to the simulation output buffers are translated by the scheduler into outgoing messages. Most other types of messages (connection management, backdoor accesses, and database accesses) are handled directly by the Dispatcher. However, certain messages that are put on the task queues invoke a non-simulated action. This preserves the ordering of simulated and non-simulated actions.
- The *Optimizer* is an optional module created by the project to recognize patterns in modeled transactions and, if desired, perform shortcuts that have the same effect. For example, if the standard initialization of a device would take a lot of time if each register write were simulated, the optimizer might recognize the standard pattern and perform a blanket initialization by directly loading the simulation state.
- The *Hardware Model Backbone* is the central infrastructure for model development, thread management, and model configuration of data paths among models written in C or Verilog.
- *Shared memory* is associated with the hardware model backbone because its structure is project-dependent, and some models interact directly with it (as in the example of a frame buffer memory array mentioned earlier).

The innovative technology in the Hardware Model Backbone is discussed in much more detail in the next section.

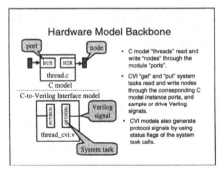

Figure 4.

6.   HARDWARE MODEL BACKBONE

The GPS Hardware Model Backbone consists of the elements shown in Figure 4. C models are constructed and enabled to communicate with Verilog using these elements. The C model API library provides constructs that allow a Verilog-like hierarchy of modules to be defined. C modules are either blocks or threads. The thread modules are analogous to `always` blocks in Verilog. They each execute as an independent thread of control in a forever loop. Block modules contain instances of threads or other blocks. Modules communicate with each other through *ports* that are connected to *nodes*. Port and instance names are unique only within the current module scope. Module names must be unique within the design. A C-language data structure is associated with a module definition, and each instance of the module has a unique copy of this data structure.

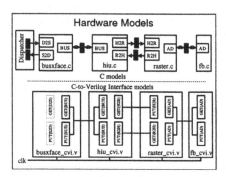

Figure 5.

Nodes are FIFO-like structures that hold an array of data values. Figure 5 shows a sample C model with a set of thread modules connected together through nodes. Nodes are represented in the figures as vertically striped boxes. When the node is created, it is allocated with a specified depth and data entry size. Nodes are roughly analogous to the wires in a Verilog module. Nodes, however, contain multiple values of the signal that would be present on the corresponding wires at different times. We call this concept "temporal buffering." Each time a thread is called it may process multiple values from its input nodes, and write multiple values to its output nodes. We call a model based on temporal buffering a "data flow model." A data flow model is a higher level of abstraction than a behavioral Verilog model because it does not directly model clock cycles, protocol signals, or even simulation time. Temporal buffering improves C model performance because it minimizes thread switch overhead.

GPS provides a standalone C simulator that is used to develop and debug algorithmic models for the subsystem hardware, and then to write and test the software drivers for the new hardware. This model becomes a reference for the desired behavior of the new subsystem hardware.

Once the C model is created, it can be translated using a tool to a set of Verilog files with hierarchy that matches the C model. For each thread module, templates for the C-to-Verilog Interface (CVI) model are written. The bottom half of Figure 5 shows the CVI models that correspond to the C models in the top half of the figure. The CVI models are written by using a set of "user-defined system tasks," implemented via the Verilog Procedural Interface (VPI), and linked into Verilog as part of the GPS simulator. These tasks are called from the initial blocks of a Verilog module that we call the CVI model. This module should have a port list matching that of the behavioral, RTL, or gate-level Verilog implementations of the block.

The CVI module acts as a placeholder for the C model in the Verilog description of the design. It reads and writes data from nodes by referencing the ports of the C model at the same instance path in C as the CVI model instance path in Verilog. The GET and PUT tasks in the CVI model have parameters to specify which port of the C model to read or write, a Verilog trigger event, Verilog signal names to be sampled or written, and Verilog status signals. Using these values and additional Verilog code in the CVI model, the clocking and protocol signal behavior of the CVI module blocks can be emulated. Protocol signals are used on a Verilog block to control the transferring of data, for example "ready," "full," "valid," etc.

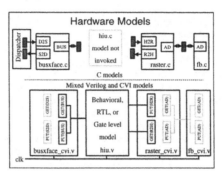

Figure 6.

Normally, the GET and PUT calls of two connected CVI models are disabled, and the C models communicate directly through the nodes to improve simulation performance. The GET and PUT calls can however be set to force communication to the Verilog signals. This can be used to validate the clocking and protocol signals of the CVI models before other Verilog implementations of the block are available. Behavioral, RTL, or gate level Verilog models can be substituted in place of the CVI model. In Figure 6 a regular Verilog model replaces the CVI model for the "hiu" block. In this case the C model thread associated with the "hiu" block is not invoked, and the GET and PUT calls of the CVI models that surround the "hiu" block are active. Synchronous time is imposed on the C model only at the boundaries with Verilog blocks. Temporal buffering can still be used in any portions of the design where C models communicate with each other.

One of the benefits of the GPS Hardware Model Backbone is that it supports standalone C simulation for concurrent engineering of hardware ASICs and software drivers. GPS C models have many features similar to Verilog, such as modules and ports, but the data flow models in GPS provide a higher level of abstraction than Verilog models. The timing and protocol signals required for Verilog are added later when defining the CVI models.

One of the key differences between GPS CVI models and NGLE "PLI shells," used in the previous generation simulator, is that models can be written with no knowledge of surrounding blocks. In other words, a block's functionality is completely specified by the C and CVI modules, and no change to connected modules is needed when a block is instantiated. In NGLE the C model had to be modified to connect it to the neighboring block's PLI shell. Also, GPS CVI models support bi-directional signals by using both a GET and PUT task on the same signal. In NGLE bi-directional signals were not supported.

In GPS the C and Verilog models can be freely mixed. The performance of the C models is maintained because signals between C models stay in the C domain.

7.   PLATFORMS AND CONFIGURATIONS

The client-server architecture together with the flexibility of the System Backbone allow GPS to be used in many different configurations of client host systems and simulation server host systems. This section describes a few of the most common configurations.

As discussed in the introduction, a primary impetus for developing GPS has been to support multiple platforms. Currently GPS is supported on HP-UX and Windows NT. Significant effort has been expended to identify platform-dependent issues and to isolate the code to just a few modules. Virtually all the source code is shared across the platforms, with some conditional compilation to handle differences in system support for such features as threads, shared memory, and sockets, and to handle the unavoidable differences in byte ordering. However, some system components are, of necessity, specifically built for one platform or the other. Perhaps most obviously, the kernel driver that implements the Interceptor is very system specific. Other Interceptor differences restrict how GPS is configured at runtime, and dictate the hardware resources required.

Another platform consideration is the host system for Verilog. In practical terms, HP-UX is still our preferred operating system for large Verilog simulations. A pure C-model simulation, on the other hand, can be executed on either HP-UX or Windows NT in a reasonable amount of time.

GPS is typically used with the following configurations:

- Pure C simulation with the test client and server running on the same host.

    This is typically used by the hardware team for early development and debugging of the C behavioral model and verification tests, and the software team for the bulk of the verification of the driver against the hardware C model.

- Large Verilog or mixed C/Verilog simulation on HP-UX, with the test client running on a necessarily separate Windows NT system or a possibly separate HP-UX system.

    This configuration is used for mainstream model verification by the hardware team. It exploits the superior capacity, stability, and performance that are available with Verilog running on HP-UX. In this mode the test client usually bypasses the Interceptor and connects directly to the server.

- Testing of a software driver via the Interceptor with a remote simulation.

    This configuration is only used when a full C model is unavailable to run on the test client's platform, or in the rare case when we desire to have the driver interact with a Verilog model.

- Testing on real hardware.

    Here the database server replaces the simulation server. Hardware team tests that use the GPS test utilities, and software team tests that use the real drivers, can be exercised. This configuration is useful for hardware prototype evaluation, manufacturing test, and field diagnostics.

8.   RESULTS

GPS has been deployed for production use with two projects, and is starting on a third project, which will fully utilize GPS. Remarkably, the first project to use the "Graphics Product Simulator" is not actually a graphics design, but is an automatic test equipment (ATE) system. This illustrates the flexibility of the C modeling portion of GPS. It is capable of modeling a wide range of designs. The ATE system design has four ASICs, each of which has been modeled with the GPS C-model API. CVI modules have been written for this design to allow many different configurations of mixed C and Verilog to be simulated. This design does not use the Test Utilities portion of GPS, but instead connects to the simulator through the client API library. The client API library allows almost any kind of address-data type bus to be modeled as messages sent to the server.

The second project to use a portion of GPS is a graphics product that was near completion and needed a way to debug the soon-to-arrive prototype hardware. The project team decided to build a "hybrid" environment which used tests ported to the GPS test utility libraries, and a special passthrough interface that allowed the GPS tests to work with an existing NGLE C model. The ported GPS tests were validated with the C model, and then used to debug the hardware. By doing this, the project was able to use the standard GPS Viewer and Talker programs to view the contents of the frame buffer and the registers in the hardware.

Finally, a new graphics product project is starting up, and has begun writing models and tests. This project is planning to use all of GPS.

We characterized the performance of GPS C models in a mixed C/Verilog simulation by comparing it to a standalone Verilog-only test bench. A block from the ATE system was chosen that had the same test sequence available as a standalone test bench, and as a GPS test. In both simulations the block being tested was modeled in RTL Verilog. In the standalone test, the stimulus was driven directly to this block. In the GPS simulation, the stimulus had to pass through C models of the other three chips in the system and then get converted to Verilog signals by the CVI modules surrounding the block. The simulation time comparison indicated that the GPS simulation was within 1% of the standalone test bench. From this we conclude that the simulation speed of GPS C models make it feasible and efficient to write most tests at the system level where they are compatible with all test configurations including real hardware.

9. CONCLUSION

We have detailed the results of our efforts to produce GPS, a next-generation graphics subsystem development and verification environment that retains the best features of its predecessor, NGLE, and also addresses new requirements. Like NGLE, GPS supports a top-down concurrent design flow. Notably, it also supports dual-platform product development, and provides a novel means of mixing C and Verilog hardware models to support full-subsystem simulation.

As we begin using GPS for product development in our R&D lab, we will face some challenges.

- We need to seek ways to minimize the resources that will be required for ongoing maintenance and support. In particular, we need to address plans for support of GPS for future versions of HP-UX and Windows. Interceptor support is of particular concern, as it requires rather unique expertise and licensing to effect the required changes to the kernel.
- We should find a way to leverage our vast portfolio of verification tests developed under NGLE. Ideas include automated porting tools and compatibility wrappers.

As we look to the future, there are a number of opportunities related to GPS.

- We will likely need to port to Linux, as we have begun shipping workstation products offering that OS.
- To improve the ease of configuration of mixed C/Verilog models we could develop a tool that supports setting GPS invocation command options and server symbols according to a succinct database of configurations. It would also be tempting to exploit recently proposed changes to the Verilog language for configuration management.
- There are a number of interesting options for C-language modeling currently being discussed (e.g. CynApps' Cynlib C++ class library, and the Open SystemC initiative). Future versions of GPS could be targeted to subscribe to the solution that prevails as the preferred standard.

- There are solutions available today for the synthesis of RTL descriptions from behavioral Verilog models. There is also talk of similar tools for C-based models. GPS could evolve to take advantage of behavioral synthesis solutions that enable a fully automated top-down progressive refinement methodology.
- Eventually, we hope that EDA vendors will offer commercial solutions that meet or exceed our requirements. There may be some opportunities to influence their developments with GPS concepts.
- We could expand the scope of our subsystem simulations to include models representing the CEC ASICs. This would give us a greater degree of system integration in our verification efforts.

10.   ACKNOWLEDGEMENTS

GPS represents the creative toil of many individuals. Besides the authors, we would like to acknowledge the engineering work of Rick Aulino, Doug Buhler, Mike King, and Lief Sorensen; and the management leadership of Don Cunningham, Ken Lewis, and Peter Brey. We would also like to thank the early adopters of GPS: the aforementioned project teams from Agilent Technologies and HP. Their feedback was invaluable, and we appreciate the risks they took in basing their development environment on a work in progress.

11.   REFERENCES

[1] Burgoon, David A., "Achieving Concurrent Engineering for Complex Subsystem Design: The Case for Hardware Functional Modeling using C," *Proceedings of the DesignCon 1998 On-Chip System Design Conference*, pp. 357-371.
[2] Burgoon, David A., "A Mixed-Language Simulator for Concurrent Engineering," *Proceedings of the 1998 IVC/VIUF Conference*, pp. 114-119.

Chapter 16

Assertions Targeting A Diverse Set of Verification Tools

Harry D. Foster
Hewlett-Packard Co.
Richardson, TX
foster@rsn.hp.com

Claudionor N. Coelho Jr.
Verplex Systems, Inc., Milpitas, CA
Computer Science Dept, UFMG, Brazil
coelho@verplex.com

Abstract: A myriad of proprietary (i.e., commercial tool specific) verification assertion languages exist today. These languages emerged due to the lack of formal language constructs supporting assertion specification in today's hardware description languages (HDL). The method described in this paper presents a unique process for unifying (or neutralizing the effects of) the many proprietary languages by using a set of predefined specification modules instantiated as assertions within the designer's HDL. This methodology creates numerous advantages and precludes the need to introduce new HDL constructs (i.e., extensions to Verilog are not required). It enables the design engineer to "specify once," then leverage the same HDL assertion specification over multiple verification processes -- such as traditional simulation, semi-formal, and formal verification tools. It also eliminates the need for the design engineer to master tool specific and proprietary language details. Furthermore, this methodology enables evaluating new verification processes and tools (containing their own proprietary languages) seamlessly for the duration of the project, without the need to modify the original HDL text.

Key words: assertions, Open Verification Library (OVL)

1. INTRODUCTION

The objective of design verification is to ensure that a design's implementation satisfies the requirements of its specification. It is the act of analysis during the course of specification (as well as implementation) that enables the engineer to uncover serious errors while they are still inexpensive to fix. To make verification and analysis economically feasible, the cost of specification at the RT-level must be dramatically reduced, and the analysis process must be automated.

Today, several categories of design verification and analysis tools for validating functional intent exist. This set includes logic simulators, testbench generators, formal and semi-formal verification tools. The first, logic simulators validate design behavior responses for a given set of input stimuli or test vectors. Predictably, the results obtained using logic simulation tools are only as good as the functional coverage quality of the set of input stimuli. Another category of tools includes those identified as testbench generators. These are used to model the design environment and generate simulation-input stimuli. In addition, these tools observe and validate proper output behavior [Begeron 2000]. The specification for proper behavior might be defined as events and assertions in the tool's proprietary

. Mignotte et al. (eds.), System on Chip Design Languages, 187–200.
© 2002 Kluwer Academic Publishers.

language. More recently, the so-called formal and semi-formal categories of tools have emerged, which are heavily proof driven and mathematical in approach. These tools include state-space exploration, such as property and model checkers, which validate user-specified properties using formal techniques without test vectors [Clarke et. al 1999]. Semi-formal verification, such as amplification tools, combine traditional simulation techniques with formal state-space exploration and model checking techniques. For these tools, the mathematical proofs are employed with a limited or bounded search at precise times during the verification process.

As engineers begin to employ more advance forms of verification to the design flow, they quickly realize that to be successful, verifiable forms of specification are required. One method of specifying the designer's functional intent is to create a set of module design assertions [Bening and Foster 2000]. As an example, consider that a possible design assertion is that a state machine's encoding is always "one-hot" after a reset, meaning that only one bit of a collection of bits is actively high at a time. If the state machine violates the one-hot assertion following a reset, then the logic design is flawed in some way. Our claim is that a module assertion monitor can be created to detect this error.

In this paper, we promote the idea of refining the design's specification (i.e., higher level requirements) into a set of verifiable RT-level assertions. We have found this technique practical and effective for capturing the designer's functional intent while providing an automatic path for validation. In section 1, we discuss current techniques for capturing assertions at the RT-level. In section 2, we introduce our assertion monitor library, which consists of a set of predefined assertion modules, that can be used for both specification and validation targeted at a diverse set of verification tools. In section 3, we present our results and experiences of applying an assertion monitor methodology to a large project. Section 4 discusses how we would like to apply the assertion monitor library to larger forms of specification on future projects. Finally, in section 5 we present our conclusions

1.1   Verification Techniques

Traditionally, engineers verify the design's implementation against its requirements using a *black-box* testing approach. In other words, the engineer creates a model of the design written in a hardware description language (e.g., Verilog [IEEE 1364-1995] or VHDL [IEEE 1076-1993]). The engineer then creates a model of the design environment (referred to as a *testbench*), which includes or instantiate a copy of the model or *device under test* (DUT). The testbench is responsible for driving stimulus (i.e., logical one and zero values) into the DUT. In addition, the testbench provides the means for observing and validating the output response values from the DUT. The specification defines the legal values or sequences of values permitted by the DUT.

One problem encountered when using a black-box testing approach is that validating proper design behavior is limited to observing output ports of the DUT. The DUT might exhibit improper internal behavior, such as a state machine violating its one-hot property, but still have a proper output response, because the design error is not directly observable on the output ports. This might be due to the current set of input stimulus, when applied to the DUT, impeding the internal problem's value from propagating to an output port. Given a different set of input stimulus, the internal error might be observable. Hence, validating all internal properties of a design using black-box testing techniques is often impractical, particularly as design sizes increase.

Alternatively, *white-box* testing can be implemented to validate properties of a design. This technique adds monitors on internal points within the DUT, resulting in an increase in observable behavior during testing. For example, adding an internal monitor to directly observe a state machine can validate the previous assertion that a state machine is always one-hot. Thus, if the one-hot property is violated, the error is instantly isolated to the faulty internal point. This overcomes the problem associated with black-box testing—the possibility of missing an internal error (for a given input stimulus) only by observing DUT output responses.

1.2 Classes of Assertions

In discussing design assertions, it is helpful to understand both verification events and design assertions. A verification *event* may be defined as an HDL expression, which evaluates to a TRUE value. For example, if the expression $(c\_req == 1)\&\&(c\_ack == 1)$ evaluates TRUE, then an *event* has occurred in the verification environment. An *assertion* is a claim we make about an event or sequence of events in a design. In other words, an assertion is a property of a design and may be classified as either *static* or *temporal*. A *static* assertion is an event that must be TRUE for all time. A *temporal* assertion has a time relationship of events associated with it, whose correct sequence must be TRUE. For example, a temporal assertion can be viewed as an event-triggered window, bounding a specific property, i.e., an event.

The following examples illustrate aspects of temporal, static, and combinations of temporal and static assertion. **Figure 1-1** illustrates an assertion for an *invariant* (or safety) property. The property (i.e., event *P*) in this example is **always** valid after *Event 1* occurs, and continues to be TRUE until *Event 2* occurs. **Figure 1-2** illustrates an assertion for a *liveness* property. The event *P*, in this example, must **eventually** be valid after the first event-trigger occurs and before the second event-trigger occurs. In this example, a property of the design is invalid if event *P* does not occur within the specified event-bounded window.

In addition to static and temporal, an assertion can be classified as either a *constraint* or a *property,* depending upon where the assertion is made. A constraint may be thought of as a range of allowable values. An assertion made on an input port of the design model being verified is an example of a *constraint* because it bounds the input stimulus to permissible operating values for that particular input port. The design cannot be guaranteed to operate correctly if its input stimulus violates a specified constraint. A property may be thought of as expected behavior in response to defined constraints. An assertion made on an output port of a design, or an internal point in the design, is an example of a *property*. For any permissible sequence of input values applied to design, its properties will not be violated if the design is functionally correct.

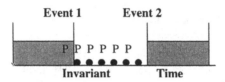

Figure 1-1 Invariant Assertion Window

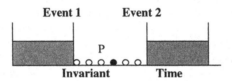

Figure 1-2 Livenes Assertion Window

1.3 Current Assertion Specification Tequniques

There are a few HDL techniques or representations currently available for specifying a property of a logic design. For example, VHDL [IEEE 1076-1993] provides a language construct for specifying a *static invariant* assertion:

> **assert** *event*
> **report** *message*
>   **severity** *level*

The *assert* statement can be used as an internal checker during the course of verification; this is an example of white-box testing.

Unfortunately, VHDL does not provide any constructs for directly specifying *temporal* assertion or *liveness* properties. In addition, with the exception of logic simulators, commercial verification tools such as model checkers, and semi-formal verification tools generally do not use the VHDL static assertion construct during verification. In other words, these tools use their own proprietary language to specify a design assertion. Moreover, Verilog [IEEE 1364-1995] does not provide any language constructs for *static, temporal, invariance,* or *liveness* assertions.

The following example illustrates different methods of capturing and validating the same design assertion targeted at (a) Verilog logic simulation, (b) the SMV public-domain model checker [McMillan 1993], and (c) general commercial property checking tools. The design assertion (or property) we specify for this example is that a specific queue in the design cannot underflow when the queue is in a valid state (i.e., q_valid is active high).

(a) **Logic Simulation:** For simulation, an HDL internal checker can be written to validate the assertion as shown in the **Example 1-1**.

Example 1-1

```
always @(posedge ck) begin
  if (q_valid==1'b1) begin
    if (!(q_underflow == 1'b0)) begin
      $display ("ERROR: QueueUnderflow");
      $finish;
    end
  end
end
```

During simulation, if the q_underflow signal is ever activated when the queue is in a valid state, the Verilog code will display an error and stop simulation.

(b) **SMV Model Checker:** Alternatively, the assertion could be specified in the temporal property language (such as Computation Tree Logic (CTL) [Clarke and Emerson 1981]]) in the HDL as a meta-comment, and then used by a public domain model checker such as SMV [McMillan 1993]. For example:

Example 1-2

//assert:qsafe **AG**((q_valid==1)→(q_underflow!=1))

This CTL Verilog *meta-comment* expresses the same assertion or property of the design as is modeled with the Verilog code in **Example 1-1**.

(c) **Commercial Property Checkers:** Many commercial tools have developed their own HDL assertion language, generally using meta-comments similar to the convention shown in **Example 1-3**.

Example 1-3

//{vendor_name}: {proprietary assertion language}

2. ASSERTION MONITOR LIBRARY

As we demonstrated in the previous section, expressing the same property of a design while targeting a diverse set of verification processes and tools currently requires many different representations. These languages and interfaces may not be natural to the designer's verification flow; prompting designers to master a large number of verification techniques and interfaces. In addition, these multiple interfaces stymie designers' efforts to evaluate new verification techniques and tools.

Our assertion monitor library was developed to provide designers, integrators, and verification engineers with a single, vendor-independent interface for design validation using simulation, semi-formal verification, and formal verification techniques. By using a single well-defined interface, our assertion monitor library can bridge the gap between the different types of verification, making the use of more advanced verification tools and techniques available for non-expert users.

OVL Assertion Library:

assert_always	*assert_odd_parity*
assert_change	*assert_one_hot*
assert_decrement	*assert_proposition*
assert_delta	*assert_range*
assert_even_parity	*assert_time*
assert_increment	*assert_transition*
assert_handshake	*assert_unchange*
assert_never	*assert_width*
assert_no_overflow	*assert_win_change*
assert_no_transition	*assert_win_unchange*
assert_no_underflow	*assert_window*

Example 2-1

```
module assert_always (clk, reset_n, test_expr);
 input clk, reset_n, test_expr;
 parameter severity_level = 0;
 parameter msg="ASSERT ALWAYS VIOLATION";

 //synopsys translate_off
 `ifdef ASSERT_ON
  integer error_count;
  initial error_count = 0;
  always @(posedge clk) begin
   `ifdef ASSERT_GLOBAL_RESET
       if (`ASSERT_GLOBAL_RESET!=1'b0) begin
     `else
    if (reset_n != 0) begin // active low reset_n
   `endif
     if (test_expr != 1'b1) begin
      error_count = error_count + 1;
      `ifdef ASSERT_MAX_REPORT_ERROR
       if (error_count <=
             `ASSERT_MAX_REPORT_ERROR)
      `endif
       $display("%s:severity %0d : time %0t : %m",
                     msg, severity_level, $time);
      if (severity_level == 0) $finish;
     end
    end
  end
 `endif
```

```
//synopsys translate_on
endmodule
```

Example 2-1 illustrates common features of our assertion monitor library. For this example we have selected the **assert_always,** which is the most general assertion. This assertion does not contain any complex sequential check, with the exception of sampling *test_expr* at every positive edge of *clk.* It is employed whenever the user wants to verify an invariant property.

The Example 2-2 illustrates using the **assert_always** to ensure that the q_underflow signal is never activated. Furthermore, this example demonstrates how to specify a logical implication, such as our previous CTL and SMV queue example (see **Example 1-2**):

Example2-2

```
assert_always   q_safe ( clk, reset_n,
                (q_valid==1) ?      (q_underflow!=1) : 1'b1);
```

For assertions requiring a more complex sequential check, the assertion monitors follow the convention illustrated in **Figure 2-1**. The *start_event* will initiate the assertion validation process, which will be performed on a specified *test_expr.* The assertion monitor will continue to validate the assertion until an *end_event* occurs.

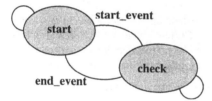

Figure 2-1 Temporal Assertion

There are two classes of sequential monitors in the assertion library. The first class is a *time-bounded* monitor. For example, **assert_change** is a time-bounded assertion that will continuously monitor the *start_event* at every positive edge of the clock. Once this signal (or expression) evaluates TRUE, the **assert_change** monitor will ensure that the *test_expr* will change values within a specified number of clocks (e.g., *num_cks*). For this monitor, the *end_event* occurs at the end of *num_cks* clocks.

The second class of sequential monitors is an *event-bounded* monitor. For example, the **assert_window** is an event-bounded assertion that continuously monitors the *start_event* at every positive edge of the clock. Once this signal (or expression) evaluates TRUE, the **assert_window** monitor will ensure that the *test_expr* remains TRUE until a user specified *end_event* expression triggers (i.e., evaluates TRUE).

2.1   Assertion Monitor Library Details

All assertion monitors within our library observe the following BNF format detailed in **Example 2-3** and defined in compliance with the standard *module* instantiation of the IEEE Std 1364-1995 "Verilog Hardware Description Language."

Example 2-3

```
assertion_instantiation ::= assert_identifier [parameter_value_assignment]
    module_instance ;

parameter_value_assignment ::= #(severity_number {,other parameter expressions},
    message)

module_instance ::= name_of_instance ([list_of_module_connections])

name_of_instance ::= module_instance_identifier

list_of_module_connections ::=                        ordered_port_connection
    {, ordered_port_connection} | named_port_connection              {,
    named_port_connection}

ordered_port_connection ::= [expression]

named_port_connection ::= .port_identifier ([expression])

assert_identifer ::= assert_[type_identifier]

type_identifier ::= identifier
```

To enable the assertion monitors during verification, the user must define the macro ASSERT_ON (e.g., +define+ASSERT_ON). During synthesis, the ASSERT_ON would not be defined. In addition, *//synthesis translate_off* meta-comments are contained within the body of each monitor to prevent accidental synthesis of the monitor logic.

There are two parameters always present in the assertion library definition: *severity_level* and *message.*

The *severity_level* (see **Example 2-1**) is an optional parameter that is used to describe the severity of a failure. By default, this parameter is set to 0, the highest severity. The way a specific tool will deal with this parameter is tool dependent. In simulation, if an error is encountered with a severity_level of 0, the simulation will halt. Severity level values greater than 0 will be displayed as warnings; however, simulation will continue to run.

The *message* is an optional parameter that is used to describe the error message that should be printed when the assertion fires.

The list_of_module_connections for all library assertions have two common port connections, *test_expr* and *reset_n*. The *test_expr* port connects the assertion expression that is to be validated. The *reset_n* port connects an active low expression that indicates circuit initialization completion to the assertion monitor. During the time *reset_n* is low, the assertion monitor will be disabled and initialized. An alternative to specifying a *reset_n* signal or condition for each assertion monitor, is for the user to define the macro *'ASSERT_GLOBAL_RESET*, which should reference a reset signal in the top module of the design. When defined, all instantiated monitors will disregard their respective *reset_n* signals, and they will be initialized whenever *'ASSERT_GLOBAL_RESET* is low.

Most of the assertions are sampled at the positive edge of a triggering signal or expression *clk*, with the exception of *assert_proposition* (which requires no *clk*).

Every assertion monitor maintains an internal register *error_count* that stores the number of times the assertion monitor has fired. This internal register can be accessed by the testbench to signal when a given testbench should be aborted. When the macro `'ASSERT_MAX_REPORT_ERROR` is defined, the assertion instance will report a problem if the number of errors for that instance is smaller than the maximum limit defined by the macro (i.e., new errors will be ignored).

2.2 Assertion Monitor Library Validation

One of the most important aspects of providing an assertion monitor library is validation through characterization and verification of correct behavior. We used three distinct methods to validate our assertion monitor library: code review, simulation and perturbation based formal verification.

In the first validation method, we attempted to reconstruct the behavior of the assertion from its description. Then, the extracted behavior was compared against the textual description for the library during code review. In the second method, a simulation strategy was devised to test the assertion library.

The third method we used to validate the assertion monitor library employed the Verplex Systems' BlackTie™ formal verification tool. Formal verification tools, such as BlackTie, usually work on the assume/guarantee paradigm for compositional reasoning, i.e. if the assumptions are true, then the property should be true [Clarke *et al.* 2000].

We constructed a very small model with two assertion monitors. The first assertion monitor is the property to be verified, whereas the second assertion monitor is a modified version of the first assertion monitor. For example, the first assertion may be modified to include a different set of parameters. This small model can be formally verified very quickly, so that several assumptions can be tested to characterize the correct behavior of the assertion monitor under test.

3. RESULTS AND EXPERIENCES

This section focuses on results from *"specifying once"* (using the assertion monitor library), then leveraging the assertions across multiple processes--simulation, semi-formal, and formal verification tools. These results are established from applying the assertion monitor library methodology to a recent HP high-end server ASIC project.

Kantrowitz and Noack [1996] demonstrated the value of creating a verification process that includes assertion monitors. In their paper, they describe a verification process developed for the DEC Alpha 21264 Microprocessor that combines assertion monitors, coverage analysis, and pseudo-random test generation. Measuring the effectiveness of their various bug detection mechanisms, the authors presented a table revealing that 34% of all design bugs were identified through assertion monitors. Likewise, Taylor, et al. [1998] revealed that assertion monitors identified 25% of their total design bugs. Clearly, a verification process that includes assertion monitors will quickly identify and isolate errors while improving the observability required for functional coverage analysis.

3.1   Effective Assertion Monitor Methodology

Capturing Assertions. From our experience in using the assertion monitor library on the HP ASIC project, it is apparent that an effective assertion methodology is one where the design engineer captures the assertion during code development. This type of methodology is preferable to augmenting the RTL with assertions after code completion. In fact, many RTL bugs are revealed to the designer during the process of creating the steps required to specify the assertion monitor arguments—prior to applying any form of verification.

Our assertion monitor library permits capturing the assertion independent of the Verilog source file (i.e., assertions can be placed in a separate file). We favor, however, embedding the assertions directly in the RTL to facilitate:

* linting, in a single step, the RTL source for syntactical errors related to assertion specification; and

* capturing design assumptions and knowledge at the point of development; which, in addition to the RTL, becomes a permanent record of the design intent.

Constraints. With our current design project, engineers translated their block-level informal interface specifications into a set of assertions. First, assertion modules were selected from our monitor library, which represented our translated set of assertions; then, these modules were instantiated directly into the engineer's RTL code. Later, when formal verification techniques were applied to the design, these assertions were treated as design constraints, the semi-formal and formal tools limited their search process to legal input behavior. During verification, new constraints were added whenever a false firing occurred on an assertion property.

Peer Reviews. An effective assertion methodology should include RTL assertion code reviews. These peer reviews permit the design engineers to describe their corner case concerns and, in the course of the review, potentially identify new concerns. We found that the peer reviews provided a useful learning experience for less accomplished assertion monitor users.

Non-Assertion Identified Bugs. For all bugs found in the course of simulation, which were identified by means other than an assertion monitors, we recommend that the designer add new assertions. This process addresses the following objectives:

* to capture the known corner case that will document a permanent characteristic of the design,

* to provide the engineer with an increased awareness on how to code assertion, and

- to ensure (given the correct stimulus) the bug can be identified in the original design, while providing a target to validate the modified design.

3.2   Assertion Monitors in Simulation

Engineers on the HP ASIC project added a combination of assertion monitors between block boundaries, or any sub-block partitions between multiple designers. This enabled the engineers to establish a "verifiable" contract on legal boundary behavior. Simulation with assertion monitors very quickly isolated interface assumptions that were violated. Many other assertion monitors were added to the design to check for illegal events (e.g., state machine transactions, queue underflow and overflow conditions, etc.). There were 1420 assertions added to the large ASIC design (42K lines of Verilog code, 830 modules) on our first project using the assertion monitor library methodology. Our assertion monitors where measured to contribute only a 3% overhead to our system level simulation (in our environment).

The design engineers were responsible for running their own block level simulations prior to delivering their individual blocks to the system simulation model. Those blocks containing a higher percentage of assertions delivered higher quality components to the system level model--as was measured by the relative number of bugs identified during system simulation on these blocks.

Another interesting point worth noting is that the assertion monitor methodology facilitates block level pseudo-random simulation sooner than might otherwise be possible. Generally, simulation must wait for the design verification (DV) group to complete their development of an entire random testbench. With our methodology, however, simulation can proceed with a partial testbench that provides legal pseudo-random stimulus and uses the assertion monitors for design and testbench validation. While pseudo-random assertion monitoring verification is occurring on a partially completed testbench, the DV group can concurrently finish development of the testbench's output validation routines.

3.3   Assertion Monitors in Semi-Formal Verification

To increase functional coverage on the HP ASIC design project, a decision was made to integrate semi-formal verification technology into the design flow. The 0-In™ Search tool was chosen for this purpose. This tool examines the simulation trace and applies bounded formal state-space search techniques to a simulation seed. Hence, a single thread through the state-space is amplified to explore interesting behavior close to the simulation trace [Switzer *et al.* 2000]. Because semi-formal verification leverages simulation and uses bounded formal techniques, it potentially can identify bugs associated with very complex assertions, whose analysis becomes intractable through full state-space search techniques.

In the abstract on this paper we claimed that our assertion monitor methodology enables the design engineer to "specify once," then leverage the same HDL assertion specification over multiple verification processes. The HP ASIC design experience with re-targeting the

HDL assertion monitors to a semi-formal environment provides an excellent example of this claim. The modules within our assertion monitor library were modified to encapsulate the related set of 0-In assertion directives. Hence, within minutes, hundreds of assertions were running through the 0-In Search semi-formal tool without modifying a single line of RTL text. Many of these assertions, at the input interface to the design block, were turned into constraints for the semi-formal search process. During semi-formal verification, a few new bugs were identified that were previously not found during traditional simulation. The essential point the authors would like to make is that our assertion monitor library enabled the integration of the semi-formal technology into the HP flow seamlessly.

3.4   Assertion Monitors in Formal Verification

Formal verification techniques also increase design coverage and design confidence due to the exhaustive nature of the technology. We used the BlackTie^{TM} tool from Verplex Systems, which is a formal RTL design verification tool that has native support for our assertion monitor library. In addition to user-defined assertions, this tool automatically extracts a set of pre-defined checks that detect errors such as bus contention, uninitialized flip-flops or latches, and full-case, parallel case problems.

During formal verification, user-defined assertions can be employed either as input constraints or as properties to be verified. The same set of assertions, specified by the designer for use in simulation and with semi-formal methods, was used for formal verification without requiring further modification. One attractive aspect of formal verification is that block-level verification can begin early in the development cycle, since a test bench is not required. The formal tool enables the engineer to explore and verify multiple design alternatives while identifying invalid assumptions concerning environmental constraints. In addition, the formal tool, using assertion monitors as properties, enables the designer to isolate implementation bugs concurrently with RTL development.

For assertion violations, the formal verification tool automatically produces a counter-example. These counter-examples were subject to simulation in our standard HDL simulation environment and also debugged in the integrated BlackTie debug environment by using a third party waveform viewer and debugging tool.

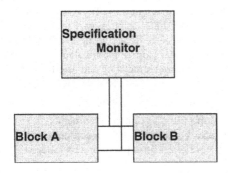

Figure 4-1 Monitor-Based Specification

4. FUTURE WORK

Shimizu et al. [2000] developed a monitor-based formal specification to overcome many of the problems associated with informal specifications currently in use (e.g., informal specifications are difficult to read and write, and cannot be functionally verified automatically). Their monitor-based specification is written in Verilog and does not require any complex state machines. Using their monitor-based specification technique, they demonstrate that a large subset of the PCI 2.2 standard could be specified and verified.

On future projects, we plan to develop monitor-based formal specifications between all major blocks of the design prior to RTL coding, as illustrated in Figure 4-1. Our approach, however, would differ from the Shimizu technique in that our monitor specifications would be constructed from various components contained within our assertion monitor library. This will provide consistency in construction format and style for each executable specification. Prior to RTL coding, contradictions in the monitor-based specification can be identified and fixed using formal verification.

5. CONCLUSION

In this paper, we have presented a method for simplifying and unifying assertion specification by creating a set of predefined specification modules that can be instantiated within the designer's HDL. We have demonstrated that our methodology does not require new HDL constructs to capture many interesting properties of the design. Furthermore, our methodology enables the design engineer to "specify once," then target the same HDL assertion specification over multiple verification processes. We presented our experience and results with the assertion monitor library used to specify and verify real designs employing traditional simulation, semi-formal and formal verification tools.

Our assertion monitor library, which includes Verilog source code and full documentation, can be freely downloaded from the **Open Verification Library Initiative** web-site (*www.verificationlib.org*). Our goal for placing the assertion monitor library in the public domain is to help establish an interface standard for assertion specification. We view our library as an empowering technology that will benefit design and verification engineers, while providing unity to the EDA community (e.g., providers of testbench generation tools, traditional simulators, commercial assertion checking support tools, symbolic simulation, and semi-formal and formal verification tools).

Acknowledgement: The HP team would like to thank Dr. K.C. Chen and Verplex's engineering for both their support of BlackTie and placing the assertion library into public domain. In addition, the HP team would like to thank David Landoll and Melonye Pratt for their invaluable support with the 0-In tools.

REFERENCES

[Bening and Foster 2000] L. Bening, H. Foster, *Principles of Verifiable RTL Design: A Functional Coding Style Supporting Verification Processes in Verilog,* Kluwer Academic Publishers, 2000.

[Bergeron 2000] J. Bergeron, *Writing Testbenches: Functional Verification of HDL Models,* Kluwer Academic Publishers, 2000.

[Clarke and Emerson 1981] E. Clarke, A. Emerson, "Design and synthesis of synchronization skeletons using branching time temporal logic." In *Logic of Programs: Workshop, Yorktown Heights,* NY, May 1981, LNCS 131. Springer, 1981.

[Clarke *et al.* 1999] E. Clarke, O. Grumberg, D. Peled, *Model Checking,* The MIT Press, 1999.

[IEEE 1076 1993] IEEE Standard 1076-1993 *VHDL Language Reference Manual,* IEEE, Inc., New York, NY, USA, June 6, 1994.

[IEEE 1364 1995] IEEE Standard 1364-1995 *IEEE Standard Hardware Description Language Based on the Verilog Hardware Description Language,* IEEE, Inc., New York, NY, USA, October 14, 1996.

[Kantrowitz and Noack 1996] M. Kantrowitz, L. Noack, "I'm Done Simulating; Now What? Verification Coverage Analysis and Correctness Checking of the DECchip 21164 Alpha microprocessor," *Proc. Design Automation Conference,* pp. 325-330, 1996.

[McMillan 1993] K. L. McMillan, *Symbolic Model Checking,* Kluwer Academic Publishers, 1993. http://www-cad.eecs.berkeley.edu/~kenmcmil/smv/

[Shimizu et al. 2000] K. Shimizu, D. Dill, A. Hu, "Monitor-Based Formal Specification of PCI," *Proc. Formal Methods in Computer Aided Design,"* pp. 335-353, Springer, 2000.

[Switzer *et al.* 2000] Scott Switzer, David Landoll, Tom Anderson, "Functional Verification with Embedded Checkers", Proc. 9th Annual International HDL Conference Proceedings, March 2000.

[Taylor *et al.* 1998] S. Taylor, M. Quinn, D. Brown, N. Dohm, S. Hildebrandt, J.Huggins, J. and C. Ramey, "Functional Verification of a Multiple-issue Out-of-order, Superscalar Alpha Processor -- the DEC Alpha 21264 microprocessor," *Proc. Design Automation Conference,* pp. 638-643, June, 1998.

Chapter 17

Predicting the Performance of SoC Verification Technologies

Gregory D. Peterson
Electrical and Computer Engineering
The University of Tennessee
Knoxville, TN
gdp@utk.edu

Abstract: Verification demands for SoC design looms as one of the most significant challenges to designers. With the substantial costs and increasing importance of system verification technologies, determining the best verification strategy is critical to SoC design and business success. This paper focuses on how a designer can apply a model to perform tradeoffs between the different types of emulation, hardware acceleration, and simulation verification tools available. The predictive power of the modeling approach is applied to usage scenarios to determine the most appropriate verification strategy to employ in current or future SoC development efforts.

Key words: verification, performance, cost, design process

1.   INTRODUCTION

Moore's Law continues to hold as electronic designs double their potential size every eighteen months. System on a Chip (SoC) designs comprised of tens of millions of gates with clock speeds approaching 1 GHz are in development and will become commonplace over the next few years. Because of the shrinking times to market, high costs in fabrication, and increasing circuit complexity, the verification task is now taking 50-80% of the overall design effort [4]. Performance demands for design verification continue to grow (exponentially) with the size of designs. With the market pressures to reduce cycle time exacerbating this situation, the verification needs of designers looms as a significant challenge.

A number of approaches exist for verifying a design before production; popular approaches include physical prototyping, emulation, hardware acceleration, simulation, and formal verification. Physical prototyping is an expensive approach and not an economically effective verification approach for SoC design. Similarly, formal verification promises the ability to prove that a given design meets its specification, but practical limitations impair this approach. Hence, although there is certainly a place in design flows for prototyping and formal verification, we focus on emulation, hardware acceleration, and simulation for verification in this paper.

Emulation systems use reconfigurable hardware (typically FPGAs) to implement essentially equivalent functionality in hardware. Although subject to constraints on routing and visibility, the designer can expect to see performance within one or two orders of magnitude of the design. To achieve this high performance for test vectors, the design must first be synthesized to the primitive

A. Mignotte et al. (eds.), System on Chip Design Languages, 201–210.

logic elements. Thus, emulators take a significant amount of time up front to complete the mapping of the design onto the primitives. The limited routing available for FPGAs, typically results in lower utilization rates of the reconfigurable hardware. Similarly, limitations on the visibility into an emulated system may necessitate re-mapping of the emulated design onto the reconfigurable hardware to achieve the required visibility.

Hardware acceleration for verification comprises custom hardware that is dedicated to specific simulation applications. The hardware accelerators often use parallel processing approaches to achieve high performance. This approach is similar to cycle simulation because the processors perform the simulation in lock-step for each simulated object at each time point. Thus, for simulations with high activity levels, hardware accelerators can achieve significant performance gains. Given the custom nature of the hardware implementations of simulation hardware accelerators, this approach can be very expensive. With Moore's Law continuing, the depreciation for an investment in this approach is significant as well.

Simulation is the most widely used verification approach and includes event-driven simulation and cycle simulation (among other approaches). Event driven simulation provides the maximum flexibility with respect to timing support and visibility, but often suffers from poor performance with respect to the number of cycles or events processed per second. Compilation of a design for simulation is normally faster than for an emulator or hardware accelerator. Simulation speed is one of the driving factors in technology innovation for design automation and a significant factor is designer productivity.

In this paper, we use a previously developed model to describe the verification performance for emulation systems, hardware accelerators, and simulators. See [6] for more detailed information on the performance model used here. We use the model to help in making quantitative tradeoffs concerning the most appropriate validation approach for a given design. Different verification strategies are explored to demonstrate how to decide the best approach for a given phase of a design and where a combination of approaches makes sense. A number of design process factors are included in the overall performance model to help optimize verification methodologies. Based on these models and their applications, we conclude with some observations concerning the best way to employ verification techniques.

$$T_{VERIFY} = t_{COMP} + \frac{N_C}{f} + N_E(t_{RECOMP} + t_{DEBUG})$$

The equation above gives a simple expression that illustrates the relationship of the verification time to the frequency of the verification engine and the number of clock cycles executed. It also includes the time required to synthesize/compile a model from its source hardware description language to FPGA primitives for emulation or machine code suitable for simulation or hardware acceleration. Similarly, this model includes the costs associated with debugging the system and recompiling the design. To simplify the model, we assume there are N_E errors that are detected during the verification. Variations on this model for emulation, hardware acceleration, cycle simulation, and discrete-event simulation are given in [6]; these applications of the model have the same general form.

Because emulators and hardware accelerators calculate the value of each gate every cycle, they are well suited for post-synthesis regression testing. The frequencies they can achieve approach that of the actual fabricated chip, sometimes coming within an order of magnitude in performance. The inherent focus on gate-level logic verification restricts the applicability of emulation, so verification provides some support for RTL models, but its primary focus is on gate level verification. The limited visibility into the design may necessitate the recompilation or resynthesis of the model to gain the required insight into the behavior within circuit blocks. With these caveats, emulation and hardware acceleration provide a very powerful, though expensive, verification capability to design teams.

For synchronous designs using a subset of HDL constructs, one simple optimization is to use *cycle simulation* as with the hardware verification techniques. This results in a simplified and faster control algorithm for the simulation kernel, at the expense of evaluating potentially extraneous events and restrictions on the timing granularity supported.

Another popular approach to simulation is to model events occurring at discrete points in simulated time, which is known as *discrete event simulation*. Discrete event simulation requires a more sophisticated synchronization mechanism, the event queue, for ensuring the proper causality holds in throughout the course of the simulation. Strictly speaking, the exercise of VHDL and Verilog models is a good example of discrete event simulation; if an appropriate subset of language constructs are used and the reduced timing accuracy acceptable, then such an HDL model can be simulated using cycle simulation techniques. Note that this model is relatively coarse, and assumes that the number of events in the simulation is approximately equal to the product of the activity level and the number of gates. If specific gates have events more often than once per clock period, then a more refined model may be needed.

After analyzing the performance claims for different cycle-based and discrete-event HDL simulator products, we estimate that cycle simulation requires approximately ten machine instructions per gate simulated, while discrete-event simulation requires approximately fifty machine instructions per event (with minor variances for each specific instruction set architecture) [6].

In the case of a parallel simulator executing on a distributed memory MIMD configuration [3], the accurate modeling of its performance requires the consideration of communications, load imbalance, and synchronization costs [7,8]. In the case of cycle simulation, performance modeling results from the analysis of synchronous iterative, or multiphase, algorithms can be applied [1,8].

Upon inspection of the terms in equation 1 above, the reader may question the means to determine several of the parameter values. The value of each parameter is determined based on the system modeled or the verification engine being evaluated. Some typical values for these terms are considered when exercising the models listed above.

Perhaps the most controversial parameter that a designer will need to include to use these models is the number of errors in the model. One reason for the difficulty in guessing the expected number of errors stems from overly optimistic designers. In reusing functional blocks from earlier designs or from third parties, estimating the error rate is very difficult. Nonetheless, the earlier errors are identified and fixed, the lower their cost.

If one considers the design of a 5 million gate SoC comprised of a number of 100K gate blocks, and if we assume that each block has a 98% chance of being implemented correctly, then the chance the overall SoC will work correctly can be found using Bernoulli trials (and assuming independent random variables) by the equation below.

$$\text{Prob[SoC is correct]} = (0.98)^{50} = 0.364$$

The above example illustrates why system level operation depends on the component blocks being tested sufficiently. Note the above equation also does not consider the interfaces between the blocks, a significant cause of errors. Hence, in practice, 90% of designs work in isolation, but only 50% of systems initially work [4].

The reader is encouraged to estimate the number of errors based on past design efforts. See [6] for more information concerning the number of errors to expect and the number of test cycles to execute.

Each detected error will interrupt the regression testing process while designers seek to identify and fix the error. In the case of very expensive emulation or hardware acceleration equipment, idle time can be quite costly when depreciation is considered (a large emulation system can cost $5 a minute in depreciation costs). In the case of emulators, hardware accelerators, or simulators on large parallel processors, each error may result in the verification tasks being removed from the batch queue, resulting in potentially long delays before the next available time slot can be used, thus artificially increasing the effective debug/recompile time. Finally, if some amount of recompilation is needed to perform debugging, the expensive verification engines are unavailable to others as well while the errors are identified. Hence the debug time may vary for the different approaches.

2.   COST MODELS

The performance models developed above for comparing the raw performance of difference verification engines can yield great insight into the potential approaches a design team could employ in helping ensure their chips operate correctly. Few design teams can attack the verification problem without some consideration of the costs involved. Given this fact, we next turn to how best to create pragmatic cost functions to support a quantitative tradeoff between the various verification techniques.

A simple cost function can be created which simply seeks to minimize the verification time, without regard to other costs. In such a case, a design team should simply choose the technology which results in the lowest runtime above.

A variation on this cost function would be to assume there exists a fixed verification budget and to purchase the mix of emulators, hardware accelerators, and simulators which will minimize the verification runtime within the budget.

Given a particular design and set of tests, one can also compute the most cost effective approach by computing the lowest cost per verification frequency. The most cost effective approach for achieving a certain number of verification cycles per second could then be chosen.

A more general notion of cost function can be supported by using the verification runtime as the domain for some function. If the function is monotonically increasing, then one simply needs to minimize the runtime as above. When the function has inflection points, then the analysis may require linear equation solvers or differential equations. Either way, the performance functions listed above are simple enough to facilitate easy manipulation and optimization.

One can compute the expected performance for a verification technology and determine how long a set of regression tests would take to complete. In contrast, determining the support, maintenance, and depreciation costs for a specific verification technology is subject to many variations with respect to cost accounting.

When considering potential cost functions, one may wish to divide the design and verification process into phases, based largely on the robustness of the components and integrated system. In such a case, one may divide the verification process into an initial development/debug phase, followed by a block regression testing phase, which leads into a system development/debug/integration phase, and ending in a system regression phase. The types and number of tests applied, the expected number of errors, and verification budget availability may change for each phase. As the design process continues, the number of errors should decrease while the number of tests and their complexity should increase. Thus, the cost and performance modeling effort may be subdivided into some number of phases with cost optimization within each phase. We explore such a subdivision of the SoC design verification effort by next exploring different design phases.

3.   BLOCK DESIGN

When design groups are developing functional blocks, the test requirements and typical usage patterns are different than during systems integration.   During block design, more debugging activities occur, with more frequent, shorter verification runs.

To explore the implications of this verification usage pattern, we consider the verification of a functional block of 100K gates. In the case of emulation, we assume a compile and recompile time of 15 minutes, a verification frequency of 100KHz, and a debug time of 5 hours per error (to take into account the possibility for re-synthesis to permit visibility to identify the cause of the error). An emulation system in this context would cost around $500K. In the case of a hardware accelerator, we assume a compile and recompile time of 2 minutes, a verification frequency of 5KHz, and a debug time of 2 hours per error (because hardware accelerators provide some support for RTL designs, but with limited visibility as with emulators). A hardware accelerator system would cost around $250K in this context. In the case of a cycle simulator executing on an 8-way symmetric multiprocessor with 1GHz processors issuing 2.5 instructions per cycle, we assume a compile and recompile time of 30 seconds, a verification frequency of 20KHz, and a debug time of 1 hour per error (to account for the greater visibility and controllability of a software simulator).   In the case of a discrete-event simulator executing on a similar hardware platform, we assume a compile and recompile time of 30 seconds, a verification frequency of 4KHz, and a debug time of 1 hour per error. The simulators and hardware would cost around $100K in this context. With these assumed performance parameters, the time to complete the verification of a block is shown in Figure 1, assuming 25 errors are identified and fixed during the verification activity. The verification time is varied over the number of test vectors/cycles executed.

As one can see from Figure 1, the parallel simulation approaches are the most efficient for smaller test vector sizes, with emulation becoming the fastest verification approach as the number of test cycles/vectors approaches the hundreds of billions to trillions. Note that these comparisons do not consider the difference in the cost of the verification approaches, only their execution time performance.

4.   SOC BLOCK INTEGRATION TEST

When designing a system on a chip (SoC), the design complexity typically far exceeds that of block design. The verification of a SoC with a number of different blocks developed and verified as above still involves a large number of interactions between blocks (the interface between components is the most problematic aspect of design and accounts for most errors). To explore the impact of verifying the integration of a large number of blocks into a SoC design, we consider a 1M gate and 10M gate design. We assume that each block has been verified as above, and that the overall system must be verified, with particular focus on interfaces. With n blocks on a SoC, there are $n(n-1)$ potential interactions to verify. We assume the emulation and hardware accelerator will once again execute at 100KHz and 5KHz, respectively, and have the same debugging times. Based on published performance claims of emulation and hardware acceleration tools and informal discussions of experienced users, we estimate the synthesis time for the emulation engine to be 2 hours for the 1M gate design and 20 hours for the 10M gate design. Similarly, we estimate the compilation time for the hardware accelerator to be 5 minutes for the 1M gate design and 1 hour for the 10M gate design. In the case of the cycle simulator and discrete-event simulator, we assume a compile time of 1 minute for the 1M gate design and 5 minutes for the 10M gate design, and that they execute at 2KHz for 1M gate and 200 Hz for 10M gate with the cycle simulator, and at 400Hz for the 1M gate and 40 Hz for the 10M gate design with the discrete event simulator. Figure 2 and Figure 3 show the results for the 1M gate and 10M gate SoC designs.

In these examples, once again the simulators perform well for smaller number of test cycles, with the emulator performing fastest for longer regression tests. It is worth noting that an emulator with 10M gate capacity costs around $11M and a hardware accelerator with that capacity around $1M, while the same symmetric multiprocessor from the block design verification example is used, with a cost of around $100K.

5.   SOC INTEGRATION TEST WITH BLOCK REUSE

For many SoC designs, a platform-based design methodology is used to reduce the number of errors, the time to market, and the need to change associated software [2]. In such a case, the SoC will consist of a number of mature blocks that make up the basic platform, along with a smaller number of new blocks that differentiate the new design from competing products. Hence, the verification of the new blocks, along with their interaction with the remaining (stable) portion of the SoC is the primary concern to designers. In such a case, the maturity of the blocks will vary greatly, and their associated verification requirements will be impacted accordingly.

6.   EQUIVALENT VERIFICATION INVESTMENT

To take into consideration the large difference in the cost of the verification technologies, Figure 4 shows the performance achieved with a $10M investment for the hardware acceleration and simulation approaches. These results assume that the regression tests can be divided into subsets and run in parallel. Once again, cycle simulation is the best approach for smaller test sets, with emulation the best approach for test sets exceeding approximately fifty billion vectors.

The number of errors detected in the design impacts the proper choice verification technology. Simulation is best for shorter regression tests involving debugging, while hardware acceleration and emulation work best as the length of tests increases and the need for debugging decreases. If the verification tasks correspond to four phases (initial development/debug, block regression testing, system development/debug/integration, and system level regression), then we may expect the number of errors found to decrease as testing progresses. Figure 5 illustrates the different performance levels for cycle simulation, emulation, and hardware acceleration with different numbers of detected errors. As expected, the emulation and hardware acceleration performs best with fewer errors and the cycle simulation performs best when there are more errors. Based on an analysis like this, a designer can determine when to use each of these verification technologies to best meet the schedule and cost needs.

7.   CONCLUSIONS

The importance of verification continues to grow with the size of designs. In this paper we focused on developing and using a performance/cost model to perform tradeoffs between the different types of emulation, hardware acceleration, and simulation tools available to designers. As a tool to help in this evaluation, some simple performance models were developed for each of these verification engines, followed by some possible cost functions to help determine which verification approach best suits the needs of a design group at a particular point in the design process. While exploring some of the results from applying these models, we investigated how each verification technique may be best suited to particular phases of design or cost/performance regimes. By applying models like these, engineers and engineering managers can make quantitative tradeoffs in determining the verification strategy to employ for a given design.

Although some typical values are listed for the parameters used in the models in this papers, readers are encouraged to insert parameters based on their design requirements and the specific hardware and software tools potentially available to them for verification. Further research remains to be completed with respect to refining these models to support more detailed probability distributions used for errors, additional exploration into "typical" parameter values, other possible cost functions, and providing better modeling support for the costs and performance of hardware/software co-verification techniques.

8. REFERENCES

[1] Vishwani D. Agrawal and Srimat T. Chakradhar, "Performance Analysis of Synchronized Iterative Algorithms on Multiprocessor Systems." *IEEE Transactions on Parallel and Distributed Systems*, 3(6): 739-746, November 1992.

[2] Henry Chang, Larry Cooke, Merrill Hunt, Grant Martin, Andrew McNelly, and Lee Todd. *Surviving the SOC Revolution: A Guide to Platform-Based Design.* Kluwer Academic Publishers, 1999.

[3] Richard M. Fujimoto. "Parallel Discrete Event Simulation," *Communications of the ACM*, 33(10):30-53, October 1990.

[4] Michael Keating and Pierre Bricaud, *Reuse Methodology Manual.* Kluwer Academic Publishers, 1998.

[5] Athanasios Papoulis. *Probability, Random Variables, and Stochastic Processes.* McGraw Hill, 1984.

[6] Gregory D. Peterson, "Performance Tradeoffs for Emulation, Hardware Acceleration, and Simulation." In *Proceedings of the 9th Annual International HDL Conference*, March 8-10, 2000.

[7] Gregory D. Peterson and John C. Willis, "High Performance Hardware Description Language Simulation: Modeling Issues and Recommended Practices." *Transactions of the Society for Computer Simulation*, 16(1):6-15, March 1999.

[8] Gregory D. Peterson and Roger D. Chamberlain, "Parallel Application Performance in a Shared Resource Environment." *IEE Distributed Systems Engineering Journal*, 3(1):9-19, March 1996.

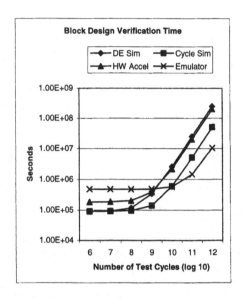

Figure 1. 100K Gate Block Design Verification Time

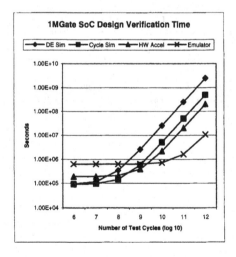

Figure 2. 1M Gate SoC Integration Verification Time

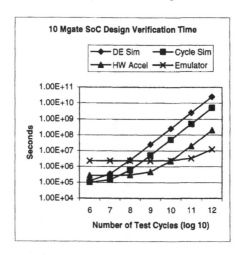

Figure 3. 10M Gate SoC Integration Verification Time

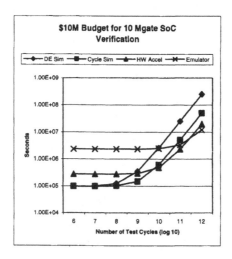

Figure 4. Equivalent Budget for 10M Gate Verification

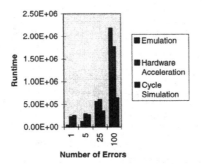

Figure 5. Impact of Errors on Verification Performance

SYSTEM SPECIFICATION

Chapter 18

Aspects Of Object Oriented Hardware Modelling With SystemC-Plus

Eike Grimpe and Frank Oppenheimer
OFFIS Research Institute

Abstract: In this paper we present an approach, how hardware can be modelled object oriented by using SystemC-Plus. SystemC-Plus is based on SystemC and includes an additional C++ class library and an extended design methodology. It allows to use object-oriented techniques and constructs for modelling hardware, which can then be automatically synthesised by a special synthesis tool that is actually under development for this purpose. For a deeper understanding of the presented work the reader should have basic understanding of C++ and SystemC.

Key words: SystemC, object oriented hardware modelling, high level hardware synthesis

1.   INTRODUCTION

Actual hardware development techniques do not longer fit the needs stemming from today's technological possibilities to integrate tens of millions of gates on a single chip. The complexity of integrated circuits is increasing at a much higher rate than the productivity of the hardware design process, opening a growing gap between the technological possibilities and the abilities to handle the resulting complexity. Therefore, new design techniques have to be developed and introduced to solve this problem.

Similar to the software crisis during the 1970's, when programs consisting of million lines of code could no longer be written and handled with the development techniques existing at that time, object oriented techniques, which were then successfully introduced into software development, could also show a proper way out of the "hardware crisis".

The use of SystemC-Plus allows to apply object oriented techniques to the development of hardware and opens a way to master more complex systems than it is possible with today's HDLs. It allows to benefit from increased reuse and flexibility and raises certain aspects of hardware design on a much higher level of abstraction than offered by RT or even behavioural level. In conjunction with an appropriate synthesis tool, it provides an automatic synthesis path starting from object oriented descriptions down to gate level, without having the need for manual refinement.

. Mignotte et al. (eds.), System on Chip Design Languages, 213–223.
) 2002 *Kluwer Academic Publishers.*

2.   SYSTEMC-PLUS

SystemC-Plus is built upon SystemC [1-4] and comprises an additional class library called OOHWLib (see section 3.1), and an extended design methodology based on a language reference manual aiming at the creation of synthesisable object oriented hardware models [5]. The development and advancement of SystemC-Plus was and still is a part of the ODETTE project (Object-oriented co-DEsign and functional Test-TEchniques) [6], which was started in summer 2000 under the leadership of the research and development institute OFFIS (Oldenburg, Germany) in close co-operation with its partners Siemens I.C.N. (Milan, Italy), IBM Research Lab (Haifa, Israel), Synopsys Leda (Grenoble, France) and the European Electronic Chips and System Design Initiative – E.C.S.I. (Grenoble, France).

SystemC was intentionally developed with the goal to allow the early creation of executable specifications of hardware components based on C/C++ as modelling language, and therefore was and still is focussed rather on simulation than on synthesis. Although SystemC is implemented in C++, its object oriented constructs such like classes only build the framework for modelling hardware, and are used to add missing hardware semantics to C++, in particular by means of a class library. C++' object oriented constructs are not intended to implement the functionality of the hardware itself, at least not when targeting synthesis. In this case the usable SystemC is limited to a language subset that is very similar to VHDL at RT or behavioural level and therefore does not provide designers with an enhanced expressiveness for modelling hardware at higher levels of abstraction compared to VHDL.

In contrast to SystemC, SystemC-Plus does allow to use object oriented constructs for modelling the functionality of hardware even when targeting automatic synthesis. For this purpose it provides an additional class library and a coding style, which together enable the designer to use constructs like class instances, polymorphic class instances, class templates and global objects (see following section) for modelling hardware and which underlay these constructs with a well-defined synthesis semantics.

SystemC-Plus was explicitly developed with regards to synthesis and therefore in principle every hardware model written in SystemC-Plus can be synthesised. Synthesis in this context means, that object oriented constructs as mentioned above are transformed by a high level synthesis tool into functional equivalent RTL or behavioural level representations, that can be processed by existing and established logic synthesis tools. A manual refinement, as needed for most higher level constructs in SystemC, like non-primitive channels, is not necessary. Since the synthesis of a SytemC-Plus does not include behavioural or RT synthesis, but relies on existing tools for this task, the SystemC-Plus synthesis subset is not completely fixed, and may depend on the abilities of the synthesis tool that is going to be used for back-end synthesis.

Though focussing on synthesis, every SystemC-Plus model can be easily simulated as used from SystemC, by compiling the appropriate sources with a common C++ compiler and by linking the OOHWLib to the executable. The resulting binary can be directly executed like every other program. The SystemC-Plus simulation is cycle accurate, that means high level synthesis will not change the temporal behaviour of the model.

3.   EXAMPLE

This example demonstrates how to use object oriented constructs in SystemC-Plus by means of a simple producer/consumer system. Producer and consumer are each modelled as an independent synchronous process running in parallel. They communicate with each other by exchanging items through a shared buffer with limited storage. The buffer must be accessed mutual exclusive. The producer process periodically creates a new item and puts it into the shared buffer, while the consumer process is waiting for new items in the buffer, gets an item out of it if available, modifies it in some way, and writes the modified item to an output port of the enclosing module. Though the example is a very simple one, it can be easily extended and applied to a variety of similar design problems which can be typically found in most hardware system.

One aspect of SystemC-Plus which is shown in the example below is the use of local objects. Local means, that an object is used exclusively within only one thread of control, typically declared as a variable in a process or in a subprogram. Both processes declare and use such objects of some user-defined class type called ItemType, representing the item being exchanged between the processes. The way of using class types such as ItemType in SystemC-Plus is very similar to the way of using class types in C++. But with regard to synthesis the use of classes in SystemC-Plus is more restrictive and their implementation must follow a certain coding style described in the SystemC-Plus LRM [6]. This coding style prohibits for example the general use of pointers which were regarded not to be suitable for efficient synthesis. Likewise most other C++ language constructs are banned, that deal with dynamic memory allocation and de-allocation, because this does not match the static nature of hardware, and would lead towards the synthesis of memories together with a complex memory management unit.

But even facing these restrictions using classes within SystemC-Plus is still a powerful instrument for modelling and allows to benefit from the classical object oriented characteristics like
- data encapsulation,
- inheritance,
- polymorphism,
  and
- communication through method calls.

A class library, that was cleanly implemented with regards to flexible use may find application in many different projects and can increase reuse significantly.

Another feature of SystemC-Plus is the possibility to use class templates. Class templates can increase the flexibility and reusability of a modelled system or component, because a class template can be easily adapted to different system requirements by just changing the actual template arguments used for instantiating it, without having the need to change its implementation. In the example illustrated in Figure 1 the ProdCons module and the class that is used for declaring the global object sharedBuffer (lines 86 - 89) are both declared as templates. The passed template arguments are used to determine the size of the buffer, i.e. the number of elements of a certain type that can be stored in the buffer, and the type of the elements to be stored. Therefore, the buffer can store nearly every number of elements of every type, may it be a simple scalar type like an integer or any kind of user-defined class type.

One of the most interesting aspects of SystemC-Plus are global objects. Global – do not mistake the term global in SystemC-Plus for the term global as common in C++ - means, that such an object is declared as data member of a SystemC module and can be accessed concurrently by different processes within the same module and even by processes within other modules. For the case of concurrent access each global object possesses built-in scheduling capabilities that guarantee mutual exclusion. It is therefore a very helpful language construct to model shared resources. A global object is simply declared by means of a class template provided by the OOHWLib (see Figure 1 line 86 – 89), which requires two template arguments to be passed at instantiation.

The first argument must be a class type that matches one of the arbiter classes within the OOHWLib class library. This argument determines which kind of arbiter is going to be instantiated for the global object, and therefore determines the kind of scheduling strategy that is applied to manage concurrent accesses. Actually three different arbiter types are provided by the OOHWLib, each implementing a different scheduling strategy: round robin, modified round robin and static priority scheduling. If more than one client at the same time, that means in the same clock cycle, requests a service from a global object that is actually not blocked by another request under execution, the arbiter of the global object will pick exactly one client, according to the chosen scheduling strategy, whose request will be granted. All other requesting clients are blocked until the service requested by the granted client has been completely finished. Arbiters do not need to be explicitly triggered by the user. Their functionality is automatically invoked when calling a method of a global object.

The second argument that is required for the global object template can be any kind of user-defined class type. This class type, or more precisely an instance of it, will implement the intrinsic functionality of the global object. In the example above a class was chosen that implements a FIFO (First In First Out) buffer, which is used to exchange items between both processes.

```
1   template<class ItemType,
2             unsigned int BUFFERSIZE>
3   SC_MODULE(ProdCons) {
4
5   public:
6     // Port declarations:
7     sc_in_clk          clock;
8     sc_in<bool>        reset;
9     sc_out<ItemType>   output;
10
11    // Producer process, periodically
12    // creates a new item and puts it
13    // into a shared buffer:
14    void producer() {
15      ItemType item;
16      // Register process to global
17      // object "sharedBuffer":
18      const idType processID =
19        sharedBuffer.subscribe(this,
20          "producer");
21      // Reset sets the variable
22      // item to some defined state:
23      if (reset == true) {
24        item.initialize();
25      }
26      wait();
27      while(true) {
28        item.buildNew();
29        // Call to global object:
30        GLOBAL_PROCEDURE_CALL(
31          sharedBuffer, // Global obj.
32          put(item),    // Procedure to
33                        // call
34          processID);   // Unique ID
```

```
35        wait();
36      }
37    }
38
39    // Consumer process, waits for new
40    // items available in the shared
41    // buffer, reads one out, modifies
42    // it in some way and writes the
43    // modified item to an out-port:
44    void consumer() {
45      ItemType item;
46      // Register process to global
47      // object "sharedBuffer":
48      const idType processID =
49        sharedBuffer.subscribe(this,
50        "consumer");
51      if (reset == true) {
52        // nothing to be done
53      }
54      wait();
55      while(true) {
56        // Call to global object:
57        GLOBAL_FUNCTION_CALL(
58          sharedBuffer, // Global obj.
59          get(), // Function to call
60          item, // Stores return value
61          processID ); // Unique ID
62        item.modify();
63        output.write(item);
64        wait();
65      }
66    }
67
68    // Module constructor:
69    SC_CTOR(ProdCons) {
70      // Declare "producer" as
71      // synchronous process:
72      SC_CTHREAD(producer,
73                clock.pos());
74      watching(reset.delayed() ==
75        true);
76
77      // Declare "consumer" as
78      // synchronous process:
79      SC_CTHREAD(consumer,
80                clock.pos());
81      watching(reset.delayed() ==
82        true);
```

```
83   }
84
85   // Declaration of a global object:
86   GlobalObject< RoundRobin,
87                 FIFO< ItemType,
88                       BUFFERSIZE > >
89      sharedBuffer;
90   };
```

Figure 1. Typical producer/consumer system modelled with SystemC-Plus

Figure 2 shows one possible implementation of the FIFO class. The most eye-catching thing is the declaration of the public methods of the FIFO class as so-called guarded methods by means of the macro GUARED_METHOD that can be found in the OOHWLib. The declaration of all public methods - excepting constructors - of a class as guarded methods is a requirement on all classes which shall be used globally. This is not just only another restriction, but a guarded method brings in some further and very useful functionality as a benefit. If a client requests the execution of a guarded method of a global object, its request will only be taken into account for scheduling by the arbiter, if the associated guard condition is true at calling time. Otherwise the request will not be taken into account, and the requesting client is blocked until this condition becomes true. Meanwhile other clients may be granted to execute other methods, that will switch the state of a guard condition from false to true and therefore unlock blocked clients.

In this particular example it makes for instance only sense to allow the execution of the put() method of the buffer, if the buffer is not already full. This condition is checked by the expression !isFull(). Likewise it makes only sense to call the get() method on a buffer that is not empty, this is checked by !isEmpty(). Note, that the functions isFull() and isEmpty() must still be defined by the user, but could be specified private or protected to improve encapsulation.

Usually a guard condition will check the internal state of an object, as demonstrated for class FIFO. But it is also possible to make the execution of a method dependent on the arguments that are actually passed to the method. For instance, if the FIFO would declare a get() method that returns x elements, the guard condition could check, whether the buffer actually holds enough elements, to satisfy a request.

Having a closer look at the implementation of FIFO, one may ask, why isFull() and isEmpty() are both specified as public, though they are automatically invoked through the guard mechanism when calling get() and put(), and could be specified protected or private as mentioned earlier in the text. This has two reasons. On the one hand, there could be still applications that would require the possibility to check the state of the buffer without having the need to put an element into it or to remove one. For such applications it seems reasonable to regard the functions isFull() and isEmpty() as part of the public interface of class FIFO, that can be called independently.

On the other hand it is also still possible to instantiate FIFO locally, as well as every other class which declares guarded methods, and in that case the guard mechanism is not invoked and the guard condition will not take effect. The reason is here, that the guard mechanism has been introduced, to guarantee that testing the guard condition and executing a method depending on that test is an atomic action for global objects. This can be simply guaranteed for local objects without the need for a guard mechanism, but requires to call the functions isFull() and isEmpty() "manually" before calling put() or get().

Note, that the guard condition "true" means, that these methods can always be called.

```
1   template<class Type,
2            unsigned int Size>
3   class FIFO {
4
5   public:
6     // Default constructor - sets all
7     // attributes to initial values
6     FIFO() {
7       emptyFlag = true;
8       fullFlag = false;
9       top = 0;
10      bottom = 0;
11    }
12
13    // Declaration of guarded method
14    // get() - returns the element at
15    // the top of the buffer, if not
16    // empty:
13    GUARDED_METHOD(Type, // Return
14                          // type
15    get(), // Signature
16    !isEmpty() { // Guard condition
17      Type tmp;
18      fullFlag = false;
19      tmp = buffer[top];
20      top = nextIndex(top);
21      emptyFlag = (top == bottom);
22      return(tmp);
23    }
24
25    // Declaration of guarded method
26    // put() - puts an element at the
27    // bottom of the buffer, if not
28    // full:
29    GUARDED_METHOD(void,
30    put(const Type element),
31    !isFull()) {
32      buffer[bottom] = element;
33      bottom = nextIndex(bottom);
34      emptyFlag = false;
35      fullFlag = (bottom == top);
36    }
37
38    // Declaration of guarded method
39    // isEmpty() - returns the value
40    // of attribute emptyFlag:
41    GUARDED_METHOD(bool,
42    isEmpty(),
```

```
43    true) {
44       return(emptyFlag);
45    }
46
47    // Declaration of guarded method
48    // isFull() - returns the value
49    // of attribute fullFlag:
50    GUARDED_METHOD(bool,
51    isFull(),
52    true) {
53       return(fullFlag);
54    }
55
56 protected:
57    // Returns the index, that is
58    // following the passed index.
59    // Treats the buffer as logical
60    // ring:
61    unsigned int
62    nextIndex(const unsigned int
63    index) {
64       index = index + 1;
65       if (index == Size) {
66          return(0);
67       } else {
68          return(index);
69       }
70    }
71
72    Type buffer[Size]; // An array to
73                       // store elements in
74    bool emptyFlag;
75    bool fullFlag;
76    unsigned int top;
77    unsigned int bottom;
78 };
```

Figure 2. Implementation of class FIFO

Another possible implementation of class FIFO would have been to first build a common class "Buffer", which declares the basic attributes and methods common for all kinds of buffers, e.g. the methods also shown in Figure 2, and then to derive FIFO from that class and to refine and add methods and attributes as needed. Choosing this kind of implementation would also allow to quickly create other kinds of buffers, like one that is implementing a LIFO (Last In First Out) strategy, by deriving them as explained for class FIFO. Inheritance is allowed in SystemC-Plus but was not demonstrated above for keeping simplicity.

What also can be taken from Figure 1 is the special style, how to access global objects in SystemC-Plus. First of all every client process of a global object has to register to that particular object. This is done in line 18f for the producer and in line 48f for the consumer by calling the subscribe() method which is predefined for every global object. The subscribe() method returns a unique id to every client, which must further be used when accessing the global object. Both actual arguments passed to subscribe() are necessary to clearly identify each client process. Another version of subscribe() allows also to pass a positive number as additional argument, that can be used to assign a certain priority to a client. But this only makes sense when registering to a global object, which is instantiated together with an arbiter implementing static priority scheduling. Otherwise the assigned priority will not take any effect for scheduling.

After registration, a client may call methods on a global object by means of the macros GLOBAL_PROCEDURE_CALL or GLOBAL_FUNCTION_CALL. The first macro must be used when calling a method with a void return type, the second one in every other case. The usage of these macros is shown in line 30ff. and 57ff. Both macros require to specify the global object to be accessed, the method to be called including all actual arguments, and the unique id of the calling client that was gained during registration. Regarding GLOBAL_FUNCTION_CALL, additionally a variable must be specified, that will store the return value of the called function. The use of the macros is necessary to ensure the proper invocation of the arbiter of a global object. A client whose request is not granted is blocked at the call site until it finally gains access.

Figure 3 shows two sample instantiations of the ProdCons module described in Figure 1 and illustrates the flexible use of templates. *subModuleA* is instantiated with a shared buffer with storage for 256 entries of type unsigned int, while *subModuleB* is instantiated with a shared buffer with storage for 16 entries of type MyClass. By using templates, a system can be optimally adjusted to specific and varying requirements and with regards to efficient resource usage.

```
1   SC_MODULE(top) // Top level module
2     // of a hierarchical module.
3   {
4     ProdCons<unsigned int, 256>
5       *subModuleA;
6     ProdCons<MyClass, 16>
7       *subModuleB;
8     // … other declarations …
9     SC_CTOR(top)
10    {
11      subModuleA =
12        new ProdCons< unsigned int,
13          256 >("A");
14      subModuleB =
15        new ProdCons< MyClass,
16          16 >("B");
17      // … other statements, e.g.
18      // port bindings …
19    }
20  };
```

Figure 3. Example instantiation of a "ProdCons" module

Templates, or more precisely generic parameters in general are not an exclusive feature of SystemC-Plus, VHDL for instance does also possess the capacity to use generic parameters and they are widely used and help to keep up flexibility. But while VHDL and other HDLs only allow to use scalar types as generics, SystemC-Plus does also allow to use complex types, i.e. class types as generics. Due to this feature it is possible to completely change the behaviour of a system or component that is parameterised with template parameters, just by passing different classes as template arguments at instantiation. Even so two classes may provide the same interface, that means the same set of public methods, the implementation of these methods and even what they are generally doing may completely differ.

Take for example a class, that implements arithmetic operations like an addition or a multiplication. Some systems that make use of this operation may require to be optimised for speed while others may require to be optimised for area. For these differing requirements two versions of the arithmetic class could be implemented and provided, one that implements fast arithmetic operations, which require more chip area and another which implements slower operations, requiring less chip area. The method interface will be the same for both implementations. If the kind of class that should be used for arithmetic operations is passed to a system, in particular a module, as template argument, only the instantiation statement has to be modified, and either the "fast" arithmetic class or the "small" arithmetic class can be passed, dependent on what kind of system is desired.

3.1   OOHWLib

The OOHWLib (Object Oriented HardWare Library) is an essential part of SystemC-Plus and includes a set of C++ classes, class templates and macros necessary for using certain object oriented features for synthesis, in particular global objects and polymorphic objects. The elements of the OOHWLib can be grouped as follows:
– class templates for declaring global objects and macros which allow to declare guarded methods,
– class templates for declaring global and local polymorphic objects,
– arbiter classes for being instantiated together with a global object,
– macros which must be used to access a global object.

The OOHWLib is an extension to the SystemC class library and is therefore fully orthogonal to it. None of the original SystemC constructs are replaced or overwritten with own implementations. It is possible to create a SystemC-Plus model without using a single element from the OOHWLib or even without linking the library, because SystemC, or more precisely a synthesisable subset of it, is a subset of SystemC-Plus, and the OOHWLib is only needed for modelling some constructs on higher levels of abstraction, as listed above.

The OOHWLib is compliant with all existing versions of SystemC, but future work, if necessary, will focus on the actual production release v2.0.

4.   CONCLUSIONS AND FUTURE WORK

We have shown, that object oriented hardware modelling is possible in principle, and that the application of object oriented techniques has a high potential for enhancing the hardware development process.

We have also presented the language SystemC-Plus, and how it combines object orientation with automatic synthesis. Furthermore we have given a concrete example that illustrates how to use SystemC-Plus.

The development of SystemC-Plus is still not fully completed due to changes in the underlying SystemC version and will be continued within the ODETTE project. Additionally, the work on a high level synthesis tool which is able to process the presented object oriented constructs is currently running. The theoretical basis for the synthesis of object oriented hardware specifications had already been laid in former projects [7,8], and have been proven in terms of prototypic tools.

Since the area of object oriented hardware modelling and synthesis is still a relatively new and innovative one, there is a lot of space left for further research. One topic that will be addressed in the future is the optimisation of the synthesis process with regard to an efficient resource usage of the synthesised hardware. This could be reached by sophisticated data flow analysis.

Another research topic will be the extension of the synthesisable subset of SystemC-Plus, and improvements and refinements of the underlying synthesis concepts for object oriented specifications.

An industrial evaluation of the new techniques and tools is also left to be done, and will be addressed within the framework of the ODETTE project. This evaluation has to show, where the concepts discussed here provide the greatest benefit for "real world" applications, and how to use them at best to enhance the design process.

5. REFERENCES

[1] Open SystemC Initiative, http://www.SystemC.org.

[2] Various contributors, *Functional Specification for SystemC 2.0 - Final - Version 2.0-P*, 2001.

[3] Various contributors, *SystemC Version 2.0 Users's Guide*, 2001.

[4] S. Swan, *An Introduction to System Level Modeling in SystemC 2.0*, 2001

[5] P. J. Ashenden, R. Biniasch, T. Fandrey, E. Grimpe, A. Schubert, T. Schubert, *Input Language Subset Specification (formal)*, ODETTE Deliverable 3.1 (confidential), 2001

[6] ODETTE – Object-oriented co-DEsign and functional Test TEchniques, IST project of the Commission of the European Communities, http://odette.offis.de

[7] REQUEST – REuse and QUality ESTimation, ESPRIT IV project of the Commission of the European Communities, http://eis.informatik.uni-oldenburg.de/research/request.shtml

[8] M. Radetzki, *Synthesis of Digital Circuits from Object-Oriented Specifications*, Dissertation at University of Oldenburg, 2000

Chapter 19

UML for System-Level Design
Extending the Object Model for Systems-on-Chips

Peter Green, Martyn Edwards, and Salah Essa
Department of Computation, UMIST, Manchester M60 1QD, UK

Abstract: UML has become the standard modelling language for object-oriented software development, on the basis of many perceived advantages. The use of UML for the modelling of complete embedded systems (hardware as well as software), potentially offers many of the same advantages. Nevertheless, closer scrutiny reveals that a number of important issues must be addressed before UML can be applied to complete embedded systems. These include the modelling of behaviour, data oriented communication, hardware modelling and IP reuse. All are briefly discussed in this chapter.

Key words: Object-oriented development, co-design, embedded systems, models of computation, hardware modelling

1.   INTRODUCTION

Object oriented (OO) approaches to software development have become increasingly popular over the past ten years, as the benefits have become widely understood. During this period specialised OO methods for the development of real-time software have been proposed e.g. ROOM [18]. The period has also seen work on the application of OO approaches to complete embedded systems, including software and hardware, and both application-specific and application-neutral[1] elements. Our earlier work on the MOOSE method is one example of this [11], MOR96], and the latter reference contains a detailed consideration of the benefits of applying the object model to mixed-technology systems, which include homogeneity, abstraction, and reuse.

The plethora of different OO software development notations that originated in the early 1990s led to a need for standardisation. This has occurred through the OMG standardising on the UML language [3], which is a graphical notation supporting OO software development. The application of UML has followed a similar path to earlier efforts, starting life as a general purpose modelling language, followed by the development of specialised extensions (or *profiles*), including a proposal for a real-time profile [19]. Now there is a significant interest in applying UML to the development of *complete* embedded systems [12], [9], [15].

This paper provides an overview of our on-going work concerning the use of OO approaches in general, and UML in particular, in the development of systems-on-chips (SoC). The basic design

---

[1] By application-neutral, we mean those parts of the system that provide the environment for the application-specific elements to execute, e.g. processors, busses, memories, operating system components etc. The term *platform* is used to describe the complete execution environment.

A. Mignotte et al. (eds.), System on Chip Design Languages, 225–233.

flow of our HASoC method, discussed in [12], is reviewed briefly and then a number of issues concerned with applying UML to SoC development in general, and particularly in the context of the HASoC method, are considered.

2.   HASOC - HARDWARE AND SOFTWARE OBJECTS ON CHIP

HASoC is a development of the MOOSE method based on an analysis of MOOSE summarised in [12]. It adopts an iterative, incremental approach to development, merging concepts from MOOSE and the Rational Development Lifecycle [3]. System functional requirements are captured in a use case model, and use cases are assigned to development iterations. Within an iteration, class and object models are developed that implement the appropriate use cases, leading to an *uncommitted* object model. The term uncommitted indicates that no decisions about object implementation in software or hardware have been taken. The model represents a collection of agents which hold state and exhibit behaviour, and which collaborate to provide the functionality of the use cases. Code in C++ is then added, resulting in an executable model that facilitates behavioural validation[2]. Subsequently the model is partitioned (resulting in a *committed* model) and mapped on to the platform[3], if one already exists. If a platform is to be developed, then the resource requirements of the committed model set the initial parameters for the design of the platform, which is carried out through the development of a OO *platform model* as described in [16]. Alternatively, if a platform already exists, the partition and mapping are evaluated, and perhaps modified. This in turn may indicate that extensions to the platform are required, which are performed via the same OO platform modelling approach mentioned above. Since the design flow is iterative, the development of uncommitted /committed models for other use cases can be overlapped with platform development/customisation. For more details, see [12].

3.   UML-RT

The notation used in HASoC is based on the UML-RT proposal from Rational and ObjecTime for real-time extensions to UML [19]. This has received a great deal of attention within the real-time community. However, on the basis of our earlier work on MOOSE, we believe that it is necessary to extend the proposal before it is suitable for mixed technology embedded systems. Nevertheless, UML-RT appears to provide a good basis for extension to the system-level, a conclusion that is also reached in [15].

UML-RT extends basic UML through the addition of concepts from ROOM. This is achieved through the specialisation of a number of concepts from the base language[4]. In particular, the UML-RT notation emphasises a hierarchical system organisation via *capsules*, a *stereotyped* form of active class[5], with specific execution and communication models. Capsules can be viewed from structural or behavioural perspectives. From a behavioural perspective a capsule typically contains a single statechart (which may be hierarchical, but may not have orthogonal components). This statechart represents the internal behaviour of

---

[2]   At present, this step utilises our existing MOOSE toolset.

[3]   The partitioning, mapping and evaluation are performed on the basis of non-functional requirements that are captured along with functional requirements at the start of development.

[4]   Most of the features of basic UML (e.g. use cases, class diagrams etc) may be used with UML-RT. However, the use of such features should be consistent with the communication and concurrency models of UML-RT.

[5]   An active class is one in which all instances have their own thread of control.

the capsule. Communicational behaviour is via *protocols*, which are named sets of signals communicated (at an abstract level) in a point-to-point fashion between capsule instances, either synchronously or asynchronously.

From a structural point of view, capsules may contain sub-capsules as well as, or instead of, the statechart. Those with only sub-capsules and no statecharts are simply containers with no intrinsic behaviour. Hierarchical refinement can be continued to any required depth. Capsules communicate via owned objects called *ports* that implement the behaviour of protocols[6]. *Connectors* between ports in different capsules show potential communications paths.

The execution model is based upon the transmission and receipt of UML signals through ports causing state transitions within the capsule's statechart. Communication is typically asynchronous[7], and ports contain incoming message queues. A capsule's thread of control chooses a message from those that have arrived and dispatches it to the state machine, which if appropriate makes a transition, executing exit actions, transitions-related actions and entry actions as appropriate. Actions can involve arbitrary computations, including the sending of messages to other capsules (peer, or sub-capsules). Once a capsule has started to process a message, it will run to completion before beginning to respond to another message. However, a capsule may be pre-empted by the execution of another capsule.

The overall approach defined by UML-RT has its origins in telecommunications [18], where state machines are extensively used in design. The use of protocols/ports provides two-way encapsulation, isolating capsules from knowledge of their environment, thus increasing their reusability, and facilitating distribution. The restricted concurrency model (one thread per capsule, run-to-completion semantics and port-based communications) has its particular form in an effort to simplify the concurrency structure of the application, reducing the likelihood of deadlock, and inter-thread interference. Whilst UML-RT is clearly applicable to a subset of real-time software systems, it is equally clear that, in its present form, extensions (or generalisations) are necessary if it is to be used successfully in the development of complete embedded systems, including both software and hardware, application and platform. The remainder of this paper discusses some of the most important issues.

4.   UML FOR EMBEDDED SYSTEMS

As indicated earlier, UML is a rich language, with many different types of diagram. Many can be used for modelling SoCs without modification e.g. use cases and class diagrams. We argue below that others, in particular capsule collaborations, must be generalised to be truly representative of a wide variety of embedded systems. Still other aspects of UML are not, as they stand, appropriate for embedded systems development, in particular, deployment diagrams, which provide an informal, 'iconified', easy-to-understand view of the platform for the benefit of software developers. However, in most embedded system developments, the hardware is not a 'given' and indeed, part of the application-specific functionality may be implemented in hardware. Hence if UML is to be used for complete system design, deployment diagrams alone are not appropriate, and the platform must be

---

[6]   More correctly, a port implements a protocol role, which is simply the view of the protocol from the owner of the port.
[7]   Although synchronous communication is also possible.

modelled in a more detailed fashion, although deployment diagrams can be used to provide a starting point. This will be discussed further below.

It is possible to argue that OO approaches in general provide strong support for defining the structure of a system through notions of association, containment, inheritance etc. However, the support for describing behaviour is rather weaker, with UML-RT only providing support for a limited form of statechart model.

Modelling a system in terms of the major concurrent elements is, in essence, equivalent to structuring the system in terms of a number of autonomous/semi-autonomous subsystems. Such subsystems are typically complex enough to be hierarchically refined. This approach is so widely adopted as to require no further comment. This also applies to the notion of subsystems delegating the responsibility for communication to some special purpose module. Both software and hardware are often structured in this fashion, and hence the overall approach of UML-RT is suitable for complete embedded systems. However, as indicated above, UML-RT is weaker in terms of the modelling of behaviour, and this issue is explored in the next section.

4.1   Modelling Behaviour

The behaviour of the major structural elements of an embedded system can be defined in a variety of ways. In particular, this can be achieved in terms of some programming language or hardware description language. In such an implementation, the capsule's thread simply looks for messages arriving through ports and processes them according to internal algorithms. Alternatively, behavioural descriptions can be developed in terms of a particular model of computation (MoC). A MoC is typically restricted in its expressiveness compared with an ad hoc description, but provides the benefit of supporting formal or semi-formal reasoning about the model, and of offering a route to the synthesis of an implementation.

Models of computation are often specialised towards particular application areas, for example, finite state machines are suitable for reactive applications such as those typically found in telecommunications, whilst variants of the dataflow model are often used in applications with significant signal processing tasks. The main point to be drawn from this is that one MoC is not suitable for all applications, and even within an application there is sometimes a need to describe different aspects of the system's behaviour with different MoC [1].

Being an OO approach, UML offers a framework for system development based on stable system structures that support abstraction, encapsulation and reuse [3]. However, if UML is to be used in the development of embedded systems, then the concept of a capsule must be generalised in such a way as to allow its behaviour to be described by MoC other than statecharts, or to simply support ad hoc behavioural definitions[8]. Hence the capsule concept must be generalised in order that specialised versions may be derived in which capsule behaviour is described by different MoC, for example synchronous dataflow (SDF), Kahn process networks (KPNs), codesign finite state machines (CFSMs), communicating sequential processes (CSP), as well as statecharts. Incorporating such models requires a reassessment of inter-capsule communications.

---

[8]   It could be argued that an ad hoc description might be obtained through the use of a trivial statechart with appropriate transition actions. However such a strategy subverts the objective of using a model of computation since the model cannot be used to reason about the behaviour.

A capsule's behaviour can be described and implemented as an SDF graph in a fairly straightforward fashion, with ports becoming data sources and sinks. More complex graphs may be partitioned across several capsules (as indicated below) with ports having to implement send and receive actors [17], although, for performance reasons, this would typically not be done unless the different capsules were mapped to different processors.

It is evident that the basic idea here is simple, although the communications mechanisms used with SDF-based capsules require further consideration (see section 4.2). However, once we allow class behaviour to be modelled via SDFs, it is necessary to consider how standard class relationships, such as inheritance and aggregation, should be interpreted. This can be done by analogy with the rules for inherited state models given by [7], and by utilising the concept of clustering in an SDF [2]. Clustering involves a subgraph R of an SDF (the unclustered graph G_U[9]) being aggregated into a single node with the same input and output arcs as R, forming a new graph (the clustered graph G_C). It is shown in [2] that if the schedule of R is known, along with the schedule of G_R then the schedule for the overall unclustered graph G_U can be found by substituting R's schedule into G_C's schedule.

Based on [7], we can use the above result to define inheritance for SDF-based classes in two special cases, which can be combined to form the most general case. In the first case, we define an abstract SDF as a high level graph whose actors are not refined to an implementable state, and hence require further refinement in a derived class. If the data rates associated with the actors in the abstract SDF are known, then a schedule can be computed for it. Derived classes may refine the abstract actors in any suitable fashion, so long as it is consistent with the data rates of the base class. Here, the abstract SDF corresponds to a clustered graph, the refinement of the abstract actors will be in terms of subgraphs, and so the result of [2] can be used to determine the schedule for full unclustered SDF of the derived class.

Alternatively, if the base class SDF is extended in such a way that it becomes a subgraph of the derived class's SDF, then a schedule for the complete, unclustered SDF of the derived class can be obtained as follows. Compute the schedule of the clustered SDF of the derived class (with the original SDF clustered into a single node), and then substitute the schedule of the base class SDF. In simple terms, what this means is that base class schedules can be used to simplify the calculation of derived class schedules.

Interestingly, aggregation (whole-part) relationships can also be realised using clustering in the same way as above.

It is simple to integrate the CFSM model of POLIS into UML-RT, given the similarities between the two execution models.

A CFSM is a composition of an input (output) automaton per input (output) signal, and a main automaton. The input (output) automata can be considered to implement port protocol roles, whilst the main automaton takes the role of the statechart. UML signals appear to be appropriate for the modelling of CFSM signals, and the multicast communication mechanism of CFSMs can be implemented via replicated ports [18].The main automaton is a conventional state machine, without hierarchy, and with restrictions upon transition actions to ensure locally synchronous behaviour [1].

In terms of interpreting inheritance for CFSMs, the rules given in [7] that do not deal with state hierarchies apply to CFSMs. This enables new states, transitions and input/output automata to be added in a derived class, and for actions associated with existing transistions to be refined or changed.

---

[9] G_U must be connected and consistent.

The work on YAPI discussed by [6] shows how an extended form of KPN can be implemented in an OO style. Processes are implemented as active objects (the granularity of processes is typically large), and the FIFOs connecting processes are realised as objects[10]. In terms of the capsule model, the FIFO is located within one of the receiving capsule's ports, and the sending port must block the sending capsule if the FIFO is full. Given that the processes in the YAPI model are coarse grain, and defined in an ad hoc fashion, inheritance is easy to specify, in terms of adding new functionality to the processes and possibly new input and output streams.

The CSP model [14] can be realised in a similar fashion to Kahn process networks, with the implementation of sending and receiving ports providing synchronous channel communication. Inheritance involves introducing additional events into the alphabet of the process implementing the capsule's behaviour. New subprocesses that respond to the new events are then combined with the original process via the choice operator.

The above provides an overview of how different models of computation can be integrated into UML-RT capsules. If this is done, then the appropriate tools can be used to analyse parts of the overall model, and to synthesise an implementation[11].

The interworking of capsules that utilise the same model of computation is straightforward. However, further work is need to determine how capsules supporting different models may be combined. The work of [10] is relevant in this respect.

4.2   Additional Communications Mechanisms

UML provides a rich variety of inter-object communications mechanisms. However, these are all message-based[12] and, as indicated in [16], messages do not satisfactorily model certain commonly occurring patterns of communications within embedded systems, particularly those concerned with data streams. Although it is possible to model such patterns with messages, this is an implementation-oriented solution that is at a low level of abstraction, and which biases the model towards a software implementation, which is at odds with the notion of uncommitted modelling. Hence we believe that a new communication mechanism should be added to UML, namely the *datastream*. This is the equivalent of a time continuous information flow in MOOSE, where the source object makes a stream of data continuously available, and the destination object reads the stream when it requires data, there being no synchronisation implicit in the datastream. If synchronisation is needed, it can be performed via 'dataless' asynchronous control messages that can easily be implemented using existing UML mechanisms. In a sense datastreams and control messages separate the transfer of data and control, which are often intertwined in software.

The use of datastreams as a communications mechanism typically implies concurrency between data source and destination, which are implemented in UML as capsules. The behaviour of the receiver must usually be implemented in such a way as to be able to process the incoming stream as it arrives (e.g. a digital filter). Clearly SDFs are one possible mechanism that can be utilised.

---

[10] During early modelling with YAPI, FIFOs are assumed to have infinite capacity. Later, the impact of finite size FIFOs is investigated.

[11] Note that a pure OO implementation may not be desirable or necessary.

[12] The term message is used in the OO software sense of making a method/member function call.

4.3   Hardware Modelling

From the foregoing, it should be clear that the generalised view of UML-RT, introduced above, is applicable to the modelling of hardware, particularly at the behavioural level. The introduction of datastreams provides for pure data-oriented communication, which is otherwise missing from UML-RT. Pure control-based communications, and mixed data and control are already available in UML-RT. Hence mappings to behavioural level hardware description languages (HDL) are straightforward, given that the mechanisms are, in fact, abstractions of common HDL mechanisms. In terms of the HASoC design flow, modelling at the behavioural level is related to committed modelling.

The integration of application-specific hardware capsules from the committed model into the platform requires refinement to lower levels of abstraction. In terms of capsule behaviour, this typically involves the transition from a behavioural description of the capsule, either in terms of some model of computation, or in ad hoc programming language/HDL terms, into synthesisable form. The difficulty of this step clearly depends on the semantic gap between the representation of behaviour and the language required for synthesis, and on the availability of tools. An example of this kind of mapping is our current work to generate an implementation in the Handel-C language from an SDF description of capsule behaviour. Handel-C can be synthesised into configurations for Xilinx FGPAs [5].

The refinement of the capsule interface must also be considered, to facilitate its eventual attachment to the platform interconnect. Techniques for refining application level descriptions to physical level ones have been proposed in order to connect hardware and software Intellectual Property (IP) [4], and these can be applied in the context of capsules in a simple manner.

Closely related to the above is the issue of IP reuse, and its use within object models. Although exploration of the partitioning options can optimise the system, for example, with respect to performance, development costs and time-to-market pressures drive developers to reuse IP wherever possible. Decisions to reuse IP are typically taken early in development, and so the question of how the IP should be represented in early stage HASoC models must be addressed. This is relatively straightforward in the case of software IP, but is rather more difficult if the IP exists in the form of hardware. However, we have demonstrated that recent standardisation work by VSIA [VSI99] on Virtual Component[13] Interfaces (VCI) provides mechanisms that enable IP described by the standard to be used in the context of UML models [8]. [VSI99] proposes that VCs are supported by a layered set of interfaces, the layers or levels corresponding to different levels of abstraction. Two of these are mandated in the VSIA model – layer 1.0 and layer 0.0. Layer 1.0 corresponds to the highest, behavioural level of abstraction which is independent of interconnect communications protocol, and all connections between VCs is assumed to be point-to-point. Layer 0.0 typically maps to RTL, and supports the use of the VC in a specific implementation context (e.g. implementing a particular bus protocol). Optionally, interface layers at intermediate levels of abstraction may be added to provide additional information. Mappings between all of the levels used to document a VC must be included in its textual description.

The VSIA standard carefully defines a range of concepts and communications mechanisms. An analysis shows how these can be interpreted in terms of concepts and mechanisms which are available in our generalised UML-RT.

---

[13] A virtual component (VC) is a block of IP, which for the purposes of this discussion can be assumed to be active in the sense of footnote 5. Hence a VC can be modelled as a capsule.

The Virtual Component Interface (VCI) defines the complete interface of the VC. At each layer, the VCI is typically made up of groups of interfaces, each of which usually deals with a common theme (e.g. data, control etc). An interface is connected to the external environment by a set of ports. Information passes through ports, which have attributes that can include direction, data format, behavioural principle (e.g. blocking write) etc. Interfaces have a protocol, which describes the sequencing and timing of transfers through its ports, although the notation for describing such protocols is not specified by the standard. However, the protocol description may be omitted for layer 1.0, on the grounds that any timing/sequencing constraints at this level are part of the functionality of the VC itself.

Hence, a VC can be modelled as a generalised capsule, an interface as a UML port, and the protocol of an interface as a UML protocol role. VSIA ports are modelled by the datastreams and messages that are handled by the UML port. Layers within the VCI can be realised via aggregation of a set of port objects, each corresponding to an interfaces within a (lower) layer of the VCI. Hence if a VC that is documented according to the VSIA standard is available for use, it can have a semantically equivalent capsule generated from its layer 1.0 representation suitable for use in early stage (uncommitted and committed) modelling. This can simply act as a placeholder in the object model specifying faithfully the interaction of the VC with peer capsules. However, if an executable model of the VC is available, it may be included into, or accessible from, the UML executable model. We have not yet, however, explored this possibility within the HASoC framework.

4.4   Platform Modelling

The earlier parts of this chapter have principally been concerned with the application-specific aspects of system-on-a-chip development with UML, although the previous section is equally applicable to the platform model. As indicated earlier, the HASoC platform model is a UML object model, and it is divided into two sub-models: the Software-Hardware Interface Model (SHIM) and the Hardware Architecture Model (HAM). The SHIM includes the operating system (as a UML component), and a virtual machine layer, which facilitates communication between software and hardware. This layer comprises a set of software objects which act as proxies for hardware objects.

The HAM is derived from a UML deployment diagram, and is another capsule model that not only represents the hardware of the system, but can support the simulation and synthesis of the overall on-chip system. For further details see [13].

5.   CONCLUSIONS

With certain extensions UML-RT can be effectively used for the development of complete embedded systems, including application-specific hardware and software, and the underlying execution environment. The extensions include the ability to use a variety of models of computation to model capsule behaviour, and progress has been made in interpreting standard OO concepts like inheritance in this new context. Further work is needed to establish how capsules described by different models can be combined.

We have argued that a data-oriented communications mechanism is necessary, and this proves to be useful at different levels of abstraction, from the level of the dataflow model of computation, through to the direct modelling of hardware. Our extended view of capsules enables hardware to be easily modelled at the behavioural level, and provides a context for refinement, simulation and synthesis. Hardware IP, documented using the VSIA standard, can easily be integrated into HASoC models, thanks to the close correspondence between generalised capsules and the VSIA VC model.

6. REFERENCES

[1] F.Balarin, E.Sentovich, M.Chiodo, P.Giusto, H.Hsieh, B.Tabbara, A.Jurecska, L.Laavangno, C. Passerone, K.Suzuki, and A. Sangiovanni-Vincentelli, 'Hardware-Software Co-design of Embedded Systems: The POLIS Approach', Kluwer 1997.

[2] S. Bhattacharyya, P. Murthy, E. Lee, 'Software Synthesis from Dataflow Graphs', Kluwer 1996.

[3] G.Booch, J.Rumbaugh, and I.Jacobson, 'The Unified Modelling Language User Guide', Addison-Wesley Longman, 1999.

[4] J-Y Brunel, W. Kruijtzer, H. Kenter, F. Petrot, L. Pasquier, E. de Kock and W. Smits, 'COSY Communication IP's', Proceedings of DAC, ACM Press, 2000.

[5] Handel-C language reference manual, www.celoxica.com.

[6] E.A. de Kock, G. Essink, W.J.M. Smits, P. van der Wolf, J.-Y. Brunel, W.M. Kruijtzer, P.Lieverse, and K.A. Vissers, 'YAPI: Application Modelling for Signal Processing Systems', Proceedings of DAC 2000, ACM Press, 2000.

[7] B. P. Douglass, 'Real-Time UML', Addison Wesley, 1998.

[8] S.Essa and P.N. Green, 'System-Level Virtual Component Interfaces (VCIs) with UML', Embedded Systems Group Internal Report, Department of Computation, UMIST

[9] J.M. Ferandes, R. Machado, H. Santos, 'Modelling Industrial Embedded Systems with UML', Proceedings of CODES 2000, IEEE Press, 2000.

[10] A.Girault, B.Lee, and E.A.Lee, 'Hierarchical Finite State Machines with Multiple Concurrency Models', IEEE Transactions on Computer-Aided Design of Integrated Circuits and Systems, Vol. 18, No. 6, June 1999.

[11] P. N. Green, P. Rushton, and S.R.Beggs 'An example of applying the codesign method MOOSE', Proceedings of the Third International Workshop on Hardware/Software Codesign, IEEE Press, 1994.

[12] P.N. Green and M.D. Edwards, Object-oriented development methods for embedded systems, Colloquium Digest, IEE Colloquium on Hardware-Software Co-Design 9th December 2000

[13] P.N. Green, M.D. Edwards, and S. Essa, 'The Co-design of SoC-based Embedded Systems using HASoC', accepted for publication, Proceedings of DATE, ACM Press, 2002.

[14] C.A.R. Hoare, 'Communicating Sequential Processes', Prentice-Hall, 1995.

[15] G.Martin, L.Lavagno, and J.Louis-Guerin, 'Embedded UML: a merger of real-time UML and co-design', www.cadence.com.

[16] D. Morris, D. G. Evans, P. N. Green and C. J. Theaker, 'Object Oriented Computer Systems Engineering', Springer-Verlag, 1996.

[17] J.L. Pino and E.A. Lee, 'Hierarchical Static Scheduling of Dataflow Graphs onto Multiple Processors', Proceedings of IEEE International Conference on Acoustics, Speech and Signal Processing, May 1995.

[18] B. Selic, G. Gullekson, and P.T. Ward, 'Real-Time Object-Oriented Modelling', John Wiley, 1994.

[19] B. Selic and J. Rumbaugh, 'Using UML for Modelling Complex Real-Time Systems', ObjecTime Limited/Rational Software white paper, 1998; (www.objectime.com/ otl/index.html).

Chapter 20

Open PROMOL: An Experimental Language for Target Program Modification

Vytautas Štuikys, Robertas Damaševičius, Giedrius Ziberkas
Kaunas University of Technology

Abstract: We present a new experimental scripting language Open PROMOL developed for: 1) delivering flexible means for representing wide range modifications of a target program, and 2) supporting white-box reuse for well-understood domains, such as hardware design. We evaluate the role of scripting and program modification in the domain. We describe the syntax and semantics of the basic PROMOL functions. We discuss the capabilities of the language to perform program modifications by widening, narrowing and isolating functionality. Examples of program modification in VHDL and other languages are delivered.

Key words: Meta-programming, scripting language, multi-language specification, design parameterization, program modification, generalization, VHDL models.

1. INTRODUCTION

1.1 MULTI-LANGUAGE DESIGN, SCRIPTING AND PROGRAM MODIFICATION

The multi-language design of complex systems, such as SoCs, is a hot topic in the EDA community. The state-of-the-art research in the area mainly focuses on the HW/SW co-design, where the hardware parts are usually described in the HDLs and the software parts in C/C++ [1-3]. The configuration of the overall system is generally described using *scripting means* of a higher-level specification language for specifying the interconnections between blocks.

In a wider context, the scripting languages (ScLs) have been used for a long time, however, only recently they have attracted a great attention. The reason of this change is the need to manage more efficiently the ever-increasing complexity of the systems. The examples are component-based frameworks, like those used in hardware design. If algorithmic languages are mainly for expressing computations and domain-specific languages are for describing domain functionality, ScLs are for gluing a system from components, whose functionality is given in other language [4-6].

Using a ScL, a designer accepts a multi-language design paradigm, which clearly implements the *"separation of concerns"* principle [7]. The application of this paradigm allows handling the variety of the different tasks in system designs separately, thus simplifying the general problem, raising the abstraction level and gaining a great deal of flexibility and reusability [2,3].

ScLs contribute not only for composing a complex system from the pre-designed components. They can serve for modifying and adapting components, too. The modification is a part of the reuse

A. Mignotte et al. (eds.), System on Chip Design Languages, 235–246.

process, which in the pure *technological* sense comprises the activities such as *finding, understanding, modifying,* and *using* in the new context artifacts (documentation, components, etc.) previously developed and used by others.

Here we consider modifications of a program at its construction phase only. In this context, we distinguish modifications which allow (1) to collect the existing instances of a component, (2) to perform a tiny modification (if needed), and (3) to represent the family of the variations as a single specification.

In the hardware design domain, the components are usually described using a HDL, such as VHDL or Verilog. Across applications there is a wide variety of components with the same functionality but slightly different characteristics, such as those for expressing the chip area, performance, energy consumption issues, etc. Each of them is a valuable asset, which should be retained as the Intellectual property (IP) component for further usage in the different context.

We can describe the "look-alike" components as a concise specification, which we can adapt through the modifications. As this kind of modifications allows expressing the existing variations at a higher level rather than changing their syntax and semantics, we call it the *generalization*. The generalization leads to the essential reduction of the number of components in the reuse libraries, and serves well for designing component-based generators [8,9].

Having in mind the above-mentioned capabilities for composing, modifying and generalizing components, we can summarize the role of scripting as a *"programming for the 21st century"* [4].

1.2   MOTIVATION OF THE NEW LANGUAGE

The related works we have analyzed can be summarized as follows: (1) meta-programming and extensions of the existing languages [10-13]; (2) component-based and generative reuse [14-17]; (3) domain-specific languages, including HDLs [18-20]; (4) scripting languages [4-6]; and (5) parameterized design [20]. Our approach has some similarities and differences in the model as well as in the implemented concepts with respect to Bassett's *frame commands* [15].

Though other authors have suggested many interesting ideas, models and solutions, nevertheless it was difficult to find a language that would suit best for expressing explicitly the composition, modification, and generalization simultaneously. As a consequence, we have designed the experimental scripting language, Open PROMOL (**Program Modification Language**), aiming at the development of the generic specifications, which specify the wide range modifications of target language (TL) programs to support the design of the generic components and generators.

The language is not dedicated to a particular domain or specific TL. The language itself does not extend a given TL directly. It only expresses concisely and explicitly the pre-programmed modifications at a higher-level of abstraction.

Of course, it may be achieved at some extent using a TL only, for example, using the VHDL meta-programming capabilities. However, by introducing an external language, we can separate concerns clearly, enhance the abstraction level significantly, and express modifications explicitly and more flexibly, thus avoiding the over-generalization of a target program.

Summary: We motivate the need for a new scripting language by the following reasons:
1. To deliver flexible means for representing the wide range modifications.
2. To support the component-based and generative reuse.
3. To express variations for describing a generic functionality more flexibly than using the meta-programming capabilities of C++ and/or VHDL.

2.   WHAT CONCEPTS DOES THE LANGUAGE IMPLEMENT?

Our main objective is to achieve higher reuse. We implement it through the *generalization* of domain commonalties and variations. While the extraction and isolation of domain *commonalties* is a relatively easy step, handling of the *variations* may require a more sophisticated manipulation. We argue that many variations of the program source code can be expressed in the generic form via the simple parameterized textual *modifications*, which have similar meaning as *if, for, case* statements in the declarative programming languages.

These variations are pre-programmed by a set of the externally parametrizable PROMOL functions, which describe the particular text *modifications* needed to generate the instance-specific target code.

The PROMOL functions are freely *scripted* into the source code, which is common for all target programs. The result is a *composition* of the PROMOL functions and the text of a TL, which is a generalization of the particular target program family, characterized by the common functionality or architecture (see *Figure 1*).

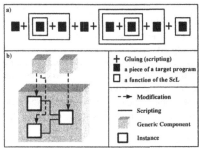

Figure 1. The interpretation of the modification and scripting concepts at a lower- (a) and higher-level (b)

According to Ousterhout [4], the main idea of scripting is that an application developer is provided with a collection of useful components, and he (she) only has to write a small amount of wiring code in order to establish connections between components. It can take various forms, depending on the nature and granularity of the components, the framework of a domain problem, and the composition model.

Components themselves are highly parameterized domain entities such as multipliers, decoders etc., which are generalized with PROMOL functions. The purpose of these functions is to perform the necessary modifications of the TL code during the generation process in order to receive a concrete instance of the component tailored to the specific needs of the developer. The combination of the modification and scripting concepts leads to the creation of parameterized systems [20], i.e., heavily parameterized architectures adaptable in terms of power, performance and area requirements.

Summary: We suggest using *meta-programming* to implement the *modification* concept, and to use *scripting* to implement the *composition* of the TL code. To achieve this, we suggest the higher-level constructs – PROMOL functions, which generate and glue together the TL code.

3.   BASIC FEATURES OF THE SYNTAX AND SEMANTICS

Open PROMOL is a functional language and consists of an open set of external functions. The context of their usage is a prescribed specification (i.e. PROMOL script). All modifications in the specification are represented as a specific composition of the external functions with the TL code to be modified [21]. Functions are called external because they represent a higher level of programming and have parameters, whose values are defined externally.

A PROMOL function has the format as follows: @ *function_name* [*argument_list*]

We present a basic set of functions, their syntax and semantics in Tables 3.1 and 3.2, respectively. The functions support the *hierarchical parameterisation*. At the highest level, the usage of a parameter may depend upon a specific condition or other parameter. Additionally, the *conditional parameterisation* yields a great deal of flexibility.

Each function has the list of arguments and returns a value, which is always a string of the TL. The arguments are either a constant, a parameter implicitly declared in the *interface* of the specification, an expression, or a composition of the external functions and strings of a TL. A constant may be either a numeric literal of the language or a string literal written in a TL. A string might be either a part of a statement or the entire construct of the TL program to be generated. The functional programming paradigm allows us to achieve a great deal of flexibility, since a TL string may be transformed gradually by several functions, until it reaches its final form. The nested functions enable to achieve a deep and flexible external modification of the TL code to be processed.

Open PROMOL is a string-oriented language. Everything (e.g., numbers, enumerated type variables, etc.) is a string. Because a particular type is recognized from the context, there are no attributes for the explicit declaration of the type. A value of the string type may be interpreted as a decimal number, a binary number or a string of the text depending upon the context of the usage.

Table 3.1. A description of the basic set of the functions (below asterisk denotes optional arguments)

Function name	No. of args	Arg	Meaning of an argument	Actions performed by the function
@sub	2	1	Expression	Parameter value substitution, expression calculation
		2*	Precision	
@if	3	1	Condition	
		2	'Then' branch	If-selection
		3*	'Else' branch	
@case	≥2	1	Selector	Case-selection
		≥2	Branches	
@for	4	1	Loop parameter	
		2	Initial value	For-loop
		3	Final value	
		4	Loop body	
@gen	5	1	Number of substrings	
		2	Separator	String generation
		3*	Substring	
		4*	Initial index	
		5*	Step	
@move	2	1	Parameter name	Value assignment
		2	Assigned value	

Function name	No. of args	Arg	Meaning of an argument	Actions performed by the function
@rep	2	1	Number of repetitions	Repetition of the text
		2	Script to be repeated	
@include	≥1	≥1	External module names	External module declaration
@macro	≥1	1	External module name	External module instantiation
		≥2*	Parameter values	

Table 3.2. Syntax and semantics of the PROMOL functions (subset)

Function name	Examples of the usage	Parameter value	The returned value
@sub	V := @sub[n*2+1];	n := 2	V := 5;
@if	X: bit@if[n>1, {_vector (0 to @sub[n-1]) }];	n := 4	X: bit_vector (0 to 3);
@case	Y <= @case[n, {B1}, {B2}, {B3}];	n := 2	Y <= B2;
@for	@for[i, 0, n-1, {L(@sub[i]) }]	n := 5	L(0) L(1) L(2) L(3) L(4)
@gen	Y <= @gen[n, { AND }, {X}, 0];	n := 3	Y <= X0 AND X1 AND X2;
@move	@move[f, {NOT}]	f := NOT	<null>
@rep	X <= "@rep[n, {@sub[sym]}]";	n := 4; sym := 0	X <= "0000";
@include	@include[gate]		<null>
@macro	@macro[gate, {AND}, n]	n := 2	2-input AND gate instance

Summary: Open PROMOL is an open set of external functions, which implement modification and scripting through the hierarchical and conditional parameterization models.

4.   MAIN CAPABILITIES OF THE LANGUAGE

The language and its processor EREBUS implement the following capabilities:

Generalization. In many cases, we can merge similar components into a single generic specification.

Abstraction. We introduce two separate levels of abstraction: a higher level is the *interface*, where parameters are defined, and a lower level is the *specification body*.

Parameterization. The language implements two parameterization models: the *conditional* (the assignment of a value to a parameter depends on a condition), and the *hierarchical* (through deep nesting and the usage of external modules) ones. Parameters are not constrained to a particular type (as, e.g., in C++ templates [10]), but can take the string values of any length and content.

Separation of concerns. We clearly separate the abstractions of the scripting language from a given TL, the interface of the generalized specification from its implementation, and the development of a specification from its usage.

Composition. A particular set of the external functions used in the specification implements an internal composition in a natural way through the concatenation of strings. The usage of external modules (via @*macro*) allows a more sophisticated composition.

Generation. There are specific functions for generating strings of a particular structure.

Extension. The language is an open set of external functions, which are independent. Hence, the new ones (if needed) can be introduced easily.

Modification. The language performs modifications of a target program using abstractions similar to that of the structural programming (i.e., *if, for, case*).

Computation. The language allows the arithmetic, relation and logic operations.

Independence from a TL. Open PROMOL treats a TL program as a simple text without any particular meaning, and uses lexical mechanisms independent of any TL syntax and the usage context to perform the necessary modifications.

Rapid prototyping. The language processor generates either a selected instance or all instances prescribed by the generalized specification.

To illustrate some capabilities, we deliver two simple specifications below. The first one represents a description (*Figure 2, b* and *c*) which after processing yields 100 different variants of polynomials in the form of the Horner scheme written explicitly (*Figure 2, d*). The specification body can be represented using different PROMOL functions, too (*Figure 2, e*).

Table a):
$$y = ((a_0 * x + a_1) * x + \ldots + a_{n-1}) * x + a_n$$

Table b):
```
$
"Enter the number of coefficients:"
{1..100} n:=4;
$
```

Table c):
```
Y = @rep[n-1, {(}]\
@gen[n, (]) * X + ),{A[}, 0];
```

Table d):
```
Y=(((A[0])*X+A[1])*X+A[2])*X+A[3];
```

Table e):
```
Y = @rep[n-1, {(}]A[0]\
@for[i, 1, n-1, {) * X + A[@sub[i]]}];
```

Figure 2. Implementation of the Horner scheme: (a) - initial form, (b) - PROMOL interface, (c) - specification body, (d)- an instance derived from the specification, (b)-(c), (e) –other description using three functions

The second specification (*Figure 3*) introduces a context of the TL used. The type of a language is treated as a parameter *lang* having three values.

Summary: The main capabilities of the language are enlisted and illustrated by the examples.

Table a):
```
$
"Enter the number of coefficients"
{1..100} n:=4;
"Select the language:
        1 - C/C++/Java
        2 - Pascal
        3 - VHDL" {1,2,3} lang:=1;
$
```

Table b):
```
Y @case[lang, {=},{:=},{<=}] \
@rep[n-1, {(}]\
@gen[n, {@case[lang, {)},{)},{)}])*X+),
       {A@case[lang, {[},{[},{(}]}, 0]\
@case[lang, {]},{]},{)}]];
```

Table c):
```
Y   = (((A[0])*X+A[1])*X+A[2])*X+A[3];
Y  := (((A[0])*X+A[1])*X+A[2])*X+A[3];
Y <= (((A(0))*X+A(1))*X+A(2))*X+A(3);
```

Figure 3. Specification expressing the differences of the TLs: interface (a), body (b), and instances for the respective language (c)

5. CASE STUDY: VHDL CODE MODIFICATION VIA WIDENING, NARROWING & ISOLATION

Sametinger [16] has described four general methods for generalizing components. We have adopted some of them for the modification of VHDL code with Open PROMOL. The first example (*Figure 4, a*) implements modifications by narrowing functionality with respect to the second example (*Figure 4, b*). The latter one illustrates the modification by widening functionality. The generated instances are given in *Figure 5, c* and *d*, respectively.

The third example below demonstrates a modification by isolating functionality. For simplicity, we present it without the explicit VHDL context. Suppose, we need to include in several different places of a higher–level design the slightly different components (fragments), which are given in the isolated files *a1, a2, a3, a4*. This might be represented in the PROMOL specification as follows:

```
@case[k,{@macro[a1]}, {@macro[a2]}, {@macro[a3]}, {@macro[a4]} ]
```

where *a1, a2, a3, a4* are file names; *k* is a parameter for the customization for particular context of the usage.

In general, by widening we mean not only the extension of the space of the parameter values, but the addition of the new parameters, too. By narrowing functionality we conceive the reduction of the number of the parameters, as well as narrowing of the application domain. By isolation we imply the splitting of the functionality into smaller parts. However, the presence of similar components makes it difficult to decide which one implements the required feature.

```
$
"Select a function"
          (AND,OR,XOR,NOR,NAND,XNOR)        f:=AND;
"Enter the number of inputs"               (2..16)
          num:=2;
$
@- this is the promol comment
@- a text between symbols $ is the interface
@- gatel is the name of the specification (file)
@- specification implements any gate function
@- (except NOT)
-- this is an instance of GATE_@sub[f]_@sub[num]
ENTITY  GATE_@sub[f]_@sub[num]  IS
      PORT (@gen[num, {, }, (X), 1] : IN BIT;
        Y : OUT BIT);
END GATE_@sub[f]_@sub[num];
ARCHITECTURE  BEH  OF GATE_@sub[f]_@sub[num] IS
      BEGIN
      Y <= @gen[num, { @sub[f] }, (X), 1];
END  BEH;
                                                    a)
```

```
$
@include[gatel]
$
"Select a function"
(AND,OR,XOR,NOR,NAND,XNOR,NOT)   f:=AND;
[f neq (NOT)]    "Enter the number of inputs"
          (2..16)        num:=1;
$
@- specification uses the external module gatel
@- the specification represents modification by
@- widening functionality with NOT gate
@- the second question appears only if
@- the condition is true
@if[f neq (NOT),
{(@macro[gatel, f, num] ), {
-- this is an instance of GATE_@sub[f]
ENTITY GATE_@sub[f]  IS
      PORT (X1 : IN BIT;  Y : OUT BIT);
END  GATE_@sub[f];
ARCHITECTURE  BEH  OF  GATE_@sub[f] IS
      BEGIN
      Y <= NOT  X1;
END  BEH;
}]
                                                    b)
```

Figure 4. The modifications by narrowing (a), and widening (b) functionality

```
-- this is an instance of GATE_OR_4
ENTITY  GATE_OR_4  IS
   PORT (X1,  X2,  X3,  X4 : IN BIT;
          Y : OUT BIT);
END  GATE_OR_4;

ARCHITECTURE BEH OF GATE_OR_4 IS
      BEGIN
      Y <= X1  OR  X2  OR  X3  OR  X4;
END  BEH;
                                                    a)
```

```
-- this is an instance of GATE_NOT
ENTITY  GATE_NOT  IS
   PORT (X1 : IN BIT;
          Y : OUT BIT);
END  GATE_NOT;

ARCHITECTURE BEH OF GATE_NOT IS
      BEGIN
      Y <= NOT  X1;
END  BEH;
                                                    b)
```

Figure 5. Instances (a) & (b) of the specified modifications in Figure 4, (a) & (b), respectively

6. EVALUATION OF THE APPROACH

From the viewpoint of the modification capabilities, the language implements the *advanced* pre-processing. It covers not only a simple inclusion (*@sub*), conditional inclusion (*@if, @case*), but also the generation of the "look-alike" strings (*@gen*), repetition (*@for, @rep*) and other functions. The external functions combined together with the text of a TL support the *scripting concept*, as well as the *external composition*, i.e. gluing of the external PROMOL modules into a target system (*@macro*).

The above mentioned capabilities can be also seen as the *external meta-programming* ones because PROMOL functions manipulate with the other (target) program. From this standpoint, VHDL allows the meta-programming at some extent, too [9, 22]. Hence, it is interesting to compare the "pure" VHDL approach with the one, which uses simultaneously Open PROMOL and VHDL.

The meta-programming capabilities of VHDL (*generic, generate, if-generate*) only partially implement the separation of concerns. As a result, the pure VHDL approach lacks flexibility for expressing and handling wide range modifications including those, which can overcome the limitations of the synthesis tools [23]. The attempts to express functionality in the generalized form may lead to the over-generalization problem [9].

On the other hand, the usage of Open PROMOL can cause some problems, which are not known in the pure VHDL approach. Those are the *naming problem* (the developer himself should care that every instance of a generic component has a unique name), and *name clashing* (multiple instances with the same name can be generated). These problems have to be solved at a higher level (e.g., by a system generator). The other problems relate to the multi-language programming itself, such as *learning* (different languages and environments have to be mastered), *reliability* (less maturity and experience of usage), *testing* (of instances as well as generic components), and *pretty printing*. These problems can be solved using the appropriate methodology.

The comparison is given in Tables 6.1 and 6.2. The accepted notations 1LA and 2LA mean the one-language approach (VHDL) and two-language approach (VHDL + Open PROMOL), respectively. The framework of the comparison is a statement of *features* (in positive sense) and *problems* (in negative sense), respectively [22].

Table 6.1. Comparison of 1LA and 2LA by features

Features	Weight
Integration	1LA ... 2LA (2LA higher)
Maturity	1LA ... 2LA (2LA higher)
Adaptability for synthesis limitations	1LA ... 2LA (2LA higher)
Rapid prototyping	1LA ... 2LA (2LA higher)
Automatic documentation generation	1LA ... 2LA (2LA higher)

Table 6.2. Comparison of 1LA and 2LA by problems

Problems	Weight
Interfacing capabilities	1LA 2LA
Naming	1LA 2LA
Over-generalization: designer's view point	1LA 2LA
Over-generalization: user's view point	2LA 1LA
Pretty printing	1LA 2LA
Dependence from a target language	2LA 1LA
Generalization depends upon algorithm and/or architecture	2LA 1LA

Summary: We deliver an evaluation of the language and comparison of two approaches: the pure VHDL and VHDL + Open PROMOL ones. We summarize the strength of Open PROMOL as a tool for implementing the multi-language-programming paradigm to describe the transformational processes (modification, generation, wrapping, etc.) in the variety of application domains.

7.   CURRENT STATE OF THE LANGUAGE AND FUTURE WORK

We use the language and its processor as an experimental tool in our research for describing modifications (program specialization, generation, etc.) in several domains, including VHDL. The users are post-graduate students in computer science. Over more than three years, the current version of the language processor has passed through the intensive experiments by more than 150 users. The future work relates to the development of the distributed version using the web-based technology. For more information, see our web site http://www.soften.ktu.lt/~stuik/group

8.   CONCLUSIONS

Open PROMOL is a functional scripting language aiming to describe a wide range of textual modifications of a target program. It uses lexical mechanisms independent of any target language syntax to perform the necessary modifications via the external functions. The PROMOL specification is a higher level description, which manipulates with a target program as data. Although there are no restrictions on the language usage, however, it suits best for well-understood domains, in which a great similarity of designs and a great deal of the repeatedly used 'look-alike' models exist. The domain of hardware design is just the case. External functions combined together with the abstractions of a given HDL extend the modification capabilities greatly. The language supports design reuse through the deep and flexible parameterization.

9. REFERENCES

[1] Jerraya, A.A., Romdhani, M., Le Marrec, Ph., Hessel, F., Coste, P., Valderrama, C., Marchioro, G.F., Daveau, J.M., Zergainoh, N.-E. "Multilanguage Specification For System Design And Codesign." In *System-Level Synthesis*, Ahmed A. Jerraya and Jean Mermet, eds. Boston: Kluwer Academic Publishers, 1999.

[2] Jerraya, A.A, Ernst, R. Multi-language System Design. Proceedings of the Design, Automation and Test in Europe (DATE 1999); 1999 March 9-12 Münich. ACM Press.

[3] Coste, P., Hessel F., Le Marrec Ph., Sugar, Z., Romdhani, M., Suescun, R., Zergainoh, N., Jerraya, A.A. Multilanguage Design Of Heterogeneous Systems. Proc. of the 7th International Conference on Hardware/Software Codesign (CODES'99); 1999 May 3-5 Rome. ACM Press.

[4] Ousterhout, J.K. Scripting: Higher Level Programming for the 21st Century. IEEE Computer 1998; 31(3):23-30.

[5] Schneider, Jean-Guy, *Components, Scripts, and Glue: A conceptual framework for software composition.* Ph.D. thesis, University of Bern, Institute of Computer Science and Applied Mathematics, October 1999.

[6] Schneider J.G, Nierstrasz O. "Components, Scripts and Glue." In *Software Architectures — Advances and Applications*, L. Barroca, J. Hall, P. Hall, eds. Heilderberg: Springer, 1999.

[7] Ossher, Harold and Tarr, Peri. "Multi-Dimensional Separation of Concerns and the Hyperspace Approach." In *Software Architectures and Component Technology*, Mehmet Aksit, ed. Boston: Kluwer Academic Publishers, 2001.

[8] Batory, D., Lofaso, B., Smaragdakis, Y. JTS: Tools for Implementing Domain-Specific Languages. Proc. of the 5th International Conference on Software Reuse; 1998 June 2-5 Victoria. Prem Devanbu, Jeffrey S. Poulin, eds. IEEE Computer Society Press, 1998.

[9] Štuikys, V., Ziberkas, G., Damaševičius, R., Majauskas, G. Two Approaches for Developing Generic Components in VHDL. Microelectronics Journal 2001; 00:000-000. Oxford: Elsevier Science Ltd.

[10] Veldhuizen, T.L. Using C++ template meta-programs. C++ Report 1995; 7(4):36-43.

[11] Benzakki, J., Djafri, B. Object oriented Extensions to VHDL – the LaMI proposal. Conference on Computer Hardware Description Languages and their Applications; 1997 April 21-23 Toledo.

[12] Barna, C., Rosenstiel, W. Object-Oriented Reuse Methodology for VHDL System Design. Proceedings of the Design, Automation and Test in Europe (DATE 1999); 1999 March 9-12 Münich. ACM Press.

[13] Czarnecki, Krzysztof, and Eisenecker, Ulrich, *Generative Programming: Methods, Tools and Applications.* Boston: Addison-Wesley, 2000.

[14] Szyperski, Clemens, *Component Software: Beyond Object-Oriented Programming.* New York: Addison-Wesley, 1997.

[15] Bassett, Paul G., *Framing Software Reuse: Lessons from the Real World.* Upper Saddle River: Prentice Hall Inc., 1997.

[16] Sametinger, Johannes, *Software Engineering with Reusable Components.* Berlin: Springer, 1997.

[17] Biggerstaff, T.J. A Perspective of Generative Reuse. Annals of Software Engineering 1998; 5:169-226.

[18] Hudak, P. Modular Domain Specific Languages and Tools. Proc. of the 5th International Conference on Software Reuse; 1998 June 2-5 Victoria. Prem Devanbu, Jeffrey S. Poulin, eds. IEEE Computer Society Press, 1998.

[19]   van Deursen, A., Klint, P., Visser, J. Domain-Specific Languages: An Annotated Bibliography. SIGPLAN Notices 2000; 35(6):25-36.

[20]   Givargis T., Vahid F. Parameterized System Design. Proceedings of the Eighth International Workshop on Hardware / Software Codesign CODES' 2000; 2000 May 3-5 San Diego. ACM Press.

[21]   Štuikys V., Damaševičius, R. Scripting Language Open PROMOL and its Processor. Informatica 2000, 11(1):71-86.

[22]   Ziberkas, Giedrius, *Analysis of the Methods of the Component-based Program Generation of the Application Domain*. Doctoral Dissertation, Kaunas University of Technology, 2001.

[23]   Chang, Kou-Chuan, *Digital Design and Modeling with VHDL and Synthesis*. Los Alamitos, CA: IEEE Computer Society Press, 1997.

Chapter 21

A System Benchmark Specification Experiment with Esterel/C

Lluís Ribas, Joaquín Saiz, Jordi Carrabina
Departament d'Informàtica, ETSE, Universitat Autònoma de Barcelona (UAB), Catalunya-Spain.

Abstract: An experiment in specifying a system benchmark in Esterel/C is presented in this paper. The selected benchmark covers a broad variety of features so that the suitability of Esterel/C to specify such systems is tested. The comparison to other system-level design languages shows the validity of this approach and envisages good chances to other approaches steaming from similar languages.

Key words: System specification languages, Esterel, system benchmarks, hardware/software co-design

1. INTRODUCTION

System complexity is increasing as demands on functionality and performance are growing to keep up with today products. Besides, the design cycle is allotted an ever decreasing time. Therefore, systems designers tend to re-usability and design flow simplification.

In this paper, we focus on the latter problem, which is currently being addressed by providing designers with CAD tools that can deal with abstract levels of design specification. To integrate the different layers of abstraction of a system design and avoid problems of specification translation, a single description language is highly recommendable. This approach, though, must consider the characteristics of the systems to design because it may occur that the selected system design language (SDL) is not suitable for describing a particular feature or behaviour of a system part. A collection of system benchmarks that covers all significant system characteristics and the cost of their specification and verification for each SDL would be of great interest to a system designer. However, the aim of this paper is not to obtain such data but only a modest approach to that end.

In a recent publication [2], a system benchmark [3] has been proposed and a comparison among some SDL done on the basis of specification cost (code length and development time). In this work, ADA [4, 5] (with OVHDL [6]), Java [7], Occam [8]/VHDL [9] and Simulink [10, 11] are used as system design languages for an embedded control of portal crane.

The purpose of this paper is to present a specification of such system in Esterel/C and compare the results with those presented in [2] in order to forecast the specification complexity for other languages inspired in this very combination of languages or language features such as ECL [12], Jester [13], or, of course, SystemC [14, 15, 16].

This work has been partially supported by the Spanish CICYT Project No. TIC98-0410-C02-02 and a researcher training grant from the UAB.

A. Mignotte et al. (eds.), System on Chip Design Languages, 247–253.
© 2002 *Kluwer Academic Publishers.*

In particular, ECL [12] stands for Esterel/C language and the results of this experiment would be directly applicable for a similar process in ECL.

In general, programming languages are preferred for system specification because of their ability to produce "executable specifications" and the system synthesis aspect is very variable. That is, programming languages act as SDL targeted to simulation rather than to synthesis. Of course, for hardware-software systems, they have a clear advantage when synthesizing the software parts but do require some sort of translation to produce the hardware parts.

In fact, there are three different approaches when designing a language to specify systems. The most simple one is to take a combination of languages such as Esterel/C or Ada/VHDL. However, this approach requires the two languages be well integrated in the design flow to avoid coherence problems and to allow a straightforward verification.

To simplify specifications and eliminate the difficulty of having two languages, most recent approaches of SDL use a single language. Some of them add new syntactic elements to describe semantics absent in the original language and some other take profit of object-oriented programming features to extend the base language with new operations and data types. Jester and ECL belong to the first type and SystemC to the latter.

Though all these languages have similar capabilities for describing concurrency, synchronous behaviour, communicating processes, and timing, Esterel has been specifically designed for synchronous, reactive systems. Furthermore, it is possible to use its formal background to verify systems and a translation to C is readily available. In addition, there was a fringe interest for us to use Esterel because of its link to POLIS [17] and, thus, to a codesign tool suite in which some system parts can be implemented in hardware.

The paper is structured as follows. The next section describes the portal crane system and its control. The following section is devoted to the system description structure in Esterel, which includes also a model of the physical system to be controlled. Finally, the last section is devoted to present the results and to outline the conclusions derived from the work.

2.   CASE STUDY: PORTAL CRANE CONTROLLER

The benchmark used as a case study for the specification experiment of this work consists of an embedded system to control a portal crane [3]. Rather than only specify the controller, the model of the whole system including sensors, actuators and the portal crane itself is described in Esterel. Therefore, a simulation of the controller is more straightforward because stimuli and reactions are taken from and applied to the system. Furthermore, the test cases are simpler to specify and easier to check.

The plant is shown in figure 1. It consists of a crane that moves a load along its track to some desired position. (A fourth-order Runge-Kutta method to solve the corresponding differential equations is used.) The embedded controller takes data from plant through position and angle sensors. The actuator consists of a DC-motor that releases a force f_c depending on VC, which is the car-drive voltage supplied by the controller. Also, there is a braking action equivalent to set VC to 0.0 and switching a relay for the car brake.

The controller must perform a sensor check on initialisation (after power on) and, then, run the control algorithm in parallel to a system diagnosis. The control algorithm is a cycle based algorithm with a fixed cycle time of 10ms. The diagnosis procedure consists of checking that the car position is within the allowed intervals (PosCarMin and PosCarMax), that the position sensor has not activated the "out of range" alarm signals SwPosCarMin or SwPosCarMax for more than 20ms during 100ms, and that the angle is not greater than a given maximum (AlphaMax) for more than 50ms during

100ms. In the two first cases, the crane must be stopped. Notice that a strict observance of the behaviour of the two latter diagnoses would assume that the wrong conditions may have been enabled in a non-continuous form during the period.

As a result, the specification of the whole system would prove the suitability of a SDL to describe a continuous environment and event-driven and synchronous tasks.

3.   SYSTEM STRUCTURE IN ESTEREL/C

The portal crane system can be divided into two parts, according to their nature: the physical subsystem, which evolves continuously in time, and the controller, that operates on a discrete time basis. In the physical subsystem we include the crane, the motor and the sensors. The sensors generate events to the controller that are, in fact, asynchronous signals. As the controller works in cycles of 10ms, it is possible to use an integration time step of 1ms to solve the differential equations that model the crane and the motor. Therefore, we assume that each tick in which Esterel divides time is a millisecond. Signals emitted by the sensors are generated at any clock cycle, thus seen asynchronous by the controller, that operates in cycles of 10ms.

The diagram of the whole system is shown in figure 2. In the remainder of this section, each component specification solution adopted will be detailed.

The modules of the **plant** and **motor** wrap calls to C functions to obtain the solution of the integration of the differential equations that model each component.

Position and **angle** sensor modules are simple FSM that update their outputs only if input variations are greater than their accuracy.

The **brake** module models the braking system of the car and switch it on so its speed be zero.

The **job_control** module is a quite complex to specify one not only because it must describe the controller behaviour but also because it is the one for which the implementation issue must be

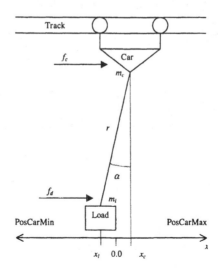

Figure 1. Crane with load

considered. There are three submodules within job_control: the initialisation, the control and the diagnosis modules.

The **initialisation** one is run when the controller is powered on and follows a sequential procedure to check the sensors. Therefore, its easily described in Esterel and can be implemented in either software or hardware, depending on which target language is used to transform the corresponding FSM.

The **control** submodule has been modelled fully in Esterel though it is based on matrix operations that imply as many as 143 multiplications and a similar number of sums. Besides, the parameters for the control algorithm are real numbers with a high variability in range (maximum 10^5) and accuracy (precision up to 10^{-12}) that makes it difficult to translate them into fixed point numbers (57 bit with 17 bits for the integer part) so a pure hardware implementation would be easier. However, the system requirements are not so stringent so that a software implementation cannot meet them.

The **diagnosis** submodule is, again, not very complex to specify in Esterel because it is limited to check if the car is positioned within the allowed range and if no boundaries or angle limits are overcome for more than a given fraction of a period. Unfortunately, these latter conditions are hard to verify. For instance, at each new cycle, the counter for SwPosCarMin (alarm signal that indicates that the car is beyond PosCarMin) must be incremented if it is detected in the current cycle, and eventually decremented if it has been present in the first one because it falls out of the current 100ms period. We decide ord that represents a 100ms period with 1 where d to implement this procedure with a 100-bit w the events have been present. However, we have also tested a probabilistic approach

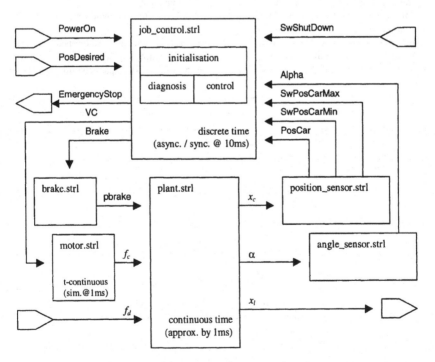

Figure 2. Esterel specification structure for the portal crane's system

	Simulink	Ada	Ada/OVHDL	Java	Occam	Esterel/C
System (controller)	60	746	6300	890	800	386(Esterel)+162(C)=548
Environment	200	101	7100			307(test cases incl.)+129=436

Table 1. Code sizes comparison (lines of source code)

	Simulink	Ada	Ada/OVHDL	Java	Occam	Esterel/C
Development	3	2	22	16	5	4
Verification		4	30		10	

Table 2. Development and verification efforts in person-days

	Simulink	Ada	Ada/OVHDL	Java	Occam/VHDL	Esterel/C
Machine/ frequency	Pentium II/ 500MHz	Sparc/ 300MHz		Pentium II/ 166MHz	Sparc/ 171MHz	Sparc/ 440MHz
Simulation ratio	3.6	0.214	100.0	2.29	23	2.1

Table 3. Relative execution time for simulation

using 16-bit integer numbers which has proved to be valid. This last approach, though not exact, could be useful regarding software or hardware syntheses of the module.

The whole system is specified as a module (**crane_system**) that instantiates all the previous modules so it can easily be combined with modules that perform test cases for the system. For control systems, like this one, it is necessary to bear in mind the problems that may arise due to the control loop. For instance, it is possible that some "causality problems" remain hidden when simulating the system in an open-loop way (i.e. without the model of the controlled system). The "causality problem" resembles an "instantaneous deadlock" (i.e. a signal dependence in the same cycle) that eventually appears when two concurrent tasks have activation conditions depending on the activation of the other. In the case of control loops, it might occur that a control signal sent to the controlled system causes it to emit a signal required to activate the sending of the first signal. The Esterel framework is able to analyse whether a program is acyclic or not. Although it is mainly a simulation issue, a system specification that shows such behaviour might contain some errors in the controlling part. Accompanying the crane_system module, there are three modules to carry the test of the system in an automated way. These system verification steps (Esterel program analyses and test case set simulation) could have been complemented by formal proofs by using temporal logic to verify module intercommunication (e.g. check whether eventually Brake and VC are set appropriately if SwShutDown has been fired).

4. RESULTS

The development of the specification of the portal crane in Esterel and C has shown the viability of this language to model whole systems with heterogeneous features. Besides, a direct link to a codesign methodology is possible because Esterel modules can be translated to C or blif (with limitations). In particular, Esterel modules can be directly used in the POLIS tool suite for system synthesis. The two main problems found in the experiment have been the interpretation of the informal specification and the lack of expertise in Esterel.

The informal specification of the crane system is rather complete but, as shown for the diagnosis module, the designer might be faced with informal specifications that are not complete or detailed enough and might have different interpretations. Furthermore, the experiment has shown that Esterel/C specifications can be done with different targets: simulation and synthesis. We have tried to generate a specification with a good compromise between the two.

As for our experience in Esterel, we believe that the inherent difficulty of building Esterel programs stems from the fact that we, as system designers, tend to think about them as sequential, procedural programs rather than as descriptions of EFSM transitions they really are. However, the cost of developing and verifying the system is similar to the ones presented in [2] for experiments alike.

Table 1 shows the size of specifications in source code lines. The second row shows the size of the specification for the controller and the third one of the environment. In the Java and occam cases, the figures shown are a combination of controller and environment code sizes. It is difficult to compare the code sizes because environment and targets are different in each case. For instance, the Java specification included a graphical user interface (GUI) of the portal crane and was mainly devoted to simulation, while the ADA/OVHDL approach was thought for synthesis and includes reusable components and a generic differential equation solver. In the case of Simulink, part of the system description is graphically done. In our case, we have limited ourselves to specify the whole system in Esterel/C to obtain a system description that enabled a rapid simulation by the xesterel program and also have considered the implementation issue by using optimised C functions. The result code lines is very similar to those required for the programming languages. Also, the development and verification time is comparable to specifications in programming languages and Simulink. We believe that the difference with Java is because of the development of the Java GUI. However, development time strongly depends on the expertise degree of actual designers. Therefore, figures in Table 2 are for guidance only.

5.   CONCLUSIONS

As shown in the previous section, the cost of using Esterel/C to model an heterogeneous system is comparable to other SDL. In particular, we did not find significant differences among all SDL for this benchmark but, if we consider the learning time for a SDL, it looks reasonable to consider other approaches that, though consider features included in Esterel, use a single, well-known language such as C or Java. Therefore, we have planned to conduct the same experiment with ECL and Jester in order to determine the gain of these approaches with respect to the use of two languages. As a result of this work, we have strengthened our initial idea that the need for some standardized metrics for system specification language evaluation would require setting up a number of system benchmarks that exercises all the aspects of system specification and design.

6.   REFERENCES

[1] G. Berry, P. Couronné, G. Gonthier, "The Synchronous Approach to Reactive and Real-Time Systems", *IEEE Proceedings*, Vol. 79, Sept., 1991.

[2] G. Gorla, W. Nebel, E. Moser, E. Villar, "System Specification Experiments on a Common Benchmark", *IEEE Design and Test of Computers*, pp. 22-32, July-September. 2000.

[3] E. Moser, W. Nebel, "Case Study: System Model of Crane and Embedded Control", *Proc. Design, Automation, and Test in Europe Conf. (DATE)*, IEEE Computer Soc. Press, Los Alamitos, Calif., pp. 721-724, March. 1999.

[4] J. Barnes, "Programming in Ada95", Addison-Wesley, Reading, Mass., 1995.

[5] A. López, M. Veiga, E. Villar, "HW/SW Embedded System Specification and Design using Ada and VHDL", *Reliable Software Technologies*. ADA-Europe 99, Springer Verlag, Amsterdam, 1999. pp. 356-370.

[6] M. Radetzki, "Overview of Objective VHDL Language Features", *Proc. FDL*. École Normale Superior, Lyon, 1999.

[7] J. Gosling, B. Joy, G. Steele, "The Java Language Specification", Addison-Wesley, Reading, Mass., 1996.

[8] Inmos Corp., "Occam Programming Manual", Prentice-Hall, Englewood Cliffs, N.J., 1983.

[9] ANSI/IEEE Standard 1076-1993, "VHDL Language Reference Manual", IEEE Press, 1994.

[10] "Simulink, Dynamic System Simulation for MATLAB", User's manual. TheMathWorks Inc., Natick, Mass. 1999.

[11] "MATLAB, The Language of Technical Computing,", User's manual. TheMathWorks Inc., Natick, Mass. 1996.

[12] L. Lavagno, E. Sentovich "ECL: A Specification Environment for Sytem-Level Design", *Proc. Design and Automation Conf. (DAC)*, IEEE Computer Soc. Press, Los Alamitos, Calif., June, 1999.

[13] M. Antoniotti, A. Ferrari, A. Flesca, A. Sangiovanni-Vincentelli, "JESTER: An Esterel-based reactive Java Extension for Reactive Embedded Systems Development", Proc. Third Forum on Design Languages, Tübingen. Sept. 2000.

[14] S. Swan, "An Introduction to System-Level Modeling in SystemC 2.0", www.systemc.org, Jan., 2001.

[15] J. Gerlach, W. Rosenstiel, "System Level Design Using the SystemC Modeling Platform", *Proc. SDL Conf*. 2000.

[16] "Functional Specification for SystemC 2.0", Synopsys, Inc., CoWare, Inc., Frontier Design, Inc. and others. Jan., 2001.

[17] F. Balarin et al., "Hardware-Software Co-Design of Embedded Systems: The POLIS Approach", Kluwer Academic Publishers, 1997.

REAL-TIME MODELING

Chapter 22

Modeling of Real-Time Embedded Systems using SDL

Jean-Philippe BABAU, Ahmad ALKHODRE, Jean-Jacques SCHWARZ

L3i / INSA de Lyon, jpbabau,ahmad.alkhodre@if.insa-lyon.fr,jjs@iuta.univ-lyon1.fr

Abstract: SDL is used increasingly for the development of real-time embedded systems. Because SDL does not have a clear interpretation of time, the associated code generators do not integrate the management of temporal constraints. In this paper, we propose a real-time semantics to SDL for the modeling of real-time embedded systems in order to prepare a real-time implementation.

Key words: Embedded systems, SDL, Real time systems, Event/Action model, and Architecture.

1. INTRODUCTION

Embedded systems interact strongly with a physical process and they are subject to strong reliability constraints, in particular at the temporal level. "A real-time embedded system is defined as a system whose correctness of the system depends not only on the logical results of computation, but also on the time at which results are produced" [4]. Due to their necessary correctness, the development of such systems implies the use of formal languages. Although SDL (Specification and Design Language) is such a formal language, increasingly used for the development of embedded system, it however does not give a clear translation of time and does not provide a complete description in which the model must be executed over the time.

In order to use the existing edition and verification tools of SDL (without any modification of SDL or formalisms multiplication), we propose a temporal semantics associated to a standardized architecture supporting the temporal constraints. To prepare the further code generation, a semantic configuration of time allowing a flexible specification of the temporal constraints and temporal knowledge of the system is proposed.

In the next part of the paper, we briefly present SDL and its time management possibilities. The third part is devoted to the model of the standardized architecture that will support the temporal constraints. The fourth part emphasizes the real-time semantics. Finally, the work as a whole is briefly illustrated with a short example.

2. SDL: BASIC PRINCIPLES AND REAL-TIME

SDL is a ITU-T standardized language and, because it is supported by an integrated development environment (objectGEODE, Tau)[3], it is widely used in industry. The code generated by the tools

257

. Mignotte et al. (eds.), System on Chip Design Languages, 257–265.
© 2002 *Kluwer Academic Publishers.*

is usually based on the services of a real-time multitasking executive. The so-formed application is then a set of communicating tasks. SDL can model concurrency and distributed systems; it also owns some specific instructions for temporal data.

The language is based on communicating finite state machines (FSM) and abstract data types. It includes the concepts of type and genericity. At the first level, the application is a system made up of blocks (subsystems) related to one another and to the border of the system by channels (Sensor, Appli, Actuator in figure 1). Blocks are composed of "substructures " (sub-block) and processes (Input, Command, Output in figure 1). A process in SDL is a communicating FSM with, maybe, several instances being executed in parallel. Communication is made via signals (IT, E, S , Com in figure 1) conveyed between blocks by the means of channels. The communicating mechanism is mono-sender/multi-receiver, yet, at the time of a transmission of a given signal, only one receiver among those waiting consumes it. In an object-based model, a process is a set of services implemented by SDL procedures. A signal is viewed as a message and when a signal occurs, the process, under some guard, executes the corresponding procedure [ECOOP 2001].

Time in SDL can only be defined and manipulated using the *NOW* instruction and the "timer"[10]. *NOW* gives access to a global clock and returns the current time. The actions related to the timer are the activation *SET (delay)* (expiry at *NOW+delay*) and the termination *RESET*. When a timer expires, it sends a signal to the waiting processes. At implementation, each action takes a certain amount of time for execution. As SDL does not specify how global time flows, the assumption, during the simulation of a SDL model, is to consider that the duration of an action can be neglected. SDL does not give a clear translation of time and does not provide a complete description in which the model must be executed over time.

This raises a problem for the development and the validation of the real-time systems. On the one hand, temporal validation (schedulability analysis) is really on a model of tasks in which each task is characterized by a

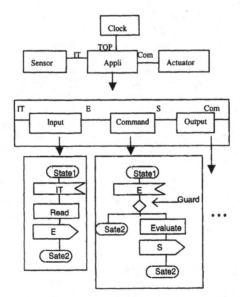

Figure 1 : SDL pattern for real-time embedded systems (reactive part).

priority level carried out from the temporal constraints and on the other hand, the SDL code generators do not integrate temporal constraints (not specified in SDL).

It is thus necessary to add real time semantics to SDL in order to build a real time code generator.

The research in this field has taken three main directions. The first one focuses on enhancing SDL by adding new structures to describe the real-time features (QSDL [5] and SDL*[8]). The second one uses SDL to model the behaviour. The model is then translated into another formalism to introduce the temporal requirement (as timed automata IF [6]). The third direction proposes to provide SDL with a temporal semantics [7]. That is our case, and we base our approach for the implementation level (within the aim of further code generation) on an architecture model.

3.   ARCHITECTURE MODEL

The first aspect it is necessary to model is the interaction between the real-time embedded system and its environment. So we give a classification of the different interactions, it is possible to find in a such system.

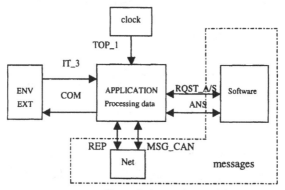

Figure 2 : interaction model

A real time system must react to stimuli (input events) coming from the interfaces with the environment and produce answers (data or output events) within a given deadline. From the physical environment, a stimuli is provided by an interrupt or by an alarm expiration (time triggered architecture). Moreover, in a distributed implementation, a system is a set of applications communicating by inter-process communication mechanisms (like pipe) or by net. To conclude, an application communicates with the physical environment via interrupts and timer and with others applications (cf. figure 2) via messages.

In the proposed architecture is based on the pattern shown in figure 2, the interrupt stimuli are called IT_niv. periodic clock signals are called TOP_n and messages are called RQST when local and MSG_net when remote. The reaction of the system produces signals, sent to the environment, called COM. The messages in reply are called ANS for local and REP for remote. The application may delegate actions to other applications by sending local or remote messages (RQST and MSG_net) and receiving the corresponding replies (ANS and REP).

The data exchanged with its environment by an application are associated with the signals (parameters of the signal) or directly read/write by the process during a procedure execution.

At the implementation stage, each category of exchange corresponds to a dedicated mode of communication between the application and its environment. For example, A polling server is dedicated to each interrupt and a periodic alarm is associated with each periodic clock signal. A mailbox, or some other queuing mechanism like pipe, socket, etc, is linked with the software communication and the exchanged data become protected shared resources.

In order to generate the corresponding code, it is necessary to classify the I/O exchanges between the application and its environment according to the type of communication used in the exchange. We have proposed typed naming rules for these signals (cf. table 1). These signals can also convey data not represented here, because it may be specific to a given application.

4.   REAL-TIME SEMANTIC

The proposed semantics integrates the "Event-Action" model of Jahanian and Mok [1] into the former architecture model. A real-time application is composed of a group of actions that operate on data by taking into account the time flow, and events rising from the computer system or its environment [9]. The temporal constraints expressed on the events are the frequency of their arrivals (minimum elapsed time between two successive events) and the response times (deadline). The temporal constraints expressed on the data are related to the life span and validity, and those relating to the actions are the execution and communication duration.

Table 1: classification of signal

Name category	Signal type	Information	Constraints
TOP_n(p,d)	Periodic Activation.	n : numero	p: period d : deadline
IT_lev(dmin,d_2)	Activation on interrupt	lev : interrupt level	dmin : minimal interval between two interrupts d2 : deadline
MSG_net(d_1,d_2)	Message from net	net : the type of net (CAN, FIP, ...)	Idem
RQST_S (d_1,d_2)	Synchronous request from other software	X	Idem
RQST_A (d_1,d_2)	Asynchronous request from other software	X	Idem
ANSWER	Application's response to a request.	X	X

At the implementation stage, the temporal constraints relating to the events and the data are derived on the launched actions by these events and on the actions which processes the data. They can be translated into activation dates of the actions (periodic, sporadic and aperiodic), waiting delays and deadlines.

4.1   Activation model

Based on the categories of stimuli defined in the architecture model, three activation modes, regarding to the type of signal, are defined. After that, these constraints, defined at application level, are derived on activation date of the corresponding actions.

4.1.1   Periodic activation

The periodic activation is simple to model in SDL by using the timer with a time-out equal to the period (figure 3): when the timer expires its time-out, it sends a signal to the process, which realizes the corresponding action.

The periodic activation must launch an action with the periodicity p according to: $@(e_1,i+1) - @(e_1,i) = p$ (where e_1 is the launching event of the action and $@evt$ represents the arrival date of the event evt).

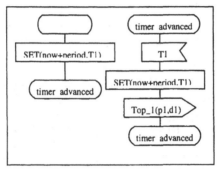

Figure 3 : periodic activation in SDL

4.2   Activation on interruption

The named signal IT_niv is dedicated to an interrupt which is characterized by its priority level (*niv*) and by *dmin*, the minimum interval separating two successive instances of the interrupt. *dmin* is defined by: $@(IT, i+1) - @(IT, i) \geq dmin$. The derived constraints on actions is that the frequency of action execution is less or equal to dmin. This rule insure that all the interrupts are taken into account by the application.

4.2.1   Activation by message (locals and/or remote)

The messages exchanged between the processes can be either synchronous RQST_S (waiting for a response synchronization in the transmitting process, figure 4) or asynchronous RQST_A (no waiting for the answer figure 5). A process can launch or finish when it awaits a message. Moreover, temporal constraints on the minimal time between two sent messages are also be expressed.

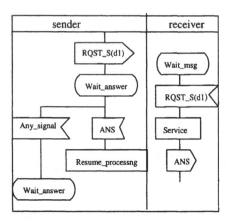

Figure 4 : synchronous message in SDL

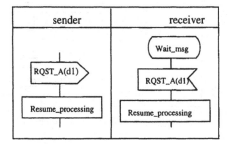

Figure 5 : asynchronous message in SDL

4.3   Deadline model

When an event e_i occurs, a set of actions is to be executed according to a specific deadline. This constraint is expressed by the following law: $@(s_i,i) - (e_i,i) = deadline$. ($s_i$: the end of the action).

A deadline is therefore associated with each input signal to the system. The constraint is then propagated in an implicit manner, in accordance with the propagation mode [2], to all the signals sent consequently to the input signal. The actions launched by these signals therefore inherit the constraint transferred by the signal. When an action is to be realized within a deadline different from the initial one, it is necessary to specify the change of deadline in the signal activating the corresponding action (figure 6).

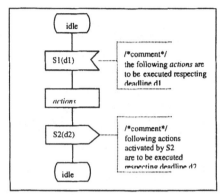

Figure 6 : deadline modification in SDL

4.4   Real-Time Policies

Once the temporal constraints and their associated semantics are specified in the model, it is possible to express specific real time policies (filtering, management of temporal faults, etc). For example, it can be necessary to proceed to the modification of the temporal constraints (increasing of a period, deadline relaxation).

Also, in the case of interrupt, it is often desirable to make some filtering in order to eliminate spurious interrupts. Such a filtering is represented on figure 7 (the example also includes the management of a temporal fault called exception).

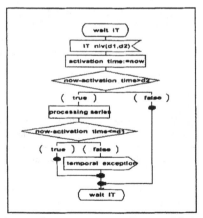

Figure 7 : interruption management and temporal fault management

5.   EXAMPLE

We now exhibit, using a classical pattern, how we use the temporal semantic extension of SDL. The example deals with a packaging unit of a wine-growing cooperative. The packaging processing

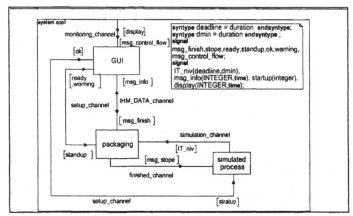

Figure 8 : modeling of packaging example using SDL

unit receives a bottle to be packed every 5 seconds (that is a maximum and the exceeding of this period produces a temporal exception). From the example, we have extracted the architecture model given in figure 6 and which presents the blocks associated to the three main basic functions (*GUI*: the monitoring system; Simulated Process: simulates the arrival of a bottle; and the *packaging* processing unit. The modeling includes the IT_4 interrupt signal (representative of a bottle passage in front of a sensor) characterized by the constraints *deadline*, *dmin* (*deadline* is the bottle packaging time and *dmin* is the minimal time between two consecutive bottle arrivals). In a slightly simplified version this interrupt is defined and managed as shown previously in figure 5.
The surrounded text box is dedicated to the declarations resulting from the semantics. If they are not taken into account by the current code generators of SDL, they will be used by the new code generator which has to be developed (*deadline* will then be regarded as a new key-word).

6.   CONCLUSION

In this paper, we studied SDL as a high level language able to model and specify real-time embedded systems. SDL has some instructions to deal with time but not with real-time. This carried us to propose an extension in the form of a real-time semantics which is based on a standard architecture, typed signals and a propagation mode. Moreover this modeling allows the description of real-time policies.
The next step of this work is to build an automatic code generation supporting the interpretation of the suggested temporal semantics.

7. REFERENCES

[1] Jahanian F., Mok A.K., *"Safety analysis of timing properties in real-time systems"*. IEEE Trans. Soft. Eng. V12 N9, Sep 1986. pp 890-904.

[2] Jean Philippe Babau et Jean Louis Sourrouille, *"Expressing real time constraints in a reflective object model "*, *IFAC Control Engineering Practice*, Vol 6 (1998) pages 421-430.

[3] J.M. Alvarez, M. Diaz, L.M. Llopis, E. Pimentel, and J.M. Troya. *"Integrating schedulability analysis and sdl in an object-oriented methodology for embedded real-time systems"*. In R. Dssouli, G.v. Bochmann, and Y. Lahav, editors, Proceedings of SDL Forum '99, Montreal,Canada, 1999. Elsevier.

[4] Stankovic J. A., *"Misconceptions about real-time computing: a serious problem for the next-generation systems"*. IEEE Computer., V21 N10, Oct. 1988, pp 10-19.

[5]   M. Diefenbruch: Queuing SDL - A Language for the Functional and Quantitative Specification of Distributed Systems, University Gesamthochschule Essen, Fachbereich Mathematik und Informatik, 1997, (QUAFOS-Project Report Q1).

[6] M. Bozga, J.Cl. Fernandez, L. Ghirvu, S. Graf, J.P. Krimm, L. Mounier, J. Sifakis *"IF: An Intermediate Representation for SDL and its Applications"*, Proceeding. of the Ninth SDL Forum, Montreal, Quebec, Canada, 21-25 June, 1999 pp.423.

[7] R. Gotzhein, U. Glässer and A. Prinz. *"Towards a new formal SDL semantics based on Abstract State Machines"*. In R. Dssouli, G.V. Bochmann and Y. Lahav, editors, SDL '99 - The Next Millennium, *9th SDL Forum Proceedings*, pages 171-190, Elsevier Science B.V., 1999.

[8] S. Spitz, F. Slomka, M. Dörfel, *"SDL* An Annotated Specification Language for Engineering Multimedia Communication Systems"*, Sixth Open Workshop on High Speed Net- works, Stuttgart, October 97.

[9] Zoubir Mammeri, "Expression et dévriation des contraintes temporelles dans les applications temps réel" APII-JESA. Volume 32-n°5-6/1998, pages 609-644.

[10] Zoubir Mammeri "SDL Modélisation de protocoles et systèmes réactifs" ISBN : 2746201666, (juillet 2000).

Chapter 23

A Framework for Specification and Verification of Timing Constraints

Eugenio Villar

TEISA Department, E.T.S.I. Industriales y Telecom. University of Cantabria, Avda. Los Castros s/n, 39005 Santander, Spain, villar@teisa.unican.es

Abstract: Timing constraint specification and verification constitutes an essential activity throughout the system design process. Currently, system design requires the use of several languages at the different abstraction levels based on different computational models. In [1], a general framework for comparing models of computation has been proposed. It represents a powerful framework for understanding, analyzing and comparing different computational models.

In this paper, this framework is extended to the specification of timing constraints. Based on this extension, different timing constraint specification means based on different computational models can be analyzed and compared. A general methodology for timing constraint verification during the system design process is also outlined.

Key words: System specification, timing constraints

. INTRODUCTION

The specification of the system at any abstraction level constitutes a key activity throughout the design process. In HW design a consensus has been reached on a common design methodology based on a few languages, i.e. VHDL and Verilog. The situation in system design is rather different and many languages based on different computational models are used at each abstraction level and each application domain [2-3].

Figure 1 outlines the general co-design methodology for HW/SW embedded systems. The process starts with the Requirements Document describing the general characteristics of the product in terms of application domain, operational environment, functionality and constraints. At this stage, the functional description is very general and refers to input and output data, data rates, input-output transformations and delays. In some cases, a general, functional decomposition of the system is provided. Constraints refer to cost, size, power consumption, etc.

From the Requirements Document, and following a Functional Design process, the system specification is developed. Functional Design can use real-time software development methodologies

Mignotte et al. (eds.), System on Chip Design Languages, 267-274.
2002 *Kluwer Academic Publishers.*

[4]. Recently, the Object Management Group has released the Software Process Engineering Metamodel based on UML [5].

The complete system specification is usually composed of two different parts, the executable specification and the non-functional requirements. The executable specification implements the functional requirements defined initially. The non-functional requirements capture all the design constraints. Among them, timing requirements are especially important as they may dramatically affect the final characteristics of the system implementation. They refer to input and output data rates and delays.

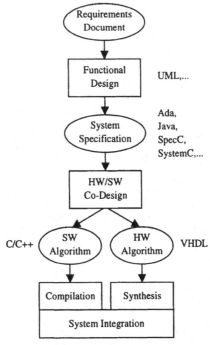

Figure 1: General system design methodology.

Once verified and debugged, the system specification is used as input to the HW/SW co-design process. After profiling, real-time analysis, partitioning and HW/SW interface synthesis, the SW and HW algorithms are generated. They are respectively compiled and synthesized and integrated on the system implementation platform [6-7].

Different languages, based on different computational models are used at each step. Some of the most representative of them are shown in Figure 1. There is no unified language today and there will probably not be one in the near future supporting all the required modelling paradigms [8].

As timing behaviour evolves in each design step identifying each abstraction level, preservation of the original timing constraints imposed has to be ensured at each step.

In general, specification languages do not support the specification of timing constraints, so, they are usually handled using separate means [9]. Timing constraint specification is particularly relevant at the higher levels of abstraction, when the design is still far from the implementation details. At these levels, untimed and/or relaxed-timed models are used [10]. At lower levels, strict-timed languages are used and it is easier to handle the timing constraints as they are embedded in the design description itself. So, for instance, a clock signal in VHDL defines a frequency constraint to be satisfied by the critical path of the logic implementation of the circuit. Most of the timing constraints on a VHDL or Verilog code can be verified directly by simulation.

Specification, analysis and verification of timing constraints for real-time, embedded systems constitutes a traditional and active research area. As a consequence, a variety of techniques for different purposes and applications have been proposed [9][11-15].

In [1], a general framework for comparing models of computation is proposed. The framework constitutes an analytical tool with which the fundamental properties of different models of computation can be understood and compared.

In this paper, a general framework for the specification and verification of timing constraints is proposed. As it is based on the general framework proposed in [1], it is independent of the particular computational model used. Thus, the framework covers any particular specification technique and language either timed or untimed. Moreover, any analysis and verification method could be based on it. The structure of the paper is the following. In the next section, the general framework for the specification of timing constraints will be described. Based on this framework, a general methodology for timing constraint verification will be proposed in section 3. Finally, some conclusions will be derived.

2. TIMING CONSTRAINT SPECIFICATION

Timing constraints can be imposed on events [9][11-12][15] or on operation delays [13-14]. Based on the framework for comparing models of computation proposed in [1], we will work on events. This is more general as an operation delay can be represented by a starting and a finishing event while there are timing constraints on events which cannot be expressed with operation delays, i.e. events generated by concurrent processes.

2.1 Event properties

Timing constraints are not imposed on concrete events on particular signals but on events satisfying some predefined properties. These properties may be independent of the value, of the tag or even of both. Moreover, they can involve one or several signals. The following would be examples of such event properties:

$p_1(s_1) \equiv$ any event e in s_1 such that $V(e) = '1'$.
$p_2(s_1) \equiv$ any event e in s_1 such that $T(e)$ is a multiple of 5.
$p_3(s_2) \equiv$ the first event e_j in s_2 after an event e_i in s_1 such that $e_i \in p_2(s_1)$.

From this point of view, an event property of a signal is a subset of that signal, that is:

$$p(s) \subseteq s$$

and, therefore, it constitutes another signal.

A timing constraint involves two different event properties which can be grouped in a pair $(p_1(s_1), p_2(s_2))$. In most cases, p_2 will refer to the events in $p_1(s_1)$. Event properties in a pair $(p_1(s_1), p_2(s_2))$ must satisfy unicity, that is, for each event $e_i \in p_1(s_1)$ there is only one event $e_j \in p_2(s_2)$, such that, $(e_i, e_j) \in (p_1(s_1), p_2(s_2))$:

$$\forall s_i, s_j \in s = (..., s_i, ..., s_j, ...) \in P,$$
$$\forall (e_i, e_j), (e_k, e_l) \in (p_i(s_i), p_j(s_j)) \Rightarrow$$
$$\Rightarrow e_i = e_k \Leftrightarrow e_j = e_l \qquad (1)$$

As an example, consider signals s_1 and s_2 in Figure 2:

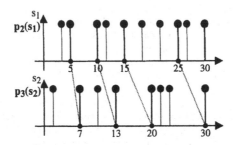

Figure 2: Pair of event properties.

Property p_2 defined previously has been applied to signal s_1 leading to the event selection shown. Property p_3 has been applied to signal s_2. The pair satisfies condition (1).

This example corresponds to a timed model of computation in which events in different signals are ordered. This would not be the case when an untimed model is used. In this case, conditions of the type "first event after an event" would require synchronization points between the two signals involved. The model is relaxed-timed as tags do not represent physical time.

Condition (1) should be verified during the verification of the system specification. If a pair of event properties used to specify a timing constraint does not satisfy unicity either the constraint is not correctly formulated or the system specification is ambiguous. In the former case, the timing constraint should be reformulated. In the latter, the specification itself may be incorrect and should be modified.

2.2   Timing constraints

A timing constraint 'tc' is defined as a condition over the tags of events satisfying certain event properties in signals s_i and s_j to be satisfied by any tuple $s \in P$, such that $s_i, s_j \in s$.

The following is the general form a timing constraint will take:

$$tc : \forall s_i, s_j \in s \in P,$$
$$\forall (e_i, e_j) \in (p_1(s_i), p_2(s_j)) \Rightarrow$$
$$\Rightarrow R[T(e_j), T(e_i)] \, op \, q \qquad (2)$$

Where:
$T(e_j)$ and $T(e_i)$ represent the tags of events e_j and e_i respectively,

$R[T(e_j),T(e_i)]$ represents the relation between the tags. As will be shown later, R involves the time distance between the events. It can be expressed directly in seconds or as the inverse in Hz, events per second or bits per second (bps),

op is a relational operator, and

q is a certain quantity expressed in seconds or seconds^{-1}, depending on R.

We will represent the distance in time required between tags by '-'. This does not require the definition of a metric in T. That is, the '-' operator will correspond to numerical subtraction only in strict-timed models of computation in which T represents physical time.

A variety of means have been proposed in order to specify timing constraints, such as specific languages [9][11-12], pragmas and attributes to the specification language [13-14], method invocations [15] and temporal logic [16]. Any of those means can be used to express the timing constraints defined in (2).

Timing constraints can refer to a minimum, a maximum or an exact distance between events. This will be defined by the 'op' relational operator used.

A timing constraint will be called a delay when it refers to events in two different signals.

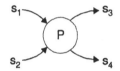

Figure 3: A simple I/O process.

So, for instance, in the process in Figure 3, the following will be delay requirements:

$$tc_1 : \forall s_1, s_3 \in s \in P,$$
$$\forall (e_i, e_j) \in (p_1(s_1), p_2(s_3)) \Rightarrow$$
$$\Rightarrow T(e_j) - T(e_i) \geq 1 \qquad \text{minimum delay}$$

$$tc_2 : \forall s_2, s_4 \in s \in P,$$
$$\forall (e_i, e_j) \in (p_3(s_4), p_4(s_2)) \Rightarrow$$
$$\Rightarrow T(e_j) - T(e_i) \leq u \qquad \text{maximum delay}$$

$$tc_3 : \forall s_3, s_4 \in s \in P,$$
$$\forall (e_i, e_j) \in (p_5(s_3), p_6(s_4)) \Rightarrow$$
$$\Rightarrow T(e_j) - T(e_i) = ed \qquad \text{exact delay}$$

A timing constraint will be called a rate when it refers to events in the same signal. They can be expressed as time values (seconds) or frequencies (seconds^{-1}). So, the following will be frequency rate constraints:

$$tc_4 : \forall s_3 \in s \in P,$$
$$\forall (e_i, e_j) \in (p_5(s_3), p_7(s_3)) \Rightarrow$$
$$\Rightarrow \frac{1}{T(e_j) - T(e_i)} \geq r \qquad \text{minimum rate}$$

$$tc_5 : \forall s_3 \in s \in P,$$
$$\forall (e_i, e_j) \in (p_5(s_3), p_7(s_3)) \Rightarrow$$
$$\Rightarrow \frac{1}{T(e_j) - T(e_i)} \leq R \qquad \text{maximum rate}$$

$$tc_6 : \forall s_2 \in s \in P,$$
$$\forall (e_i, e_j) \in (p_8(s_2), p_9(s_2)) \Rightarrow$$
$$\Rightarrow \frac{1}{T(e_j) - T(e_i)} = er \qquad \text{exact rate}$$

In an I/O process, timing constraints can be classified depending on the kind of signals involved. Thus, an I/O constraint will refer to the time between an input event and an output event, such as 'tc_1'.

An I/I constraint will refer to the time between two input events, such as 'tc_6'. It can be a rate or a delay. An O/I constraint will refer to the time between an output event and an input event, such as 'tc_2'.

An O/O constraint will refer to the time between two output events. It can be a rate, such as 'tc_4' and 'tc_5' or a delay, such us 'tc_3'.

I/I and O/I constraints have to be satisfied by the environment in which the process operates. We will call them domain timing constraints. I/O and O/O timing constraints have to be satisfied by any implementation of the process. We will call them functional timing constraints.

3.   TIMING CONSTRAINT VERIFICATION

As has been commented already, condition (1) represents a powerful way to identify ambiguities either in the specification of the timing constraints or in the system specification itself. Once these ambiguities have been removed and the system specification verified, the system design process can start.

During system design, the initial timing constraints have to be verified at each design step.

Let us represent the set of timing constraints at any step of the design process by TC^i, TC^0 being the initial set of timing restrictions. Let:

$$P^{TC^i} \subseteq P$$

represent the subset of behaviors of P satisfying timing constraints TC^i.

Let us consider I/O process:

$$P \subseteq S^{N_I} \times S^{N_O}$$

with $N_I + N_O = N$, where N_I is the number of inputs and N_O is the number of outputs.
Let us call:

$$I^{TC^i}$$

the set of input signals to the process satisfying the domain timing constraints of TC^i, and:

$$O^{I^{TC^i}}$$

the corresponding set of output signals. We will say that the process is time-closed when:

$$P^{TC^i} = P$$

that is, any behavior of P satisfies the whole set of timing constraints.

We will say that the system is time-closed when the corresponding process SYS is time-closed. We can ensure that the design process exhibits a correct timing behavior when at a certain step the system is time-closed. Any further transformation maintaining the timing characteristics of the system will also be correct. It is clear that time-closure can only be ensured when a strict-timed computational model is used.

From this point of view, timing constraints evolve from the initial set of timing requirements TC^0 through the high-level, untimed and/or relaxed-timed models of the system. At these levels, they have to be verified using estimations.

When the design reaches a concretion point where a strict-timed model can be used, time-closure should be ensured. From this point, any design step maintaining the timing characteristics of the system will ensure design correctness.

4.   CONCLUSIONS

In this paper, the framework for comparing models of computation proposed in [1] has been extended to the specification and verification of timing constraints. The framework is useful in the analysis and comparison of different means of timing constraint specification developed for different computational models. It covers any particular specification technique and language either timed or untimed.

Based on the framework, a general methodology for timing constraint verification during the design process has been developed.

In any case, this is a preliminary work to be extended further with more detailed mechanisms for both specification and verification of timing constraints.

5.   REFERENCES

[1] E.A. Lee and A. Sangiovanni-Vincentelli: "A framework for comparing models of computation", IEEE Trans. On Computer-Aided Design of Integrated Circuits and Systems, V.17, N.12, December, 1998, pp.1217-1229.

[2] E. Villar and M. Veiga: "Embedded system specification", in "Embedded systems design and test", edited by J.C. López, R. Hermida and W. Geisselhardt, Kluwer, 1998.

[3] D.D. Gajski; F. Vahid; S. Narayan and J. Gong: "Specification and design of embedded systems", Prentice-Hall, 1994.

[4] K. Shumate and M. Keller: "Software Specification and design: A Disciplined Approach for Real-Time Systems", Wiley, 1992.

[5] "The Software Process Engineering Metamodel (SPEM)", OMG document number: ad/2001-06-05, http://www.omg.org/uml.

[6] S. Kumar, J.H. Aylor, B.W. Johnson and W.A. Wulf: "The codesign of embedded systems", Kluwer, 1996.

[7] J. Staunstrup and W. Wolf (Eds.): "HW/SW co-design", Kluwer, 1997.

[8] A.A. Jerraya, M. Romdhani, C.A. Valderrama, Ph. Le Marrec, F. Hessel, G.F. Marchioro and J.M. Daveau: "Languages for system-level specification and design", in "HW/SW co-design", J. Staunstrup and W. Wolf (Eds.), Kluwer, 1997.

[9] B. Dasarathy: "Timing constraints of real-time systems: Constructs for expressing them, methods of validating them", IEEE Trans. On Software Engineering, V.SE-11, N.1, January, 1985, pp.80-86.

[10]   E. Villar: "Specification of complex HW/SW embedded systems", in "Design of HW/SW embedded systems", E. Villar (Ed.), Servicio de Publicaciones de la Universidad de Cantabria, 2001.

[11]   F. Jahanian and A.K.-L. Mok: "A graph-theoretic approach for timing analysis and its implementation", IEEE Trans. On Computers, V.C-36, N.8, August, 1987, pp.961-975.

[12] C.-C. Lien and C.-C. Yang: "Frame representation for specification of timing constraints in real-time systems", Information and Software Technology, V.34, N.7, July, 1992, pp.467-477.

[13] L.Ko, C. Healy, E. Ratliff, R. Arnold, D. Whalley and M. Harmon: "Supporting the specification and analysis of timing constraints", proc. of the IEEE Real-Time Technology and Application Symposium 1996, IEEE, 1996, pp.170-178.

[14] R.K. Gupta and G. De Micheli: "Specification and analysis of timing constraints for embedded systems", IEEE Trans. On Computer-Aided Design of Integrated Circuits and Systems, V.16, N.3, March, 1997, pp.240-256.

[15] V.F. Wolfe, L.C. Dipippo, R. Ginis, M. Squadrito, S. Wohlever, I. Zykh and R. Johnston: "Expressing and enforcing timing constraints in a dynamic real-time CORBA system", The International Journal of Time-Critical Computing Systems, 16, 253-280, Kluwer, 1999, pp.127-155.

[16] V. Cingel: "Timing constraint verification using temporal logic", in P. Prinetto and P. Camurati (ed.): "Correct hardware design methodologies", Elsevier, 1992, pp. 429-440.

Chapter 24

A General Approach to Modelling System-Level Timing Constraints

Marek Jersak, Dirk Ziegenbein, Rolf Ernst (jersak I ziegenbein I ernst @ida.ing.tu-bs.de)
Technische Universität Braunschweig
Braunschweig, Germany

Abstract: Timing constraints are an integral part of the design of embedded real-time systems. They affect most system-level decisions, in particular hardware/software partitioning, allocation and scheduling. Modern embedded systems execute a large set of tasks on a heterogeneous architecture in an increasingly dynamic environment. This necessitates the specification of timing constraints which consider unknown and dynamic situations with event jitter and burst. Different system-level analysis and implementation techniques assume different types of constraints as well as specification models and target architectures. It is thus important to combine those specialised solutions for system-level design of complex and heterogeneous embedded systems. In this chapter, we propose an efficient representation for timing constraints that allows to combine different specification, analysis and implementation techniques for complex embedded systems.

Key words: timing constraints, timing analysis, jitter, burst, system-level design

1.   INTRODUCTION

Many embedded systems are operated in a real-time environment and have to satisfy a set of timing constraints to function correctly. In many applications these timing constraints are hard, i.e. they lead to functional failure if violated. For such systems, it is imperative that satisfaction of timing constraints is guaranteed under all operating conditions. Even for systems with soft timing constraints, where violation leads to degradation of performance, a good understanding of possible timing as a result of different operating conditions is highly desirable to find a cost-efficient implementation.

Embedded systems are quickly becoming tremendously complex, executing a large, heterogeneous set of tasks in an increasingly dynamic environment. This necessitates the specification of sophisticated timing constraints which go beyond the traditional periodic rate constraints and individual process deadlines. In particular constraining event jitter and event bursts must be possible, since jitter and bursts negatively influence timing and buffer requirements for connected system parts. Jittery and bursty system behaviour results from resource contention, execution dependencies, scheduling decisions and from uncertain timing of the system environment. Another consequence of system complexity is the increasing use of different specification languages, each best suited for a specific application domain, leading to multi-language designs.

Timing constraints are typically validated by executing large numbers of test vectors. Testing or simulating the whole state space is not feasible for all but the simplest systems or system parts. More

275

Mignotte et al. (eds.), System on Chip Design Languages, 275–283.
2002 *Kluwer Academic Publishers.*

recently, analysis techniques such as schedulability tests for software processes have been used for timing verification. Individual analysis techniques are restricted due to assumptions about specification models, target architectures and types of timing constraints. In summary, there exists no single technique which is universally applicable to all mixes of tasks, timing constraints, target architectures and scheduling policies. Consequently, a combination of modern system-level analysis, hardware-software partitioning, allocation and scheduling techniques has to be used to handle complex systems.

In the following the main requirements to specify timing constraints for complex, dynamic systems, realistic event models and a mix of design techniques are described.

Expressiveness and Ease of Use: Modelling of timing constraints has to be expressive yet easy to use. It has to go beyond the traditionally specified periodic rate constraints or deadlines for individual processes, and additionally allow to model constraints that are required to model highly dynamic systems with jitter and bursts. At the same time, difficult to understand formalisms which in theory can express very complex constraints should be avoided, if no techniques are available for their verification. Instead, it should be possible to extend the types of constraints that can be specified to allow adaptation to emerging analysis techniques.

Language- and Technique-Independence: Specification languages abstract the timing of an implementation. In untimed languages, e.g. data flow or C, only the (partial) ordering of operations is modelled. In perfectly synchronous languages, e.g. Simulink [1], time is idealised into discrete time steps and zero delay execution. Timing constraints are not part of either of these languages but rather are provided in an additional natural language document. They need to be formalised early in the design flow to be applicable to system-level design techniques.

It should be possible to specify timing constraints in a design technique-independent way in order to combine different system-level analysis, hardware-software partitioning, allocation or scheduling techniques, which can even be provided by different sources.

Source Classification: Timing constraints can be divided into constraints imposed by the environment in which an embedded system is supposed to operate and constraints that are a result of design decisions. The former include I/O latency constraints, maximum input sampling jitter or minimum throughput constraints. Design decisions, in particular scheduling and allocation of a certain system part, constrain the timing for the remaining system. Similarly, in a 'divide-and-conquer' approach new timing constraints have to be specified for each subsystem. Consequently, the source of each timing constraint should be maintained in order to support an iterative design flow.

In the remainder of the paper, we first compare related work and then present our timing constraints specification in Section 3. In Section 4 we show how to combine our specification with a system representation targeted at system-level analysis. This is followed by two examples in Section 5, one targeting a particular timing analysis technique, the other showing the impact of constraining event jitter and bursts on synthesis.

2.   RELATED WORK

There is a large number of system-level analysis and scheduling techniques for embedded real-time systems. Traditional scheduling techniques, e.g. Rate-Monotonic Scheduling, are restricted to periodically arriving events, periodic deadlines and periodic rates. They usually assume independent processes (or tasks) and allow analysis based on Worst-Case Execution Times. For an extensive overview of existing scheduling techniques and schedulability tests see Fidge [2]. Ernst [3] provides a similar overview for techniques used for hardware/software codesign. As has been shown e.g. by Gerber [4] or Yen [5], best-case values are needed to analyse real-time scheduling anomalies in distributed systems. This requires using *intervals* where values are delimited by an upper and lower bound. Other work, e.g. by Tindell [6] or Gresser [7], additionally acknowledges the fact that realistic systems exhibit communication jitter and bursts. Our goal is to specify timing constraints such that different techniques can be applied, extended and combined as appropriate.

Many mathematical formalisms have been developed to model reactive real-time systems, including timed process algebras, temporal logic or timed constraint programming languages. A brief overview is given in [8]. All of them offer ways to specify timed system function and to reason about functional correctness in the presence of time. However, these languages do not seem to be suitable for system-level synthesis, since system properties are heavily idealised to enable reasoning. Such idealised properties are hard or impossible to implement. Therefore, reasoning is only valid for system simulations which satisfy those assumption but not for an actual implementation. Due to their mathematical soundness, those languages are also rather complex.

For example, the timed concurrent constraint language (tccp) [8] allows to specify timing mechanisms, e.g. time-outs or watchdogs, in terms of constraints. However, tccp assumes maximal parallelism and unit reaction to events. Both restrictions facilitate reasoning about system behaviour, but cannot realistically be implemented. A synthesis path from tccp is thus far from clear.

Amon [9] formalises hardware timing-diagrams by using event logic to constrain the timing of events relative to each other. His approach is relatively flexible in identifying the events involved in a constraint, without yielding very complicated expressions. However, the description is too detailed from a system-level perspective, and also requires a specific system representation (OE-graphs).

Dasdan [10] provides a comprehensive classification of timing constraints and of event models including jitter and bursts. Min-max intervals are used for their specification. Our approach uses a very similar classification, but focuses on a more general and design-flow independent way to specify timing constraints.

Emerging system languages such as SystemC [11] or SpecC [12] allow to annotate timing information to processes and communication for the purpose of simulation or IP exchange. However, the constructs are not suitable for modelling timing constraints. Recently, Rosetta [13] has been introduced as a requirements specification language. It uses terms to provide a multi-faceted specification that an implementation (typically hardware) has to satisfy. One view is via the 'constraints' domain. However, this domain currently supports only execution time constraints for individual processes. This is not sufficient for system-level design, when processes and communication have to be scheduled on a heterogeneous architecture.

Recently the SPI model has been developed which enables efficient non-functional system-level analysis, in particular of timing and memory requirements [14]. In section 4 we will couple our constraints model with SPI and show how analysis benefits from the combined representation.

3.   TIMING CONSTRAINT MODELLING

The first question to ask is 'What can be constrained?' We assume here the widely used notion that as time passes, certain points in time (events) can be identified. The model of time can be discrete or continuous, however points in time themselves are atomic and have zero duration.

We view a system as a set of processes with dedicated ports (input or output) for communication. We define a token to be the atomic unit for communicated data. From the perspective of system-level modelling, analysis, allocation and scheduling, the following points in time are interesting.

– The starting time of a process.
– The completion time of a process.
– The point in time, when a process starts reading or writing tokens at a particular port.
– The point in time, when a process completes reading or writing tokens at a particular port.
– If a specification language supports buffered communication channels, then the point in time when a token becomes available for reading at a particular process port can be distinguished from the actual reading of the token. The situation is different when writing tokens. Written tokens are immediately committed to a channel.

We now introduce a small set of parameterised timing constraint macros. By choosing parameter values appropriately, a large set of constraints with intervals, jitter and bursts can be specified.

Latency Constraints: Latency constraints are used to limit the propagation time for causally dependent tokens along a certain path. The acceptable latency L is bound by a [min,max] interval (*Figure 1*). A token td is said to be causally dependent on token ti, if it was produced by a process execution which either read ti or a token which is causally dependent on ti.

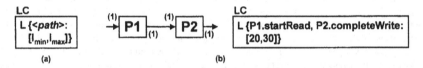

Figure 1. *Latency Constraint:* general form (a) and example (b). The acceptable latency L along path *<path>* is bound by a [min,max] interval. In the example, P1 and P2 read/write one token per activation. The LC has to be satisfied from the point in time when process P1 starts reading one token, till the point in time when process P2 completes writing a causally dependent token. The acceptable latency interval is between 20 and 30 time units.

Rate Constraints: Rate constraints constrain the timing of consecutive events of the same type. The acceptable period P and jitter J are bound by [min,max] intervals. *Figure 2* shows the general form. Depending on the choice of parameters, different types of constraints can be modelled. *Figure 3* shows some examples.

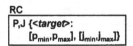

Figure 2. *Rate Constraint:* general form. The acceptable period P and jitter J are bound by [min,max] intervals.

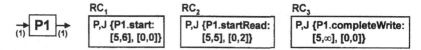

Figure 3. Rate Constraint examples: starting time with acceptable period range between 5 and 6 time units (RC1), periodic read start with acceptable jitter between 0 and 2 time units (RC2), sporadic write completion (RC3). The minimum distance between individual write events is at least 5 time units, the maximum distance is not bounded.

Burst Constraints: Burst constraints are used to model the activation of processes that display bursty behaviour. We have adopted the terminology used by Tindell [6] and extended it with an explicit lower bound for intervals. The acceptable outer period *Po* (between bursts), inner period *Pi* (within one burst) and burst length *N* are bound by [min,max] intervals. The general form and an example are shown in *Figure 4*.

Figure 4. Burst Constraint: general form (a) and example (b). The acceptable outer period *Po* (between bursts), inner period *Pi* (within one burst) and burst length *N* are bound by [min,max] intervals. In the example, P1 completes writing bursts of 10 to 20 tokens at least every 200 time units but not more often than every 100 time units. The separation of tokens in each burst is between 2 and 3 time units.

Synchronisation Constraints: Sometimes otherwise unrelated events have to be synchronised to occur within the bounds of a time interval *S*. Explicit synchronisation is necessary if no global clock is assumed. The general form and an example of a synchronisation constraint are shown in *Figure 5* and *Figure 6*, respectively.

SC

S {<*target*>(<*syncTarget*>):
[s_{min}, s_{max}]}

Figure 5. Synchronisation Constraint: general form. The <*target*> event has to fall within [s_{min}, s_{max}] of the <*syncTarget*> event. Both values can be negative.

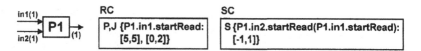

Figure 6. Synchronisation Constraint example. P1 hat to start reading input *in1* periodically every 5 time units, with an allowable jitter between 0 and 2 time units. Reading of input *in2* has to be started earliest 1 time unit before, and latest 1 time unit after reading of *in1*.

4.   COMBINATION WITH THE SPI MODEL

In the previous section we showed the expressiveness of our timing constraints model. In order to facilitate system-level analysis of timing without being bound to a certain specification language or to a certain analysis technique, we combine our timing constraints specification with the SPI system model. The SPI (System Property Intervals) model is an internal representation that was specifically developed to facilitate system-level analysis of non-functional system properties [14]. In this section, only the basic concepts of SPI, which are necessary to understand this paper, are introduced informally.

SPI abstracts a heterogeneous functional specification into a unified representation consisting of processes that communicate via directed channels. During abstraction, functional details are omitted and only those *system properties* necessary for non-functional system-level analysis are captured. These include activation functions, data rates and data on channels. Execution and communication latencies can be annotated but are implementation dependent. Key to functional abstraction for analysis is the possibility to specify all properties as *intervals*. For example, a data rate interval bounds the number of produced or consumed data, capturing conditional communication. Functional abstraction and the use of intervals imply that SPI is not executable. Virtual processes and channels are used to model the system environment and to represent additional information, in particular scheduling dependencies. Virtual elements do not have a direct functional correspondence in an implementation but influence system-level decisions.

Timing constraints can be specified in SPI, but only in form of latency path constraints (called SPI LCs here to distinguish them from the LCs in our constraints modelling). This restriction keeps the model simple and general. It is possible to express other types of timing constraints using SPI LCs and virtual elements, but this leads to constructs that can be difficult to understand and harder to analyse. Expressing complex timing constraints separately and combining them with the SPI representation of a system as proposed here is a much more efficient, modular and flexible approach. Analysis techniques that comprehend the semantic meaning of our timing constraints can be applied directly or only with minor transformations. On the other hand, it can be advantageous to map our timing constraints to SPI LCs, since an analysis technique based only on SPI LCs is automatically able to evaluate any other form of timing constraints, making this a very general approach. The mapping is demonstrated by the example in *Figure 7*.

Figure 7. Rate constraint macro and its mapping to the SPI model, where only latency path constraints (called SPI LCs here) are available. The mapping also requires virtual SPI elements (denoted by dashed lines). The SPI LC on channel *cs* forces a periodic execution of process *Pc* every 5 time units. *Pc* consumes one token from *cs* and immediately produces one token each on channels *cs* and *ct*. The token on *ct* is consumed at completion time of *P1*, which must happen within the SPI LC interval of [0, 2] time units on *ct*, accounting for the acceptable jitter.

5. EXAMPLES

Our first example shows how our timing constraint specification can be mapped to existing analysis techniques, and how design decisions affect timing constraints. The task graph representation in *Figure 8*a is used in a response time analysis for static priority scheduling by Yen and Wolf in [5]. In this analysis, a task graph with deadline d and period range $[p_{min}, p_{max}]$ is assumed. Virtual processes r and c with pre-defined delays are used to model different earliest release times and different deadlines for individual paths through the task graph.

An equivalent system using the SPI model and our representation for timing constraints is shown in *Figure 8*b. Due to the RC, process $P1$ has to be started periodically within $[p_{min}, p_{max}]$. The SC delays the start of $P2$ by at least r. LC1 states that $P3$ has to complete within the deadline d after $P1$ has started, while LC2 states that $P4$ has to complete earlier than d by at least c.

The mapping from *Figure 8*b to *Figure 8*a is trivial. Therefore, if we can arrive at a system description as in *Figure 8*b, the analysis technique described in [5] can be used.

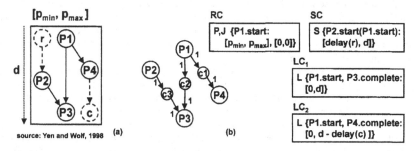

Figure 8. Existing analysis technique (a) and equivalent representation using SPI and our timing constraints (b)

To show how scheduling decisions affect timing constraints, and why it is important to maintain the source of a timing constraint, suppose we are trying to schedule $P1$ to satisfy $LC1$ in *Figure 8*b. The maximum execution time allowed for process $P1$ also depends on the worst-case execution time of process $P3$, which can be longer than its core execution time (i.e. $P3$'s execution time without interrupts) because of preemption by higher priority processes. Now assume that the highest priority has been assigned to process $P3$. Its execution time now equals its core execution time because it no longer can be preempted. Thus, $LC1$ can be replaced by a new latency constraint $LC1' = [0, (d - core_{P3})]$ that is valid for the path $\{P1.start, P3.start\}$. However, $LC1'$ is only valid as long as the priority assignment for $P3$ is not changed. This dependency has to be maintained.

Our second example shows how to constraint bursts and jitter. In *Figure 9* we model a video phone connection via a shared bus. The camera C sends images to the encoder En, which encodes each image into a number of packets (between 15 and 50). Each packet is then transmitted via the shared Bus to the decoder Dec, which reads the packets and decodes each image. The image is then sent to the display Dis. Note that this specification is multi-rate, since for each execution of En and Dec, the Bus function has to be executed between 15 and 50 times.

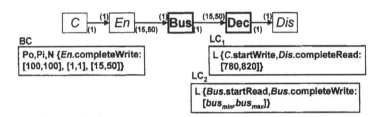

Figure 9. Video phone connection example with camera *C*, bursty packet encoder *En*, packet *Bus* with jittery delay, packet decoder *Dec* and display *Dis*. LC1 has to be satisfied for a real-time transmission. LC2 limits the jitter on the *Bus*.

The encoder *En* is constrained by burst constraint BC to send all packets belonging to one image in bursts with an inner period (i.e. spacing between the packets) of 1 time unit. A new burst of packets corresponding to the next image is produced every 100 time units (the outer period). The precision of this constraint strongly suggest an implementation of the encoder in dedicated hardware.

Let us assume that the video phone connection can be considered real-time if each image taken by camera *C* is displayed on *Dis* within about 800 time units. Therefore, latency constraint LC1 between 780 and 820 time units is specified for the path from camera to display. The bounds of LC1 ensure that the images have to arrive at the display at a sufficiently regular rate for pleasant viewing (as opposed to an LC with wider bounds).

Now suppose that we are designing the decoder *Dec* and that we can influence the scheduling of the *Bus*. The bus delays each packet for a time between bus_{min} and bus_{max}. The range of the interval depends on other traffic on the bus (not shown) and on the bus scheduling strategy. The larger the maximum delay on the bus, the less time is available in the worst case for the decoder to decode an image. Furthermore, the larger the jitter on the bus, the more often the decoder will have to wait for additional packets to complete decoding a picture. Consequently, for an efficient implementation of the decoder, minimizing the jitter on the bus is desirable. This requirement can be specified using an appropriate latency constraint LC2 which has to be satisfied by an appropriate bus scheduling strategy.

6.   CONCLUSION

In this paper we showed that a small set of timing constraint macros at a natural level of abstraction is sufficient to model a large variety of timing constraints required by modern system-level analysis and implementation techniques. The macros presented are language- and methodology-independent and thus facilitate the combination of multiple design languages and techniques, which is becoming essential because of rapidly growing embedded real-time system complexity. We demonstrated our approach in three ways: - by combining our timing constraints specification with the SPI model, which is a representation specifically targeting system-level timing analysis independent of design languages or analysis techniques; - by showing how our constraints specification can be mapped to an existing analysis technique; - and by motivating why constraining event jitter and bursts is important for synthesis.

REFERENCES

[1] The MathWorks, Inc., "Using Simulink, Version 3", Jan. 1999
[2] C. J. Fidge, "Real-Time Schedulability Tests for Preemptive Multitasking" in *Real-Time Systems Journal*, vol. 14, 1998
[3] R. Ernst, "Codesign of Embedded Systems: Status and Trends", in *IEEE Design & Test of Computers*, Apr. 1998
[4] R. Gerber, W. Pugh and M. Saksena, "Parametric Dispatching of Hard Real-Time Tasks", in *IEEE Transaction on Computers*, Mar. 1995
[5] T. Yen and W. Wolf, "Performance Estimation for Real-Time Distributed Embedded Systems", in *IEEE Transactions on Parallel and Distributed Systems*, Nov. 1998
[6] K. W. Tindell, "An Extendible Approach for Analysing Fixed Priority Hard Real-Time Systems", in *Journal of Real-Time Systems*, Mar. 1994
[7] K. Gresser, "An Event Model for Deadline Verification of Hard Real-Time Systems", in *Proceedings 5th Euromicro Workshop on Real-Time Systems*, Oulu, Finland, 1993
[8] F.S. de Boer, M. Gabbrielli and M.C. Meo, "A Timed Concurrent Constraint Language", in *Journal on Information and Computation*, to appear
[9] T. Amon, "Specification, Simulation, and Verification of Timing Behavior", *Ph.D dissertation, University of Washington*, 1993
[10] A. Dasdan, "Timing Analysis of Embedded Real-Time Systems", *Ph.D dissertation, University of Illinois at Urbana-Champaign*, 1999
[11] Open SystemC Initiative, "SystemC", http://www.systemc.org/
[12] D. D. Gajski et al., "SpecC: Specification Language and Methodology", *Kluwer Academic Publishers*, Mar. 2000
[13] Systems Level Design Language community, "Rosetta Reference", http://www.sldl.org/
[14] D. Ziegenbein, K. Richter, R. Ernst, L. Thiele and J. Teich, "SPI - A System Model for Heterogeneously Specified Embedded Systems", *IEEE Transactions on VLSI Systems*, to appear 2002